BRASS

BRASS

Jane Byrne and the Pursuit of Power

Kathleen Whalen
FitzGerald

Contemporary Books, Inc.
chicago

Library of Congress Cataloging in Publication Data

FitzGerald, Kathleen.
    Brass, Jane Byrne and the pursuit of power.

    Bibliography: p.
    Includes Index.
    1. Byrne, Jane, 1934-   2. Chicago, (Ill.)—
Politics and government—1950-   3. Chicago
(Ill.)—Mayors—Biography.   I. Title.
F548.52.B95F57   1981   352′.00092′4   [B]   80-70633
ISBN 0-8092-7006-4   AACR2

Published by Contemporary Books, Inc.
180 North Michigan Avenue, Chicago, Illinois 60601
Manufactured in the United States of America
Library of Congress Catalog Card Number: 80-70633
International Standard Book Number: 0-8092-7006-4

Published simultaneously in Canada by
Beaverbooks, Ltd.
150 Lesmill Road
Don Mills, Ontario M3B 2T5
Canada

This book is lovingly dedicated to
Meghan, Garrett, and Fitz
and to the memory of my father,
Tom Whalen.

Contents

Acknowledgments

I wish to thank members of the Burke family for their time and trust. I wish to thank Aileen Byrne, Maureen Byrne Gill, and Mike Dwyer, Bill's uncle, for sharing with me their precious memories of Bill.

To my friend, Mary Agnes Dalton, who was never too tired or too busy to do another interview and who was always ready to help me think and understand. To Joan Thompson and Annette Brownlee, who cared enough to criticize and whose literary comments and insights were invaluable in the preparation of the manuscript. To Sister Marguerite Green of Barat College, who reviewed the entire manuscript and whose suggestions I treasure. To Myra Althardt, who generously prepared the manuscript again and again.

To those who cared for my children—Bernice Moreschini, my sister Molly, and my cousin Carol. To the other members of my family, Ellen and Tommy, who never wavered in their support.

To my mother, Catherine Whalen, who characteristically

gave her support, her criticism, her enthusiasm, and her belief in me. To my mother-in-law, Bridget FitzGerald, who also supported, cared, and believed.

To Jodi Bornstein of Contemporary Books, whose help, on a personal level as well as on a professional level, was invaluable.

To Alice Ryerson of the Ragdale Foundation, who graciously provided an environment for writing and a belief in the writer.

Foreword

In the late fall of 1977, Jane Byrne, Commissioner of Consumer Sales, Weights, and Measures, was accusing the Bilandic administration of improprieties related to taxi fare increases. Charges on both sides were becoming more and more acrimonious. Contrary to the prevalent flow of opinion, I found myself admiring Bilandic's adversary.

One morning I received a call from Donna Fitzpatrick, whose home in Lake Forest we had purchased. Out of the blue she asked me what I thought of Jane Byrne. I told her that I thought Jane was one hell of a woman, that she had nerve, and that what she was doing was terrific. I waited for Donna to disagree with me. Donna said, "Oh, well, she's my sister." Donna had not prefaced her question with the fact of their relationship, and if I had told her that I thought Jane Byrne was crazy, I'm sure that my relationship with Donna would have been quickly terminated.

Within a few months Jane Byrne declared her candidacy for mayor of Chicago. The following fall, in October 1978, my husband and I were invited by the Fitzpatricks to a fund-raiser for Jane in Lake Forest. It was at that time that I was first introduced to Jane Byrne. I did not become active in her campaign but followed it through her sister. I became fascinated with Jane and wanted to know what made her tick. While she was beating the bushes for votes, winning the primary, and becoming mayor of Chicago, I was completing work on my dissertation at Northwestern University.

This work involved analyzing power relations within the Catholic Church. I had had extensive experiences within the Church, and this was an opportunity to look at what I had experienced on an abstract level. While there is absolutely nothing abstract about power in the Church, I came to an understanding of how widely and how deeply Catholics are affected by their unique relationship with their priests. Catholics have experienced authority and obedience all their lives; it is a basic part of the Catholic culture. When Catholics come to their own power (not necessarily within the Church), they bring to it their own history, and exercise power in a very Catholic way.

I had known something about Jane's education and her family. I watched her come into her own in a very Catholic way, in a very Irish way; yet she was a woman, and what was true for a man was not necessarily true for a woman. I just did not know what to make of her and found myself looking at her closely and analyzing what she was saying within the context of Irish-American Catholicism.

With that phone call from Donna I began to realize that I had known the family over the course of many years. I had taught from 1958 to 1962 at St. Joseph School in Homewood, Illinois, where Father Joe Burke, Jane's uncle, was the pastor. I had known him well and had become acquainted with his brother, Monsignor Ed Burke. His powerful presence was strangely tempered by an elusive, haunting melancholy. Ed Burke was vulnerable in a way that his younger brother, Father Joe, was not. At the time that I was on the far south side, my sister, Ellen, was attending Barat College with Carol Burke,

Jane's younger sister. Currently, my son, Garrett, is in kindergarten with Bill Fitzpatrick, Jane's nephew.

In addition to the Chicago associations, my family had known the Byrne family in Cleveland for many years. Marie Whalen, a cousin, had worked with Bill and Tommy Byrne at the Byrne foundry, Basic Aluminum Casting. Our families had known each other for a long time and had many common friends.

I felt that writers all over the city were sharpening their pencils, clipping articles from the press, and sitting down to write their books about Jane Byrne. I knew that I could write about her, not necessarily better than they, but in a way that many others could not.

I have attempted to make sense of Jane Byrne's life. Approximately 300 people shared with me their memory of Jane, her family, and her first husband. A number of these people were interviewed many times. A rather curious phenomenon developed during the course of collecting data, interviewing, assimilating and integrating the material, and finally writing. I was told over and over again that the Burke family absolutely did not trust anyone, and many people felt that Jane's apparent mistrust of people stemmed from a deep family trait. I did not find this to be true.

Members of Jane's family were interviewed many times. I also interviewed cousins, neighbors, friends, and acquaintances. Mrs. Aileen Byrne, Bill Byrne's mother, and her daughter, Maureen Byrne Bill, were likewise most generous and patient as I returned to them for further information about Bill. Never at any time were any conditions placed on their sharing of information. No one ever requested to read the manuscript; no one ever asked what I was doing or how I was treating an issue. There were no demands, no conditions, no constraints. In a very few instances they shared with me an incident or a view that they did not want published but wanted me to know about so I would understand the background. These proved to be of a minor nature and did not in any way affect the content of the book. The manuscript was not submitted to the family for their approval, agreement, nor endorsement. The work is entirely my own and represents only *my interpretation* of the various people, circumstances, and events that are a part of Jane Byrne's life.

I formally requested an interview from Jane Byrne. She refused, saying that she was under contract with another author and could not legally give me an interview. Whether or not this is true, I don't know. I personally feel that she and Jay will go to Palm Springs and write her memoirs when she leaves office. Originally, I felt disappointed that I was not going to be able to interview her. As I began a careful analysis of her words, I realized that she was becoming more and more guarded and less open in her statements about herself, her history, her feelings.

She had given marvelous interviews to Paul McGrath, Milton Rakove, Myra MacPherson, and Elaine Markoutsas, wherein she revealed much about herself. I feel that even if she had agreed to my interview, she had become so much more defensive that she probably would not have shared with me as she had with the others who interviewed her before or immediately after she became mayor. I have drawn extensively from their work.

I have attempted to articulate those traditions and values, the history and culture of the Irish-American Catholic upper class from which Jane Byrne derives. I have attempted to set forth her own personal history, with particular emphasis on those people and events that influenced her growth and development as a woman. I have attempted to describe Bill Byrne, the nature of their marriage, and the extent to which his death traumatized her. I have hypothesized her pursuit of power as a replacement for her husband and as a method of sublimating her grief. I have described her political behavior in light of her relationship with Richard Daley and against the backdrop of Chicago Machine politics. I have described her campaign, the choices that were forced on her, and the fact that the system is bigger than the individual.

There are those who may ask what right we have to look closely at a public figure's life. What right do we have, as Shana Alexander so aptly phrased it, to splash around in another person's life? I would postulate that we do not have a right *not* to know, for we, as an informed body of citizens, must understand not only what our elected officials do, but also why they are doing it. We have entrusted them with the safekeeping of our society; to judge their stewardship objectively demands that we know who and what they are. Marc Pachter, in *Telling Lives: The Biographer's Art*, states:

> If certain lives have the power to touch or to transform our own (quite literally, in the case of the political world), to exalt or to terrify us, then we, with the biographer as our representative, have a right to make sense of those lives, to their innermost nature.

This work is classified as an interpretive biography. It rests on the solid foundation of months and months of research. There was a great gathering of facts and details, of evidence and clarification. This data base, the vast amount of information that has been collected about Jane Byrne's life, is not an end in itself, but rather has served as the doors and windows through which I have peered into Jane Byrne's life. What I have heard, what I have seen, what I have felt, I have shared.

It may be said that this work is a meeting of two women. I have brought myself—my own history, experiences, education, thoughts—to the meeting. The interpretation I have given to the raw data of Jane Byrne's life is bounded by my own limitations, predispositions, and the state of my own maturity. And others will write their own books, bringing themselves to their own unique interpretation of this fascinating woman.

Perhaps more than my entrée into the family and friends, perhaps more than my own educational and professional experiences, the fact that I am part of the very distinct Irish-American, Catholic culture and share with her a similar background and have internalized many of the values with which she lives has enabled me to interpret her life with somewhat greater clarity and insight than those with greater distance.

At this time, no one can judge Jane Byrne's effectiveness as a mayor. I can only judge her effectiveness in attaining her goal. Whether she uses her power wisely or foolishly will be left to history to judge.

Chronology

May 24, 1933	Margaret Jane Burke was born
June 1951	Graduation from St. Scholastica High School
June 1955	Graduation from Barat College
December 31, 1956	Married William Patrick Byrne
December 31, 1957	Daughter Kathy born
May 31, 1959	Lieutenant Byrne died
September, 1960	Joins Kennedy presidential campaign
August, 1964	Hired for first city job, Chicago Commission on Urban Opportunity personnel department
March 4, 1968	Appointed Commissioner of Consumer Sales, Weights, and Measures
January 1973	FTC begins antitrust investigation into Checker cabs
January 1975	Jane Byrne appointed co-chairman of Chicago Democratic Party

January 1976	Taxis put under Department of Sales, Weights, and Measures
December 20, 1976	Mayor Richard J. Daley died; Jane's powers over taxis increased
December 1976	Jane Byrne dumped from position of co-chairman of Chicago Democratic Party by George Dunne
July 7, 1977	City Council voted taxi fare increase
July 27, 1977	Taxi memo from Jane Byrne notarized
November 10, 1977	Jane's memo published
November 21, 1977	Jane Byrne fired by Bilandic
March 17, 1978	Jane Byrne married Jay McMullen
April 24, 1978	Jane Byrne announced candidacy for mayor
February 27, 1979	Jane Byrne won primary, 51 percent
April 3, 1979	Jane Byrne won mayoral election, 82 percent
April 16, 1979	Jane Byrne's mayoral inauguration

An Irish Wake

The third weekend of October brought Indian summer to Lake Forest. Temperatures were in the middle and upper seventies. The evenings had been cool, the days warm, and the right combination of moisture had transformed a million trees into gold, crimson, and deep, deep purple. Little bands of Mexican gardeners, emerging from the rumbling Italian landscape trucks from Highwood, had already made their weekly assault on the dead leaves and the dried mums, leaving the broad green lawns and winding drives in perfect order.

Late in the afternoon of October 21, 1978, the last of the San Francisco sourdough bread had been sold at the Wine and Cheese Shop. Janowitz had rolled the last tenderloin and butterflied its last rack of lamb for the evening dinner parties. The owners of The Left Bank were putting away the hot dog buns and sweeping their floor. Marshall Field was locking its big brass doors. The Country Squires and Mercedes were pulling into St. Mary's parking lot, hoping to be on time for the five o'clock evening Mass.

Over on Lake Road at Chernie and John Hewitt's large gray

mansion, preparations for the first fund-raiser of the campaign
had begun. Station wagons from the catering company were
pulling into the long circular driveway. Trays of cold meat,
hors d'oeuvres, thirty pounds of jumbo shrimp, cases of liquor
and mixes, Swedish meatballs, and other hot dishes were being
carried into the Hewitts' pantry. In the large marble foyer a
cash bar had been set up across from the ticket table. The black
help in their white uniforms were arranging the shrimp on the
cracked ice, placing them carefully on the large silver servers.

Although they had been in it for only two years, Chernie and
John Hewitt loved their big stately home. There were more
than twenty-five rooms and the concrete walls were thirteen
inches thick. Because the McLennan-Reid Bridge that crossed
the ravine next to their property had been deemed "structur-
ally unsound," the city had dismantled it, reducing the few cars
that normally came that far north on Lake Road to practically
none.

The elegant gray mansion was designed in 1912 by Howard
Van Doren Shaw. Shaw had designed Market Square, the heart
of Lake Forest's shopping, and many of the more elegant and
prestigious homes in the area. The Hewitt home was very much
a part of the history of Lake Forest. However, like so many
other homes, its beach had been eroding for years. The Hewitts
still had 150 feet from the three French doors leading out from
the gold leaf and walnut library, beyond the slate patio with
the graceful statue of Rebecca at the Well, to the edge of the
bluff and their own private beach.

Chernie Hewitt was a small woman in her late thirties who
wore her thick black hair in a high bouffant style and favored
black sweaters, black pants, and black evening dresses. She was
a product of the Chicago public schools—Taft, Sullivan, and
Jones Commercial. She had met John while working for him
and moved quickly from employee to wife and business partner.
John was tall, fair, clean-shaven, open-faced. Through a series
of brilliant moves he had purchased small companies that were
total liabilities, poor risks, and turned them into profitable
enterprises.

They were not to the manor born. What they had was not

given to them at birth but had been worked and fought and struggled for. They suffered no illusions about themselves—where they had been, where they were going.

They were proud of their new home and had graciously lent it for use by the St. Mary's Parents Club yearly social. Although the three younger Hewitt children were still in the Montessori School, their oldest had started at St. Mary's and the others would be there soon. Chernie had become friends with Donna Fitzpatrick through the fund-raisers at St. Mary's. Donna and her husband John were avid supporters of St. Mary's School. John Fitzpatrick had been elected to St. Mary's School Board and took an active interest in his children's education.

The Fitzpatricks were a thin, handsome couple with five black-haired, freckled-faced children with big, deep Irish eyes. Wherever Donna went, the five were with her, frequently in their green Chevy wagon. In the summer of 1978 they could be seen on their way to St. Mary's or to Baskin Robbins in their big wagon with a wrinkled green and white bumper sticker, "We Believe Jane Byrne."

Donna's sister, Jane, was running for mayor of Chicago, and although they didn't think she had a chance, she was Family and would receive their unquestioning support. Donna told Chernie that she would like to hold a fund-raiser for her sister but that their house was not big enough. Chernie immediately offered their large home since there would be such a crowd.

The Hewitts had their own reasons for supporting Jane Byrne. Among their holdings were two relatively small manufacturing companies, Congress Packaging and S.K. Smith. They were located on the north side of Chicago in the 33rd Ward. More than one hundred people were employed there, mostly women, with a large representation of black, Latino, Pakistani, and Polish heritages. Chernie had been hearing more and more of the women talking about Jane Byrne. They were meeting her on the el platforms, at PTA meetings, in the churches and stores, block clubs and street corners. This was the woman who was gutsy enough to blow the whistle at City Hall, and just maybe she was gutsy enough to win.

Chernie and John were familiar with the informal system of

taxation controlled by the building inspectors in Chicago, who would make their monthly inspections in their big black Lincolns. The Hewitts had similarly situated friends who also owned companies in Chicago. These friends were required to make surreptitious regular payments to the electrical and water people from City Hall. Everyone had had it. Running a business was hard enough—inflation, taxes, headaches. They couldn't do anything about that, but just maybe they could stop the harassment. Just maybe there was something about this Jane Byrne.

John Hewitt had been an active, lifelong Republican. He had conducted political workshops for the Republican Party in LaGrange, a suburb west of Chicago. Before lending his home and supporting this maverick Democrat, Jane Byrne, he would have to know more about her and her politics. Jane and her husband, Jay McMullen, together with Donna and John Fitzpatrick, went to the Hewitt home early that fall and spent the afternoon discussing their outlooks and beliefs.

John Hewitt was impressed with Jane's honesty, her convictions, her intelligence, yet remembers Jane being "extremely restrained and nervous, steeling herself to convey confidence." Jane struck Chernie with her intensity and vitality and gave the impression of one being "driven" by some force within herself. Turtlenecked Jay was relaxed, smiling, suave—in John Hewitt's words, "the perfect counterpoint to Jane's intense personality." The Hewitts decided they could and would support Jane Byrne in every way possible. A fund-raiser would be held October 21, 1978, at the Hewitt's home. Earlier that fall Jane's brother Edward and sister Mary Jill had both held parties for Jane in their respective neighborhoods in Chicago. Neither had been intended to raise money but to introduce her to their friends and neighbors, hoping to recruit support and political workers for the campaign. Both had relatively good showings, despite the potential for political reprisals. And Jane herself had held a party in her apartment that summer for more than three hundred people. She asked for no money at that time, either.

Now, with the Hewitts' support, Donna and John Fitzpatrick could plan an impressive, important event. There were only

"*A city thriving under the leadership
of its young, yet utilizing the
many accomplishments of its elderly,
while providing a safe and worthy
habitat for both.... This is the
responsibility of us all.*"

Jane Byrne

*You are cordially invited to meet
Jane Byrne
Mayoral candidate - City of Chicago
on Saturday, October 21st
6:00 - 9:00 p.m.
at the home of
Mr. and Mrs. John Hewitt
1345 Lake Road
Lake Forest, Illinois*

*Donation: $20.00
per person*

*Please respond by
October 17th*

four months left until the Democratic primary, and all the big money, Republican and Democrat, was supporting the Machine candidate, the incumbent mayor, Michael Bilandic. Although she had announced her candidacy in April 1978, Jane was still not taken seriously. During the month of September the *Chicago Tribune* mentioned her only twice.

Jane needed the money. She needed the support. She needed the coverage. What better way than a sophisticated, elegant party on the North Shore, in Lake Forest, where many of the Chicago business and industry elite made their homes. This was surely to attract attention from the media, to assure that Jane be perceived not only as a viable contender, but also as a formidable one.

Jane Byrne's ties to Lake Forest were established thirty years before when she drove daily north from Chicago to Barat College, a Catholic women's college placed incongruously in the middle of a wealthy Protestant community. Her three younger sisters followed her to Barat; her father, William Burke, served for many years on its board of trustees. It was to the sisters of the Sacred Heart at Barat College that she and Bill Byrne drove after their wedding Mass. It was to Barat that she returned when Bill was killed.

So it seemed appropriate to have a party of that magnitude and significance at a large, elegant Lake Forest mansion by the lake.

Five hundred invitations were ordered, divided among the Family, and sent out. Tickets were $20 each. A large response of perhaps seven or eight hundred people was easily anticipated, for the Burke Family was large and had been born and bred in the Chicago area. Of the six Burke children, only Billy did not live nearby. The others—Jane, Carol, Donna, Mary Jill, and Edward—had all married into large Irish families that provided a network of friendship and support. Their many, many contacts were in business, in law, in politics. All in Chicago. Donna wrote and designed the invitations. They were on off-white heavy-textured paper with a thin, bright green border and brown script.

The inside quote, attributed to Jane, was also written by Donna. Laughingly, Jim Wolf, Mary Jill's husband, who was an attorney, warned Donna that someone would look up the quotation and find out that it was from Patrick Henry or somebody, and she'd get into trouble.

As the time for the party drew closer, Chernie felt certain that they would have a bigger crowd and was afraid Donna had not ordered enough food. Two days before the party Chernie ordered more of everything so they would not run short. She had also called the Lake Forest Police, notifying them of the large party, requesting permission for on-street parking until midnight for a distance of some blocks around the house.

Because of the wonderful weather, the Family waited expectantly, excitedly for the crowd. By 6:00 the food, drinks, and the impeccable staff in their crisp white uniforms were all in order. The band was due momentarily. Jane, her sisters, Donna and Mary Jill, and Chernie Hewitt were all in black. Sophisticated, classic black.

The band, the Pete Baron Jazztet, rode together that Saturday evening from the South Side. They had often played at the Exchange Pub for Tommy Fitzpatrick, John's older brother, and he had referred them to Donna and John for the party. At 6:10 they hurried breathlessly into the big house, apologizing to John Fitzpatrick for not being on time. It didn't matter, for no one was there yet. Except the Family. The Burke women and their husbands, Edward and his wife. The in-laws. All Family. John led them into the large empty dining room, to the left of the library off the foyer.

By 6:20 Pete and the members of the band were in their striped shirts and straw hats, the instruments were in place, and they began to play, the sounds echoing through the empty dining room. The Hewitt children, already in their pajamas, tiptoed into the room and sat on the floor until they were escorted back upstairs by the housekeeper. A member of the band said, "This is what the American dream is all about."

By 6:35 Jane and Jay were stationed in the library. She wore a soft, loose, black silk dress, high black heels, and a single strand of pearls, creating a stark, almost severe image. Her hands were as cold and icy as her darting blue eyes. Jay wore casual dark slacks and a turtleneck. They were joined by Edward, quiet, relaxed, unassuming, the counselor in residence, the ascetic campaign manager. A Richelieu designing the future court of his monarch.

By 6:45 Chernie Hewitt began to feel a knot in her stomach. A practiced hostess, she knew what was considered "fashionably late." But by this time, with so many people coming, there ought to have been some there already. She and Donna avoided each other for the time. The Dixieland music filled the large empty rooms. The bartender recounted the bottles, stirred the ice, straightened the napkins. John Fitzpatrick had a beer, walking solemnly in the black and white foyer, avoiding the ticket-taker's eyes.

By 6:55 the first of the guests arrived, commenting that the house was hard to find, the bridge was out, the streets were not well lit. The Family clutched at this excuse many times before the night was over. Donna went to the library door, motioned for her sister. Jane emerged dutifully, nervously greeted the newcomer, and retreated quickly to the sanctuary of the library. She would repeat this pattern just seven more times that evening.

Chernie Hewitt had grave misgivings. She paced back and forth in front of the large French windows, peering nervously down the long drive, hoping that the crowd would find its way. Her eyes held a fixed gaze, oblivious of those who had already arrived.

By 8:20, the pastor from St. Mary's, Father Brett, arrived, and Donna ushered him around to meet the few guests. The shrimp and hors d'oeuvres were passed again. Glasses were refilled. Tall Jim Wolf, glass in hand, was rocking on the balls of his feet, laughing nervously. People were reintroduced to each other. A middle-aged man propped himself against the bookcases, for his feet hurt and he was bored. He began reading book jackets.

A few of the women were seated on the deep velvet sofas in

front of the unlit fireplace. They would reach for a hand to assist them up and over to the shrimp and canapés, for the plush apricot carpeting was so deep and so thick that one sank into it as if in quicksand. One of the women, visiting from Cleveland, had been active in the Democratic Party for forty years. She was anxious for a taste of Chicago politics and for a chance to meet Jane Byrne. She spent the evening in polite dismay, dividing her attention between Father Brett and the shrimp.

A small clustering was back in the conversation area near the bay windows overlooking the lake. The women sat with their arms folded, ankles crossed. A few of the men stood near the shrimp, looking over each other's shoulders, glancing in the direction of the library, hoping to see the candidate again. A young couple were trying to engage in small talk, stabbing the shrimp with little colored toothpicks.

By 9:30 the scope of the disaster was evident. The cracked ice under the jumbo shrimp began to form into a big snowball. The little egg salad, creamed cheese, and crab canapés sat. The band played harder. The large apricot living room grew larger. Mary Jill, Jane's youngest sister, whispered to herself, "My God, there's no one here." Of the five hundred invitations, they could have realistically expected seven to eight hundred guests; fewer than twenty came.

Those who came were embarrassed. An old friend of the Family felt the night was "cold, dark, depressing." An older woman whispered to her daughter, "No one thinks she has a chance, and no one has bothered to come." The band played on. A few couples began dancing. Donna and John sat anxiously on the arms of the velvet sofas, taking turns with Father Brett.

Edward stood with his arms crossed, leaning against the door to the large living room off the foyer. Remembering who was there, remembering who was not there. Or was he hearing the death knell of a candidacy?

The evening, rather than being a significant political event, took on the ambience of an Irish wake. Jane became less the salty, terse "gutsy broad," the member of Daley's inner circle blowing the whistle on her enemies, the candidate who was "sick and tired" of Bilandic's jogging and who wanted to return the city to its vitality and pride. She became the proud bereaved widow holding herself within herself, not laughing, not crying, lest the rest of the Family lose heart. She had a role she had learned only too well in former times. Andrew Greeley has called the Irish-American Catholic wake "an extraordinary phenomenon, both heartless and reassuring, melancholy and rejoicing, unbearably painful and stubbornly hopeful." This night was all of that and even more.

The women in black, the priest, the heaviness, the futility of it all. Dignity in the face of disaster. The rituals, the rubrics, the familiar patterns of conversation: Mary Jill whispering to Donna, "I can't believe this is happening." Donna looking to John; John looking to Edward; Edward silently entering the closed library.

At 10:00 P.M., finally surrendering, Chernie moved away from the windows, shrugged her shoulders, and joined the group in the bay. The Family sat back. The caterers set up flat aluminum pans of chili and Swedish meatballs in the dining room. John Fitzpatrick asked the band to stay. They agreed. Dinner was about to be served. Respects were to be paid.

The small gathering was ushered into the large empty dining room. The smells of the chili and ham floated across the room. John Hewitt stood before the band and stated simply, "I have not known Jane Byrne for a long time. Yet I have found her to be a vital, energetic person. She has demonstrated a high level of intelligence, leadership, vigor. While she is not the front runner, she is someone of strength. I have walked the streets of Chicago, and I know the people want change. I have confidence that they will support Jane Byrne."

Jane appeared small and frail next to John and the band. No charisma, no strong public presence, but simply a thin, intense woman in black, resembling more the widow about to thank the priest and the people who had come to the cemetery than a pretender to the throne of Richard J. Daley. Her eyes gazed directly, intently, at the small group clustered before the chili. Her thin hands gestured gracefully, almost prayerfully, as she spoke about the poverty and despair, the neglect and anger boiling up in the streets of Chicago. About the twelve-year-old with needle marks on his arms, about the terror and crime at the Robert Taylor Homes, about the corruption in and lack of response from City Hall. She said that Chicago was more than the exclusiveness of Beverly and Sauganash, more than Lake Shore Drive and LaSalle Street. She spoke about change and about the strengths of the neighborhoods.

The listeners were neither voters nor large contributors. They would not be there to work the precincts and wards. Yet they were there—perhaps really only able to support her morally. She owed them something—they had come.

She spoke with the same intensity, the same low, clipped, uninflected sentences, phrases, words that were later to become her trademark. She was the teacher, quickly leading a group of bright students to her way of thinking, without coercing, without patronizing, simply stating the facts as she knew them to be.

Her statements met with respectful discreet applause. The band gave one last enthusiastic volley and Jane led the way around the chili and meatballs and back to the library. The guests headed for the living room with their plates, making their way gingerly across the thick carpet and sinking back into the deep velvet sofas. The candidate did not reappear.

The good-byes and thank-yous and well wishes were made as Donna and John hurried for the coats. The trumpet, drums, and bass were carefully packed in the trunk and the musicians headed south on Route 41 for Hyde Park. The caterers began scraping the dishes, putting the leftovers into plastic containers for Chernie to take over to the children in the religious education classes at St. Mary's after the 8:45 Mass the next morning. The glasses and ice and bottles and ashtrays were gathered and cleaned and put away for another day.

After the guests departed, the Family drew together to review what had happened, what had gone wrong. To draw strength, humor, support, and criticism from each other. To reinforce their solidarity, their "Burkes against the world" philosophy, which is reminiscent of Ben Bradlee's writing of John Kennedy: "He loved his brothers and sisters with a tribal love. All Kennedys were born gregarious, but under siege, it could be the Kennedys against the world." This was the time to let Jane know once again that she was not alone in her ambitions and that they would support her 100 percent in whatever she wanted to do, simply because she was one of them.

Deep within herself, at a level that neither Donna nor Mary Jill, that neither Jay nor Edward, could ever inhabit, Jane knew where she was going. The disaster of the evening was not a disaster to her. It was simply what happened—nothing more, nothing less.

The quality of Jane Byrne's ego was of such toughness, of such texture and fiber, of such magnitude, that her deepest belief was in herself and in herself alone. Not for a single moment did she doubt that she would win. Not a glance to the left or to the right, but straight ahead to the election and the big chair waiting for her on the fifth floor of City Hall. While the Family did not share that vision, that total obsession, they knew of its presence and did not question it.

Jane Byrne did not have the luxury to show embarrassment, to lose her confidence, her control, to acknowledge that the party was a fiasco. The Family took its cues from her, as they had done so many times before. Mary Jill stated, "We always just looked to Janie to come up with something. She always plunged right ahead. She never turned tail and ran." And that night, there was her pride, her control, her determination. She had a job to do. She was going to win and she knew it. She could not afford to lose her nerve. Loss of nerve had never plagued her before; it was not going to start then.

Leaving the large, imposing gray house shortly before midnight and walking in the thick gray fog down to Lake Road, the guests were filled with a sense of ambivalence, of Celtic fatalism, of confusion. Would Jane Byrne end up a footnote in some future history book of Chicago? Would people someday ask, "Who was that blond gal who ran for mayor back in the seventies?" Was the evening an exercise to feed Jane's vanity?

To satisfy social obligations to the Family? To accommodate a curiosity about a Lake Road home? Or was this a preamble to a a whole new epoch in the history of Chicago?

As the guests slowly drove their Buicks and Lincolns north on Lake Road, they could see in their rearview mirrors the lights burning brightly in the old gray house by the lake.

2

Wednesday's Child

The day was cloudy and cool, with temperatures in the low sixties. Wednesday, May 24, 1933. Katharine Burke gave birth to her second child, a girl, Margaret Jane, named after her two grandmothers, Margaret Burke and Margaret Nolan. Margaret—*margarita,* the pearl—hard, opaque, found inside an impenetrable protective shell. They called the child Janie; Margaret was too formidable a name for a small child.

Margaret Jane came into the world with the caul on her face. The caul, part of the membrance holding the baby within the mother's womb, was torn away in the struggle of birth and the child carried it with her as she entered into the world. The caul, sometimes referred to as the *veil of birth,* is thought to bestow luck, fortune, blessings on the child. It was once thought to endow the child in later life with psychic powers. In the nineteenth century, and until recent times, Irish seamen would buy a child's caul; its magic powers were believed to be an infallible preventative against drowning. When sold, the power of the caul passed from seller to buyer. Janie—a Wednesday child, "full of woe," with a caul to bring her luck, fortune, and blessings. The Fates ordered for her a bittersweet life.

The year 1933 signaled a turning point in this country. The entire nation, paralyzed by the horrors of the Depression, was just beginning its slow, painful recovery. 1933 was also a turning point in Chicago. Mayor Anton Joseph Cermak was assassinated on February 15, 1933, and Edward Kelly was elected mayor of Chicago, beginning a tradition of Irish mayors that Margaret Jane Burke was to continue nearly fifty years later.

When Jane was born, the family lived on the north side of Chicago at 6503 N. Claremont. Then they moved to a better address—first in Sauganash Park and then in Sauganash proper to a red brick center-hall colonial. Sauganash, on the far northwest side, is one of the most desirable areas of the city in which to live. It is as if the city were tipped and all the movers and shakers who had to live within the city bounds rolled into Sauganash. Those who had no children could live on the Gold Coast or the near north side, but those with families desiring a suburban environment lived in Sauganash.

The streets in Sauganash do not have the rolling contours and cul-de-sacs of the suburbs but are as straight and carefully zoned as the rest of Chicago. The tudors and colonials run from moderate to magnificent, with many overpowering their tiny lawns. There is probably more power and influence per square foot in Sauganash than in any other neighborhood in Chicago. In Sauganash live the judges, commissioners, police and fire chiefs, and members of the boards that decide the fate of the city. The power people live in Sauganash.

Throughout America life was getting better and, in Chicago, the Burke family was growing. Joining Janie and her older brother, Billy, was Edward, born fourteen months after Jane. For five years there were only the three, then three more girls—Carol, Donna, and Mary Jill—in the next ten years. The younger girls were quite different from the three elder. When they were born Katharine was in her middle to late thirties and had suffered miscarriages. Perhaps she was more comfortable and secure; perhaps some of the intensity of the mother-daughter symbiosis had been dissipated through Jane. Carol, Donna, and Mary Jill were freer, less needing to control, and were able to see the world not as a hostile, cruel enemy that needed reining, but as a nice place in which to live, to grow, to fall in love, marry, and bear lots of children.

As happens in many large families, the need for order and control is so great that the children fall into a lockstep formation behind the eldest; the alternative is utter chaos. In such families the same face, the same voice, the same expression appears on six or eight or ten different bodies. Not so with the six Burke children.

No line formed behind Billy (never referred to as William), the eldest. Billy was the colorful son, a rebel. Friends remember Janie and Billy "snapping at each other all the time." He always had some deal in the works, but no one ever really knew what he was up to. At one time, he sold religious goods to churches in the Chicago area. He told the pastors that his Uncle Ed had sent him, which assured him of an immediate sale, until Uncle Ed found out about it. Perhaps because the parents were younger, had more energy and were less distracted, perhaps because too many expectations were placed upon him, Billy eluded, avoided, and escaped family demands. Bill received a good education, married, and yet knew too well the demands that were to come his way if he remained in Chicago. He took his family of ten children to California; this was a highly irregular move for a Burke.

Janie's younger brother, Edward (never Eddie) was thin, handsome, and reserved. Edward, avoiding fights with the older ones, was sensitive and quiet. It was a rare Catholic family that did not send one of its children off to the service of the Church. Edward was the natural choice for the priesthood and after eighth grade he entered Quigley Preparatory Seminary.

Chicago priests are like no other priests in the world, and some astute sociologist will someday discover that it is because of Quigley Seminary. Quigley sits in the middle of Rush Street, where there are more nightclubs, taverns, saloons, bars, and hookers than on any other street in Chicago. The only comparison would be if the Archdiocese of New York had constructed its minor seminary in Times Square. Each day hundreds of adolescent seminarians make their way past the glitter of Rush Street to the big monastic classrooms to learn that which boys who want to be priests must know. It is left to speculation whether they learn more inside or outside the classroom.

After Quigley Edward went on to St. Mary of the Lake Seminary to study philosophy and theology among the lakes, hills, and trees of Mundelein, Illinois. He withdrew before ordination and, as so many who have had extensive training in a seminary, entered law school at the University of Notre Dame.

The Burkes were active members of Queen of All Saints Catholic Church. Prior to the 1960s, the local parish met the needs of its people on every conceivable level. As well as providing a place to worship and to receive the Sacraments, the parish was the social and political center of the neighborhood. Each parish, like each family, had its own personality, flavor, and scent. The pastor set the tempo of his parish; his personality was perhaps the single most important factor in determining its tone.

Frank Dolan, the Right Reverend Monsignor Francis Jerome Dolan, was the pastor of Queen of All Saints from 1934 to 1969. When most pastors were constructing churches, Frank Dolan was building a basilica. He was powerful and able to deal well with his Sauganash parishioners.

When most pastors were seen as solitary, without family, Frank Dolan had his brother, Father Walter, with him in the parish. Another brother, Father Jim, who, when not serving in the Navy or on the Archdiocesan Mission Band, also lived with him. While there was no doubt that the monsignor ran the parish, the rectory was the Dolan family home and, as such, was as open to the neighborhood people as any other home on the block.

The Burke family were among those closest to the Dolans. Bill was an usher and frequently, after the Masses, the ushers and their families joined the Dolans for breakfast. Year after year, the Fourth of July was celebrated at the rectory with hot dogs, watermelon, lemonade, and fireworks. A group of twenty to thirty families took their vacations together at Houghton Lake, Michigan—the Burkes among them.

Katharine Burke liked the Dolans—she liked the kind of priests they were and what they stood for—power, class, ambition, family-centered, and "pure as the driven snow" in their personal lives. They were priestly priests—not a breath of a whisper about women, about drinking, or about money. Frank Dolan had power and knew how to use it. He built a multimillion-dollar church-school-rectory-convent complex on eighteen acres that made other parishes' facilities look like a house of cards. Stone from Wisconsin and Indiana, slate from Vermont, onyx from Morocco and Pompeii, marble from Siena, mosaics from Florence. Monsignor Dolan prevailed upon Cardinal Meyer to request the Pope to elevate his church to the rank of basilica, or "regal church," one fit for the Pope himself.

From the Dolans, the Burke children, as well as others intimate with the Dolans, learned about power, power that was familiar and not to be feared: a big man in black pants who grilled hot dogs and rowed a small boat across a Michigan lake but who, despite the familiarity, was always addressed as Monsignor Dolan.

The Dolans were priests, special, with power sanctioned by the authority of God Himself. The lessons learned about power, authority, and style—about people who had power, authority, style—were invaluable, especially to Jane Burke, who one day would pursue and create her own power, authority, and style.

To understand a Catholic politician, to understand Jane Byrne, it is imperative to understand the result of years of intensive training that affect one's thought processes and the result of the mental gymnastics and moral juggling that are an intrinsic element of Catholic education of the '40s and '50s. These patterns and ways of thinking are virtually impossible to eradicate, even long after one has ceased to practice the faith. Those who stormed out of the Church as the altar was turned around and Latin was put on a shelf can never really stop thinking as a Catholic, any more than a zebra can change its stripes.

Catholicism is a burled-walnut religion, with swirls of contradictions, paradoxes, ironies. A Catholic learns to think in contradictions, in nuance and shadow. A typical Catholic statement made by Jane Byrne is, "I don't change my mind; facts change my mind." When charges were made that she accused Michael Bilandic of conspiring with the taxi industry to increase fares, she stated, "I did not say that he committed a *conspiracy*. I said that he engaged in *conspiratorial acts*." Nuance, precision, slicing the acts of the will so thin that you can see through them.

The substratum of Catholic thinking as taught before Vatican II lies in the concept of Original Sin, which holds that babies come into the world as spiritual cripples. In the '40s and '50s a young Catholic, five or six years old, heard the story about the beautiful garden, apples, snakes, and the gates of the garden banging shut.

And as the child matured, at around age eight or ten, he learned the meaning of original sin: a darkening of the intellect, a weakening of the will, and a strong inclination to evil—the cold, hard fact of life as sure as poppies grow in Flanders Field. People aren't smart; they are weak and they will always be drawn to sin.

This is the basic human condition, and no amount of reform, no legislation, no marching, no movements, are ever going to turn men's feet from clay to ivory. Those who perceived Jane Burke Byrne as a reform candidate, a reform mayor, knew nothing of what she learned from the Benedictine Sisters in the classrooms on Keene Avenue in the 1940s.

From Queen of All Saints Grade School Jane went on to a nearby Benedictine high school—St. Scholastica, located on Ridge Road close to Evanston. The same Benedictine sisters that staffed Queen of All Saints also taught at St. Scholastica. The Benedictine Order is the oldest order in the church, a down-to-earth order with the motto *ora et labora*—pray and work. Nothing abstract, like the *veritas* of the Dominicans, the poverty of the Franciscans, or the obedience of the Jesuits. Just prayer and work.

Katharine had a miscarriage and nearly died of a hemorrhage when Jane was sixteen. She depended upon and confided in her eldest daughter. Responsibilities for the younger girls, worry about and fear of the possible loss of her mother made Jane even more serious. She had little time for frivolity or small talk. For Jane, life was serious business over which she needed to have control.*

Many years later a cousin was going into the hospital for a D and C. She had been hemorrhaging for many days, and her doctor wanted to perform this relatively simple surgical procedure. Jane said to her, "Why that's sheer nerves. You just control yourself. You don't let people make you sick. I have days when I'm running from morning to night, there's tension all day long. No way are they going to make me sick. You just control yourself." The cousin went ahead with her surgery.

She joined the debating club and became a member of the Chicago Catholic Forensic League. She loved the controversy, debate, and discussion but, according to a former teacher, did not want to expatiate—she waited until she was sure before stating things. She was cautious, in control at all times, providing evidence and statistics for her point of view; establishing a criteria of judgment; developing a probable solution.

To be a Catholic—a young educated Catholic—in the '40s and '50s meant that you were part of a way of life that perhaps the world will never know again. Catholicism was more than a subculture, a group that was somehow out of step with the rest of society like the Amish or the Beatniks; it was a coculture, a group that existed beside the mainstream yet distinct from it. You were part of the "one, holy, Catholic, and apostolic Church"—you were right and all the others were wrong. It

---

*It was at this time that Jane decided to become a doctor. Janet Towne, a young obstetrician, cared for Katharine. Jane was impressed by Dr. Towne and wanted to follow in her footsteps.

gave you a strange confidence mixed with an insidious insecurity because you knew you were different from most people.

The Benedictine Order has long been known as the Keeper of the Liturgy. They were first and foremost a monastic order, and at St. Scholastica, the girls were encouraged to enter into the spirit of the Liturgy. At noon the nuns chanted their office (the ancient compilation of psalms and prayers to honor the Blessed Virgin) in a small chapel, and many of the girls would attend—Prime, Tierce, Sext, None, Vespers and Compline, Matins and Lauds (the names of the hours of the office). Repeated day after day, week after week, year after year.

The Liturgy, the rituals and rubrics of the Church, the oils and candles, bread and wine, the incense and the clanging of the thurible. The squeaky confessionals, the purple on the statues during Lent, the fasts and abstinences, the sacrifices and penances—always the same, never different. "Beauty, ever ancient, ever new," St. Augustine wrote. *The Catholic Girls Guide*, the missals with the five colored ribbons, packed full of holy cards. Things you could see, taste, and smell.

At St. Scholastica, Jane learned the meaning of public celebration—the coming together as a people to share in prayer, liturgy, song, and movement. When she became mayor one of the most dramatic aspects of her administration was the enlargement of the Special Events calendar. She instinctively knew of the need that the public had to celebrate their public life, their lives as citizens of the City of Chicago. October Fest, Chicago Fest, fireworks, food along Michigan Avenue—like a huge lawn party—for the Fourth of July. Her detractors accused her of a "bread and circuses" mentality. It is certainly true that it may be easier to throw a party than to resolve the problems in the schools and in the neighborhoods; however, the street is the public forum, and life in an urban environment can easily erode the individual, the quality of life slowly decaying, with people locked in helplessness. While people are waiting for change, they must gather as a people and celebrate the beauty and vitality of the city. This she learned from the Benedictines.

Blue serge uniforms, crisp white blouses, beanies. Order, control. Jane marched in step with the other girls, perhaps more seriously, more severely, for she had a purpose. Consequently, she was so aloof and so private that when the staff was compiling the yearbook, *The Scholastican, 1951*, they had nothing to say about Jane Burke. They didn't know her despite the four years together. There were only 149 girls in the class and Jane Burke had eluded them.

The captions accompanying the other 148 Scholasticans' yearbook pictures reflect the character of a girl, a Catholic high school graduate, in 1951—the values and standards that were important, the way you were supposed to be in order to become a successful Catholic wife: "A lady to the fingertips . . . cute as a kitten . . . a baby face and sweet . . . laughing and loyal . . . ."

For Jane Burke the editors of *The Scholastican* finally came up with: "Neat and nice . . . doctor to be . . . success assured . . . cool poise." Jane was going to be a doctor. Despite the fact that she was a quiet, serious student, she could not hide her ambition and drive from her classmates.

Curiously, she took a small part in the senior production, *Murder in a Nunnery.* She played one of the students. The attraction she had for acting at first appears contradictory to her shy, serious, no-nonsense ways. But Jane Burke, as an adolescent, was conscious of the impression she was making on others. Psychologists call this *impression management,* or the ability to monitor, to watch and control the picture of yourself that you are conveying to others. Such people, *high self-monitors,* are able to adjust their performances skillfully when signals from others tell them they are not having the effect they desire. Skilled impression managers are professional actors, trial lawyers, salespeople, artists, and politicians. Jane was very much controlling her public self. She revealed only what she wanted her classmates to know about her: she was cool and she would succeed.

During Jane's junior year in high school, her Uncle Ed, Chancellor Burke, conducted the official Chicago Archdiocesan

Pilgrimage to Rome, and he took Jane and her cousin along with him. This was the year 1950, the Holy Year, when the Pope opened the golden doors of St. Peter's Basilica, which were opened only every fifty years. In addition, Pope Pius XII had declared 1950 the Marian Year, for it was the year that he pronounced the dogma of the Assumption, the infallible declaration that the Mother of God was assumed body and soul into heaven.

They sailed from New York on the *Queen Elizabeth* on April 14, 1950. On board, Uncle Ed said Mass every day. A familiar-looking man served as altar boy and frequently took up the collection in the small chapel. He was Bing Crosby and Jane, without any introduction from her uncle, confidently approached him, introduced herself, and asked for his autograph. Jane's cousin, a year older, stood back, watching Jane, thinking, how like her, always plunging ahead, never sitting back and waiting for someone to take her by the hand. Spunky Janie, so much like Aunt Katharine. Her own mother, Ethyl, had died the year before. She thought of the very special relationship Janie and Katharine enjoyed, so unusual, so close, but not too dependent on each other. She finally went up to Bing and got his autograph. Five days later the ship dropped anchor in the English Channel. They transferred to a tugboat in the channel and made their way to Cherbourg, the port beyond the *cape de la Hague*.

Three glorious days in Paris with Uncle Ed. Paris, the City of Light. The city of churches and art and wine and history. On to Versailles with the famed Hall of Mirrors. They left Paris for Lourdes on a train through the Pyrenees. There Uncle Ed said Mass at the grotto. They witnessed the Procession of the Sick, where hundreds of the lame and the halt carried candles and sang the familiar Lourdes hymn to the Blessed Mother. They took the famed Lourdes baths as a protection against illness and disease.

On to Marseille, where beggars stood with children in rags, and sailors and merchants thronged the docks and narrow streets that ran back into each other. Then away from the noise and frenzy to Nice, Monaco, and finally to the unspoiled, beautiful seacoast town of Rapallo, where they rested a day before approaching the Eternal City on April 29.

Roma. They were met by Bishop Primo, head of the Chicago Seminary in Rome. They stayed near Santa Maria del Lago, the American church in Rome. Uncle Ed was right at home, and his two nieces observed him in his element: saying Mass at the side altar at St. Peter's; being met and entertained by all the important bishops and monsignori of Rome; knowing the best restaurants; touring the catacombs, the basilicas; meeting the Pope, a frail, ascetic man carried into St. Peter's like a king on his throne. The pomp, splendor and power of Rome—and Uncle Ed was at the center of it all.

Jane watched Uncle Ed closely. Careful not to let him know that she was watching, she saw him move with style and grace, she saw big and important people defer to him, she saw her uncle more comfortable in Rome than he had been sitting around their kitchen table. Jane began to understand the convolutions of power and she began to understand that people—simple people like her own Uncle Ed—seek power, hold power, and use power.

On May 1 they traveled to the Pope's summer residence, Castle Gondolpho. It was May Day, and on the way they were rammed by a Communist bus. From Castle Gondolpho they drove on the Appian Way to Anzio Beach where they saw the GI Cemetery and the shrine to Maria Goretti, the young Italian girl who gave her life to protect her purity. They stayed at a convent in Assisi and went to Mt. Subiaco, the cave in which St. Francis of Assisi slept. On to Florence, Milan, Switzerland, Lake Lucerne in the Swiss Alps, to the Benedictine Monastery of Einseidel, the birthplace of Gregorian chant, where they saw the monks pray Vespers.

Finally, on May 10, Uncle Ed and the rest of the tour set sail for New York from Le Havre. The *Queen Elizabeth* seemed remotely familiar. Jane's cousin became seasick. Jane, maintaining her exquisite control, did not.

Jane brought back with her a Papal Blessing for all the nuns at

St. Scholastica; to show her classmates, she brought the special lace mantilla, a black veil that covered her face out of respect to His Holiness. It was similar to that which widows in Spain and Italy wear. The veil of birth, the veil of respect, the veil of widowhood were to be the marks of Jane Burke's young life.

Throughout the four years at St. Scholastica Jane kept to herself, separate from her classmates. Her particular combination of shyness and aloofness made her difficult to approach. Her father was then vice-president of Inland Steel; her uncle was chancellor of the archdiocese; her mother ran the fund-raiser for the school. On the school days they didn't have to wear the uniform, Jane dressed better than any of the other Scholasticans. She drove her own car while most of her classmates used the CTA. Jane was different, a cut above those whose fathers delivered milk or mail, whose mothers worked at Illinois Bell or taught third grade and wore cloth coats.

There was, and perhaps still is, a unique advantage in attending an all-girl high school. During adolescence, when girls discover that they should not be too smart or too aggressive lest they scare away the boys, Jane and the 148 other girls in her class did not worry about hiding their talents under the proverbial bushel. They could be as smart and as aggressive as they wanted because they were their only competitors.

They knew that the Benedictine nuns were smart, educated, articulate women who made decisions, called the shots, set the tone, and demanded the most, both academically and spiritually, from the girls. They didn't defer to a man for decisions or tiptoe around his ego to avoid bruising it. There was no such thing as compromising their energies and ambitions—*ora et labora*. You pray and you work, or, as Katharine Nolan Burke told her own four daughters: "Low aim, not failure, is the worst."

3

All Her Geese Were Swans

On March 29, 1979, between the Democratic primary, February 27, 1979, and the regular mayoral election, April 3, 1979, the Chicago Women's Democratic Committee held a luncheon for Jane Byrne at the Conrad Hilton Hotel. On the committee were women with such prominent Chicago political names as Daley, Elrod, Hartigan, Hynes, Pucinski, Foran.

Jane's sister, Donna, and her daughter, Laura, sat with Jane at the head table. Jane noticed that her sister was unduly quiet and withdrawn that afternoon and called her that night to ask her why she had a "puss" on her during the luncheon.

Donna replied righteously, "You must be different now. How could you be nice to all those people who were ready to stab you in the back just a few weeks ago?

Jane answered her sister softly, "Donna, I know that I really didn't have a friend in that room. Some of the people that I care about most weren't there . . . Mother and Bill." Donna heard her sister's voice break on the other end of the phone.

Adrian Rich has called the loss of the daughter to the

mother, the mother to the daughter, the essential female tragedy. Katharine Marie Nolan Burke was the mother who never saw her eldest daughter become mayor of Chicago, the mother whom Jane believed sent the wonderful snow that devastated the incumbent mayor in the winter of 1979, the mother who dedicated her life to her children, especially to her four girls.

Katharine was the strong, controlling center of the Burke family; she was a power person, a model of strength, force, dominance, and control. Her eldest daughter, Jane, emulated and absorbed her mother's values and her mother's ways to a far greater degree than did her other three daughters.

A friend of Katharine Burke was once asked why none of the four Burke girls ever went into a convent. "Because marriage and children were much too important to them," she said. The home, the family, loyalty, sticking together—the Burkes. Their identity as a family was impressed on them, and they in turn made it clear to others that they were the Burkes. Relationships they held with others outside the family were always tenuous. Neighbors were either "in" or "out" with the Burkes. A Burke motto was, "I'll forgive but I'll never forget"; when their door closed, it stayed closed.

Katharine's mother, Margaret Jane Crane, married John Francis Nolan at Holy Name Cathedral in Chicago. They had five children. Shortly after the birth of their youngest, Margaret died. Margaret's two daughters and a number of her granddaughters were to suffer traumatic births and miscarriages—a shadow cast over the lives of three generations of women who valued and needed many children.

After Margaret Nolan died, Katharine was placed in St. Mary's Boarding School in Nauvoo, Illinois, the home of the Mormons. She was only twelve. A great-aunt, whom the children called Nana, came from Ireland to help John Nolan raise the other four. For all practical purposes, Katharine's family had crumbled. At a time when Katharine most needed a mother, her mother was gone. Years later, when a neighbor was considering sending her own teenage daughter to a boarding school, Katharine told her, "I would never put a daughter of mine in a boarding school"; she never did.

Katharine Nolan's years at the school were long and lonely. She took possession of a small window seat and there she would sit and read. The tragedy of her mother's death, the austerity and rigor of the school, and the many hours by herself with only her books threw Katharine more and more into herself. She became an intensely private person, as frequently happens when one lacks personal privacy—sleeping in rows, eating in rows, sitting in rows, praying in rows, all dressed alike, as individual as blackbirds sitting on a telephone wire.

Perched on her window seat, which she claimed at the beginning of each year, Katharine threw up a wall of privacy that never came down. The things she could not learn from her mother she tried to learn from books. She read and she remembered what she read.

According to Pablo Picasso, women are either princesses or doormats. Katharine determined she was not to be a doormat, nor would any of the daughters she was to have. She believed that the world was a cold, cruel place and to survive you had to control. She knew doormats did not survive; people wipe their feet on doormats.

To be a princess, Katharine determined that she would marry well, have a large family, and hold them close to her. She would tell them what she had read, what she had thought, and what the world was like. As they grew and had to face the world, she would always be close to them, for Katharine knew only too well how cold and cruel life was without a mother. She never forgot how she felt when she was alone, with herself as her only friend.

Katharine met Bill Burke one Saturday evening after a football game at Notre Dame. They both had other dates at the time. Both were living in Chicago, and he called her when they got back. They dated, fell in love, and were married on August 31, 1929. She was twenty-four; Bill was twenty-six.

The first years of their marriage were difficult. Money was scarce; there were three babies, Billy, Janie, and Edward; Bill was trying to establish himself professionally. He was smart, ambitious, not afraid to work hard, and quickly made his way up through Inland Steel—from clerk to vice-president. Sociologists would call the Burkes *upwardly mobile*; the son of an Irish blacksmith now a vice-president of Inland Steel. His wife moved with him.

Katharine was a small intense woman with as many contradictory sides to her character as her eldest daughter Jane has. Perhaps because she was not a beautiful woman she was terribly conscious of her appearance. Perhaps because she spent so many years dressed in the ugly dark uniform, dressed like a little nun, dressed like a doormat, she wore designer clothes—from Gucci or Saks—drove a Cadillac, and had her hair and nails done weekly. The respectable woman—the right clothes, the right schools for the girls, the right people and the right places. Bill provided the resources for her expensive taste and needs.

Yet, amid all the display of wealth and social status, it was to her children that Katharine's energies and love went. The world of Sauganash and Queen of All Saints Parish saw her as the wife of a prominent successful executive; yet if she could be coaxed to attend a neighborhood luncheon, she was the first to leave to get back to her home. She had dedicated herself totally to her children, to her girls. She was aloof, reserved, a private woman without many women friends. It was to her family that she gave herself, not to outsiders.

Katharine loved to tell a story about how Billy, her eldest, would come in from school, see the girls and Edward, hear the radio blasting and the dishwasher going, smell gingerbread in the oven—people, food, noise, commotion—and would ask, "Where's everyone?" Katharine was not in sight—and the rest didn't count.

It was with her oldest daughter, Jane, that Katharine established a special bond, the bond between a mother and her oldest daughter. Some of that consummate energy flowing between herself, as the eldest daughter, and her own mother, which was so cruelly and so abruptly halted at her mother's death, began to flow again after fourteen years with the birth of her own daughter Jane. Donna, Jane's younger sister, described Katharine and Janie as "two peas in a pod." Equals in their intensity, in their aloofness and privacy, in their perceptions, in their looks and manners, in their needs to be princesses, in their destiny for tragedy, and in their ability to survive and to land on their feet.

Katharine was intolerant of people who were soft, weak. Whiners and crybabies had no place in her home. She believed if you did wrong, you faced up to it; if trouble came, you bore it with strength. During the campaign a reporter asked Jane if she ever felt like crying and she said, "Many times. But my mother always taught us not to cry in public. If you must cry, you cry at home." In 1979 Jane said to Maggie Daly, "Someone once told me that you should cry into your pillow . . . never cry in public. The bad times are your times . . . not everyone's."

A friend of the family commented that Katharine "had marvelous eyes. She could control all of her kids with her eyes. Her displeasure was shown on her face." She disciplined with swiftness, with fairness, with affection, and she never let her children lose face. Katharine was exasperated, impatient, sometimes upset, but never mean.

Donna was eight when all the girls in the neighborhood had Toni dolls. The hair was made of a synthetic fiber that could be combed, washed, set, and fashioned in various styles. Donna told a friend, Marilyn, that she would fix her doll's hair if she would leave it overnight. Donna cut the doll's hair off to the scalp, handed the doll back to Marilyn the next day, and told her she had no idea what had happened. Donna threatened her sisters and the other girls in the neighborhood not to tell on her.

Katharine asked Donna what had happened and Donna denied any knowledge of the haircut. Katharine called Mary Kenny, a playmate of Donna's, from next door and asked her what had happened. Mary could not lie to Mrs. Burke. Katharine then took Donna upstairs to her bedroom and made her stand in front of a picture of the Sacred Heart of Jesus. "Now, Donna, look at Jesus and tell me what happened to Marilyn's Toni doll." Donna told her mother the truth. Katharine, with a mother's sense of justice, made Donna give Marilyn her own Toni doll in restitution.

A few weeks later Donna was playing with a friend when Jane pulled up in her sports car and said to Donna, "You'd better get in fast . . . you're in trouble now . . . just wait until you get home." They got home quickly and Jane slammed the door to impress her predicament on Donna. Donna walked into the dining room and found a new Toni doll on the table, larger than the one she had had to relinquish. Donna had learned her lesson and had made amends. It was time to forgive Donna. It was over, no more to be said.

When Donna was sixteen, with her first driver's license, she was stopped in her mother's car by the Wilmette Police for speeding on the Edens Expressway. The car was filled with girls and they had been joyriding around Loyola Academy, a boy's high school, which Donna was forbidden to do. Donna had to appear with her mother at the Wilmette Police Station. She was led to a back room where she had to look at graphic pictures of automobile accidents. They drove home in silence. Donna was planning to go to a party that evening and presumed that she would not be allowed to go. As they drove into the driveway, Katharine told her to get ready for the party. It was over. Donna had learned her lesson and there was no need to drag out her humiliation.

The Irish have an expression describing a parent who thinks extraordinarily well of his or her children: "She thinks all her geese are swans." Katharine did think her six geese were swans. Perhaps if she overestimated them, it did them no harm; while she encouraged them to be the most they could be, she was realistic about their talents and put no undue pressure on them to excel in areas for which they were intellectually or emotionally ill equipped. But she did put pressure on them to be all and everything they could be. She always told her children, "Whatever you want to do, you go after. Only one person will stop you from getting what you want and that is yourself."

Katharine had her own code of behavior that she instilled in her children and expectations to meet that code were high. Katharine taught her children not to disparage another's character by repeating the phrase: "He who pilfers from me my good name robs me of that which does not enrich him, but makes me poor indeed."

The image Katharine Burke showed to the public was very much an extension of her private person. She was not a warm, affectionate woman to her neighbors, yet she was aware of her responsibilities to them and of her obligations as a neighbor. Charity, to Katharine, was loving your neighbors as God loves them, but not necessarily feeling affection, just doing the kind and right thing. As Mary Gordon said in *Final Payments*, "Catholics . . . knew that Charity was a fire in the heart of God and never confused it with that Protestant invention, philanthropy."

Neighbor Mary Kenny, who grew up with the Burkes, described the relationship of her mother, Anne, with Katharine as stemming from "some ancient tradition" of neighborliness. It was never intimate, never taking out of the house what belonged inside, but they were always there, simply there, when they needed each other.

Anne's husband, Jim, had a heart attack when all three of their children were out of town. As the ambulance pulled into the drive, Katharine rushed into the kitchen with a large roll of cash, telling Anne, "Take what you need; you need cash at a time like this." Concerned that Anne was alone, Katharine called the hospital every half hour.

Shortly before midnight Jim's condition stabilized. Anne left Ravenswood Hospital at 12:30 A.M. Their doctor followed her home in his car. As she turned the corner onto their street, she saw all the Burkes sitting on their front steps. Katharine offered to have one of them stay with her that night so she wouldn't be alone. The ancient tradition of neighborliness—not intimate, simply there.

Katharine's life was comfortable but not without its barbs and hooks. She suffered miscarriages and came close to death when Jane was in high school. She depended greatly on her eldest daughter and shared with her many of the anxieties of this frightening experience, for she had no power or control over her own life. Dr. Janet Towne, a young obstetrician and gynecologist, cared for Katharine during this period. Katharine and Dr. Towne grew to be friends and Jane instinctively admired this woman who so expertly and so professionally saved her mother. Jane grew to emulate Dr. Towne and decided that she, too, wanted to be a doctor. Katharine completely supported her daughter's ambition and made arrangements for Jane to watch a surgical operation.

The one quality that truly endeared people to Katharine was her sense of humor—dry, ironic, subtle. Katharine was never mean, nor did she use her humor to hurt people. Perhaps through her humor Katharine was able to show the affection that she was unable to express physically. It would be difficult to imagine someone as well read and as fond of language as Katharine Burke lacking a keen sense of humor. Friends often came into the Burke home and sat around the coffee pot, which never ran dry, laughing with Katharine. It was her humor that protected her from bitterness when her own mother died and from disillusionment when she had miscarriages of her own.

Katharine's father, John Nolan, later moved in with her, Bill, and their children. She was good to her father. They loved going to the races and loved to gamble. Bill did not approve of the races because he thought they were in poor taste; Katharine enjoyed them immensely.

Katharine did think alcohol was in bad taste. She did not drink and neither did her children. She didn't even like to have alcohol in the house; it just was unnecessary and was too closely associated with a loss of control. If anything, a loss of control lacked taste. Her daughters agreed with her to the extent that Jane once lashed out at her father for enjoying himself too much at a friend's wedding. Bill was feeling no pain, playing the piano and leading the guests in song. It was getting late and

Katharine could not get Bill to leave. Jane could not get him to leave either. They finally got him home, and the next morning Jane went down to the recreation room where her father had his bar and threw out all the liquor. She was angry with her father for his behavior the previous night. He smiled at his wife, shrugged his shoulders, and went out into the garden. Katharine said nothing to her husband.

When Jane was director of Consumer Affairs, the Burkes held a tea in honor of Mayor Daley, who was seeking reelection. It was one of many big, expensive political parties they held in their backyard. Talk was that the Burkes were trying to buy a big City Hall position for Jane, but she already held a big City Hall position. Everyone on the block was invited to meet the mayor. At the end of the block lived a young woman, about Jane's age, who was retarded. When she came to the front door dressed in an inappropriate outfit, an Andy Frain usher turned her away, thinking that the woman would only embarrass the Burkes and would add nothing to the party. Katharine heard about the incident, ran down the street after the woman, and gently brought her back to their home. She was doing the right and kind thing and suffering no embarrassment—it was just plain Christian charity.

But Katharine Burke was also a power person. She had no illusions about its sources, its expression, its use. The Family was her main source of power. People who disliked her called her a snob, an elitist, ignoring those who could not help her or her family. A classmate of Edward's stated, "You could be introduced to her twenty million times, and unless you were loaded [with money], she'd never remember your name." Katharine could not be bothered wasting her time socially on those who didn't count. This was an area of her life that was not impinged on by the constraints of Charity, for Katharine had no fear of the ambiguities of power.

Michael Novak, in *Notre Dame* Magazine, viewed the rise of Catholics to positions of political power:

Those who relish the responsibilities of power, who do not fear its ambiguities, who can contain their own moralizing until they understand the stakes, may be more able to act . . . their heads are clearer, their speech is plainer, and their instincts are sharper.

Katharine Burke's head was clear, her speech was plain, and her instincts were very, very sharp. She evoked strong feelings: there were those who admired, respected her; there were those who detested, distrusted her. Many feared her; few understood her.

Katharine lived vicariously through her children. When Jane became interested in politics, Katharine would listen to her by the hour, fascinated at hearing about a world that was so foreign to her. Monsignor Dolan commented, "Katharine would be in seventh heaven if she could see Janie as the mayor now. How she would have enjoyed it!"

On January 18, 1974, Donna talked to Katharine at 10 P.M. Donna had been out of the hospital only four weeks after the birth of her son, Edward. Donna's husband, John, was out of town, and Donna was home alone with the three children. At 4:30 A.M., Jane called from the hospital. They had taken Katharine there after a severe heart attack. She was sixty-eight years old and they didn't know if she was going to live. The family gathered quickly. Edward never left her side. She appeared to stabilize when she suffered a second, more critical, attack.

As the doctors met with the family and spoke to them in obtuse medical terminology, Jane interrupted, "What you're saying is that she's dying and it's just a matter of hours." The doctors said she was right. She cried and then, characteristically, took charge and began to plan her mother's funeral. At 4:30 P.M., January 21, 1974, Katharine Burke died.

Edward drove to his office, closed the door, and wrote a eulogy to his mother. He delivered it from the altar of Queen of All Saints Church, January 24, 1974. As he spoke, his voice began to break. Jane cleared her voice loudly. Edward straightened up and finished it without tears.

God bless you, Kate—

You have touched each of our souls with an enthusiasm for life,
With a striking dry wit when we were despondent,
With your capable and assuring presence when we were sick,
With unyielding iron when we would falter,
With a refuge when we were afraid,
With pride when we accomplished,
With protection when we were destroyed,
With understanding when we were confused,
With humor and an encouraging shrug when we did not succeed,
With wisdom when we were in doubt,
With stinging truth when we were wrong,
With a flattening word when we were boastful,
With an appreciation of the honor and respect and love due "your father,"
With an understanding of good and evil, and children and family, and life and death and God,
With an abiding and sad and fearful loneliness now that we are without you and, finally, with a toughness to endure.
God bless you, Kate, and we, all of us, thank you.

4

The Grieving River of Memory

Jane once commented, "My father was not as strong as my mother. We used to call him 'the businessman.' He was soft and kindhearted."

Bill Burke was warm, affable, and affectionate. While the saying goes, "The father is the head of the house, the mother is the heart of the house," many, many Irish families do not fit that model. Friends, when they came to the house, received a welcoming kiss from Bill and a hug from him when they left. In family pictures, the children are on his lap, at his knees, touching, and loving.

At the *Delta Queen* dinner given on October 15, 1979, in honor of President Jimmy Carter, the mayor of Chicago, after introducing the judges and senators, amid the Secret Service men and white-jacketed waiters, asked, in a hushed voice, "Now, Daddy, will you stand for the people?" And Bill Burke, enfeebled by illness, stood with tears rolling down his face as ten thousand people cheered.

The Burkes were north-side Irish in every sense of the word. Bill Burke held a number of jobs as a young man. He had been in the police department for a short time and had worked as a court reporter with another smart, ambitious Irishman, Richard Daley. Although they went their separate ways, their paths and the paths of their children were to cross many times in the future.

On the north side of Chicago, many of the fathers who had joined the police or fire department saw to it that their sons did not. Their sons went to college, attended law or medical school, went into business. North-siders did not need the intense, exclusive identity with other Irish to survive; their Irishness was left in the top drawer and conveniently pulled out when necessary, but not worn every day. They thought, if it helps, use it, but they did not let it strangle or isolate them.

Many south-side Irish families remained in the police or fire department to the third and fourth generation. Daughters married friends of their brothers in the department, and their sons grew up eager to join the department.

To begin to understand the nature of the influences that shaped Jane Burke Byrne, it is necessary to understand the subtle but significant cultural and social differences between the north-side Irish and those Irish who lived on the south and west sides of the city. There were not as many Irish on the north side; consequently, they never developed the clannishness, the social intensity, the identity with other Irish that the south- and west-side Irish did. The north-side Irish were more urbane, cosmopolitan, less vocal in their identity with the Auld Sod.

On the Phil Donahue Show, Jane stated, "I am not Irish Catholic." Obviously, she did not mean that she was not Irish and that she was not Catholic, but in effect was saying, "Don't judge me that way. I am primarily myself. My ethnicity is my own business. Don't generalize about my people and don't extend those generalizations to me."

However, if she were south-side Irish, she would have sat and beamed because Phil Donahue had acknowledged her ethnicity. However, if the Burkes had been south-side Irish, there would be less likelihood that Jane would be mayor today; what was expected of a "girl," a good Irish Catholic girl, living on the south side was well articulated and did not include becoming mayor. She would have felt, to a far greater degree, social pressures to conform to a more traditional woman's role.

The north-side Irish were uncomfortable with the chest pounding, shillelagh swinging, the jigs and reels of the south-side Irish. Her uneasiness with all the cultural trappings was blatant during the 1980 St. Patrick's Day Parade. Chicagoans were accustomed to Mayor Daley, in a dark suit and bright green bowler hat, surrounded by politicians of every racial and ethnic mix. "On St. Patrick's Day, everybody's Irish!" he would shout.

In 1980 Chicagoans heaped abuse on Jane Byrne, marching in a full-length fur coat, topped off by a Kelly green silk peak cap. She began the parade with Ted Kennedy, her choice for the Democratic candidate for President. The crowd grew hostile as it shouted, "Where's Mary Jo?" at Kennedy. The mayor and the senator put a distance between each other as they marched down State Street, hoping to dissipate some of the anger of the crowd. The mayor and the senator, waving awkwardly and smiling nervously, were embarrassed, uncomfortable, and not unmindful of the possibility of violence. Jane's father, the son of Irish immigrants, had to be escorted home by her bodyguards. St. Patrick's Day, 1980, was a fiasco. The lion tamer had momentarily forgotten what she was: the lions were ready to attack. Being a professional Irish woman was just not her "thing"; the crowd knew it and resented her attempts to fill the shoes of Richard Daley.

That she does not care for a public display of her ethnicity does not mean Jane Burke Byrne is any less Irish than those who do. Her ambivalence about being Irish is very characteristic of many, many Irish. The very word Irish conjures up conflicting feelings of pride and embarrassment, of aggressiveness and submission. Chesterton wrote in the *Ballad of the White Horse*:

> The great Gaels of Ireland
> Are the men that God made mad
> For all their wars are merry
> And all their songs are sad.

Pete Hamill, in the *Dayton Daily News*, commented on the Irish in America: " . . . the myth of the melting pot was apparently true. The Irish appear to have melted away . . . [yet] why does the Irish past come flooding back to so many people, like a dark grieving river of memory and history and resentment?"

The dark, grieving river of memory is not far from Jane Byrne, for in the late 1800s Bill Burke's mother and father, Jane's grandparents, made their way from Castlebar, County Mayo, to Chicago. Bill's mother, Margaret Burke (a Burke before and after her marriage), initially went to St. Louis with her brothers and sisters. Her brother, Pat, ran unsuccessfully for mayor of St. Louis in November 1944, the only Democrat to lose in the city when Franklin Roosevelt was elected President for his third term. Pat had been a deputy sheriff and a business agent for the Milk Wagon Drivers and Inside Dairy Workers Union in St. Louis. Aloys P. Kaufmann, former mayor of St. Louis who defeated him, stated, "Patty Burke was an honorable man from everything I know . . . losing to me didn't kill him." Margaret Burke's other brother, Jim, was active in Democratic party politics and served as Justice of the Peace in St. Louis.

Margaret Burke and her sisters, Cecilia and Nora, came to Chicago from St. Louis. Cecilia Burke, Jane's great-aunt, became executive secretary to William E. Lee, head of the Chicago Federation of Labor. Margaret and her sisters first found work as hotel maids in Chicago.

Chicago hotels—the places where the rich and powerful would meet and dine and show themselves off to the rest of the world; where the Irish would make their beds, iron their clothes, wash their dishes, empty their garbage, polish their coppers and brass. In *Working Girls*, Carl Sandburg saw them as:

> going to work . . . with little brick-shaped lunches wrapped in newspaper under their arms . . . with a peach bloom of young· years on them and laughter of red lips and memories in their eyes . . . and the feet of these move slower and they have wisdom where the others have beauty.

Many years later Margaret Burke's granddaughter, Jane Burke Byrne, would preside over dinners and luncheons and banquets as the mayor of Chicago in the same hotels that her grandmother had cleaned and scrubbed. As she dined, entertained, and was entertained in these great hotels, Jane would not forget the "dark grieving river of memory and history and resentment."

Michael Burke was born in a village in Mayo about twenty miles away from where Margaret was born. There he learned the trade of a blacksmith—the fires, the heat, the molding of iron, the heavy hammers, the pounding, pounding, pounding. The fire, the iron, and the pounding taught Michael secrets about the world, about himself, and about Ireland and America that he would teach his sons—secrets they would not have to learn the hard way, as he did.

Margaret Burke and Michael Burke, although born only twenty miles apart, had to come to Chicago to meet and marry. In 1899, a daughter, Ethyl, was born. Edward and Margaret May followed; neither lived to see their second birthday. Then William Patrick and another son, whom they called Edward after the son they had lost. The last child was named Joseph.

They lived on the north side of Chicago, on Rockwell Street, in St. Sylvester's Parish. They were a close, happy family and would spend evenings around the piano singing of "happy wars and sad love songs." Whether the Burkes had little or whether the Burkes had much, they sang in their rich Irish tenor voices. The tradition of the piano on Rockwell Street continued for many years. When Ed and Joe brought home their priest friends to see Margaret and Michael, the first thing they did, after a round of drinks, was head for the piano.

Ed and Joe decided to enter the priesthood. At a time when the Irish were positioned in the bottom half of American society, there was no swifter, no bolder, no smoother way up than through the priesthood. The priesthood meant power, prestige, authority, dignity—a way out of the social and mental bogs the Irish seemed destined to inhabit forever.

No higher creature walked the earth than the priest. To have two boys called to the priesthood was like winning the daily double. And the mother of a priest became a special creature of her own. There was something sacred; an aura of holiness and Sacraments surrounded women who had given birth to one of God's holy priests.

A cult developed around a priest's mother such as Margaret Burke. She was treated with deference and with respect by the nuns and laypeople. She never again in public referred to her sons except by their proper titles, Father Ed and Father Joe. In her own way, her vocation was more precious, more womanly, and more like the Holy Mother of God herself than the vocations of all the nuns in the world.

Ed Burke was no run-of-the-mill seminarian. He was brighter than most. He was big, handsome, had a deep Irish tenor voice, and knew how to handle himself. A certain power, authority, assuredness radiated from him; that particular combination of intelligence, drive, and innate political instincts characteristic of Ed Burke would later characterize his niece, Janie, his brother Bill's oldest daughter. In his early twenties, while his classmates were struggling with philosophy, scripture, and the fine points of moral theology, Ed Burke sailed through his studies, eager to get on with the business of being a priest.

The Jesuits who taught at Mundelein Seminary took notice of Ed and made sure Cardinal Mundelein also took notice. Ed was ordained ahead of his class of 1932. This was an honor, a way of setting apart those few whom the cardinal liked. It was part of the cardinal's system of rewards, marking Ed for greater things.

After a few months' assignment at St. Edward's Church in Chicago, Cardinal Mundelein sent Ed to Rome; he saw in this bright young man all the qualities of a great man of the Church like himself. Parish life was too narrow, too small for the talents of an Ed Burke.

In 1932 Ed went to Rome with another classmate who was to study the history, the antiquity, and the parchments and remnants of the early Church. Ed went to study Canon Law. After their first year, Ed's classmate had learned of the catacombs and early martyrs, of Aramaic and Sanskrit, and of Saints Polycarp,

Athanasius, and Jerome. But Ed had learned where all the real bodies were buried; he had learned where the buttons and levers were and who pushed them and how to get them to push them. He knew that the important things were not found in books. What he learned between classes about Vatican life was to serve him well for the next thirty years. One of his classmates in Rome was a young ambitious priest from St. Louis, John Patrick Cody. They would meet again. After three years in Rome, Ed received a doctorate in Canon Law and was ready to return to Chicago.

With loud, eerie blasts, the steamer slipped out of Le Havre. The young priest loosened his high starched collar, planted a heavy black shoe on the bottom rail, and watched France disappear in the wake of the ship. The year was 1935.

He was glad to get out of Europe and back home again. Europe was in trouble. Germany was rumbling with news of a super race and Adolf Hitler. Cardinal Mundelein had a name for him—"the Austrian paperhanger"—Hitler, trying to fill the world with blue-eyed, thin-lipped blonds. Who the hell did the Germans think they were? His thick Irish neck reddened as he thought of their arrogance. He tugged at his collar and walked slowly on the narrow gray deck to the starboard side of the ship.

The steamer made its way out of the channel, past Dorset, Devon, and Cornwall and onto the open seas. The winds picked up. He turned his black collar up around his neck and strained against the wind to look north, toward Cobh in Cork Harbor.

Five days later the steamer pulled into New York Harbor. He could see the New York skyline and the Statue of Liberty welcoming him home—the huddled masses yearning to breathe free. The hell with the huddled masses—the Burkes were on their way up, he thought to himself. They had been huddling long enough; it was time to stand up and be counted. He was anxious to see Joe, who was ordained in 1934, and Bill, who by now had three kids—Billy, Janie, and Edward—and, of course, the folks.

As fate would have it, a dancer committed suicide by jumping off a New York building soon after Ed disembarked. Ed, who was walking by, gave her the Last Rites and covered her with his suit coat. A New York paper carried the headline the following day: "Priest Brings Peace to Troubled Dancer's Soul." Ed Burke, at the right place, at the right time.

Cardinal Mundelein was waiting for Ed to return home. Ed was assigned to the chancery office in 1935. He became vice-chancellor in 1938, a year before Cardinal Mundelein died; and in 1943, at the age of thirty-six, he was appointed chancellor. By this time, Cardinal Stritch had taken over and was relieved to find the chancery in such good hands.

The chancellor is the executive officer of the archdiocese, in charge of the day-to-day operations. John Gregory Dunne describes the role of a chancellor in his novel, *True Confessions*:

> He was a combination lightning rod, hatchet man, and accountant. Someone to fend off the pastors and take the heat off the Cardinal. Young enough not to be infected with old ideas about how to run a parish or to have formed friendships that could not be broken. If necessary. Tough enough to talk decimal points with a Protestant banker or lean on a contractor. If necessary. In other words, a man to do the dirty work . . . [yet] one false move and you became an expensive luxury.

There were two Catholic Churches in America at this time: the Church in Chicago and the Church in the rest of the country. The Catholic Church in Chicago did not exist in a political vacuum; it was made up of the same Chicago people, from the same backgrounds, who shared the same biases and who knew how to make things work. Take a good ward committeeman, put a Roman collar on him, and he could run the parish; give the pastor a shirt and tie and he could deliver the votes. Take a monsignor from the chancery and he could run Streets and Sanitation; the man who ran the sewers could keep the cardinal happy. If Chicago was the "City that Works," the Catholic Church in Chicago was the Church that worked. And it worked, in large part, because of the energy, skill, and political instincts of Ed Burke.

The scholarly Monsignor John Tracy Ellis attempted to analyze the reasons the Church in Chicago worked as it did. He stated that since 1924 the cardinals "allowed things to happen among their clergy and laity while they have maintained a vigilant, masterly inactivity." Cardinals Mundelein, Stritch, and Meyer sat back reflectively, staying out of the way, and events did begin to happen in Chicago that were to affect the course of the Church deeply in this country.

Monsignor George A. Kelly, in *The Battle for the American Church*, stated that there were "certain factors uniquely packaged in the Chicago environs: charismatic and overpowering energy in the priestly leadership; educated and classy laity waiting to be motivated for a cause; a good cause at the right time; a freewheeling, independent style of behavior typical of the Windy City itself; and relatively permissive bishops."

Out of these came many movements and programs that brought the laity into the direct work of the Church. But these programs did not happen because Chicago had a messiah complex or because the cardinal was looking the other way. Monsignor Jack Egan commented, "Everything that developed in Chicago that was good had Ed Burke's fingerprints on it." Father Bill Quinn, while acknowledging that Cardinal Stritch was "extremely permissive and very trusting of other people," stated that "he was also very shrewd. He had a very long view of the Church—nothing was going to solve all of the problems and nothing was going to ruin it either."

To look at the Church in Chicago during those years is to take off the back of an old gold watch and look with amazement at the many little dials and wheels and disks whirling and spinning in their own little orbits, while the big hand keeps going around. Ed Burke and a man very different in temperament, in outlook, and in personality, Monsignor George Casey, kept things running. Casey and Burke did not care for each other. There was the Burke camp and the Casey camp—the balance of power, which Father Roger Coughlin views as "fundamental to the growth of the diocese and the health of its organization. One man would have been afraid to do what the division of power allowed to happen."

George Casey was in charge of finances. He was quiet, reflective, and conservative, both politically and personally. Ed Burke took care of the organizational end: policies, personnel, and programs. Ed was flamboyant, decisive, a man with style and flair. His mind was quick, fluid, able to grasp a situation immediately and act decisively. Indecision was tantamount to mortal sin.

Ed Burke gained the reputation as a liberal because of the exciting programs that had his fingerprints on them. Ed Burke was not a liberal; he was a pragmatist. Forty years later his niece, Jane Burke Byrne, would also be called a liberal, a reformer. She was neither; like her uncle, she was a pragmatist. If it would work, he went with it. He had an intuitive sense of who was a winner and who was a loser. If he liked you, the way you looked, if you were the right nationality and could be counted on to be loyal to him, you were in. And he would go to the ends of the earth, even to the cardinal, for you.

In the winter of 1954 a young priest, Father Jack Egan, who had been working on the Cana Conferences, took an interest in the Puerto Ricans living in the Woodlawn area. After visiting a home with twenty people and no heat, he began the Woodlawn Latin-American Committee, which soon found itself in debt for $10,000. On a cold Saturday morning Jack called Ed Burke, who said, "Get right down here."

When he arrived at Ed Burke's office Ed said, "Let's go up and see the cardinal." They knocked on the cardinal's door and found him typing at his desk, suspenders down around his pants. Ed said, "Father Egan was in to see me about the Puerto Ricans. Jack, tell the cardinal about it."

Jack Egan went back to Woodlawn with $5,000 and a promise of more money if things began to move. Jack was in. He was loyal. He could be trusted. He didn't go to Casey.

Ed Burke was highly complex with many contradictory qualities: hard and soft, trusting and suspicious, prayerful and proud, generous yet calculating. A cameraman found that he had forgotten to load his camera after a photo session with a group of active laypeople. Ed, the group's moderator, sensing his embarrassment, kidded the group and got them to pose again. The photographer did not lose face.

During the Casey-Burke years the chancery has been called a honeycomb of intrigue. The stakes were high—power. The Irish in Chicago were drawn to power as sure as the needle on a compass points north. Power in the Church—pure, unadulterated power, pure raw power, untainted by money or sex. Ed Burke used people, but it was fair play: he used people, was used by them, and everyone knew the rules.

A priest commented, "Life was good in those days. Those guys had their bottoms in butter." Ed Burke lived high. He loved the good life—good food, vacations, parties, rich and influential friends. Life was for the living. He was not a monk with a vow of poverty—a lot of money passed through his hands. There were "drop days" at the chancery, when the pastors came to pay their respects to the monsignors and leave them a "little something." Ed spent money lavishly, but what he took in with his right hand went out with his left. He spent money on himself, and he was more than generous to many. Many inner-city convents could not have existed without his help. He took care of priests who needed special attention. Many a family was grateful to Ed Burke for their rent or their gas bill money.

If Ed Burke had a weakness in his pursuit and exercise of power, it was his soft heart, which his closest friends call his undoing. One cold dull January morning, an assistant to Father Jack Egan, Katie Murphy, was tired and depressed. Ed Burke, walking through her office, noticed her despondency and asked her what was wrong. She said she was just tired and had been working too long. He reached into his coat pocket and handed her a round-trip ticket to Florida and reservations at a Miami Beach hotel. He told her to clear her desk, go home and pack, since he could not use the tickets.

He picked up the entire bill for Katie's holiday and called her boss, Father Egan, to tell him not to give her any trouble. When Katie returned after two weeks in the sun, she went in to thank Monsignor Burke. He did not want to embarrass

Katie, for he knew how she felt about accepting the tickets. As she walked into his office, he said, "Thanks for going Katie; you made me feel now that I should go because you look so rested and relaxed."

Ed Burke never became a bishop. It is said that Cardinal Spellman wanted Ed to go to New York but Ed didn't want to leave Chicago. It is said that his name was to go to Rome but Cardinal Stritch didn't want to lose him. It is also said that Ed did not become a bishop because Stritch was not a bishop-maker, except when Joliet became a separate diocese. A priest friend, explaining why Ed never became a bishop, said that he had no bishop to sponsor him. He recalled the Gospel story of the cripple lying beside the pool of healing water. When asked by Jesus why he had been lying there for so many years and had never gone in, he said, "I have no one to put me in, Lord." No one made Ed Burke a bishop. (A Chicago priest remarked, "If Ed had been the bishop, you couldn't take your eyes off the baton. You couldn't look at your toes or miss a beat. You'd be out, out if you missed a single beat.")

In the late '50s financial matters in the archdiocese ran amok. There were stories of gross mismanagement, laymen abscond-ing with vast sums of money, money disappearing in high places. Cardinal Stritch was called to Rome and made Pro-prefect for the Congregation of the Faith, the Vatican's way of kicking him upstairs. Cardinal Stritch never filled the position, for he died before he got to Rome. On November 16, 1959, Albert Meyer, a serious, reflective scholar, became cardinal of Chicago. He did not care for administration, nor for the flamboyant Irish style of Ed Burke. Casey was more in keeping with his tastes. And Ed Burke, despite all his wheeling and dealing, was an extraordinarily sensitive man. Meyer did not give compliments ; Ed took this as disapproval.

One morning, Albert Cardinal Meyer rang Monsignor Burke and asked him to come up to his office. As Ed walked in, the cardinal stated, "I have several good parishes which I'm sure you'd like; but if you don't want any of them, you can stay around here." He was out. It is said that Meyer had to bring in five to do the work of Ed Burke.

Ed Burke—Right Reverend Monsignor Edward M. Burke, chancellor of the archdiocese of Chicago, domestic prelate since 1946, protonotary apostolic since 1957, chairman of the cardinal's Committee for the Spanish-Speaking, chairman of the Archdiocesan Commission on Sacred Music, chief justice in the Archdiocesan Marriage Court—was out.

In 1961 he became pastor of St. Bartholomew, a white, Irish, Italian, German, Polish, working-class parish on the north side of Chicago. Ed Burke was only fifty-four when he went to St. Bartholomew and he was not about to roll over and play dead. The young priests at St. Barts were excited about Monsignor Burke becoming their pastor—his reputation as a liberal, as an innovator, was legend. Pope John XXIII was throwing open the windows in the Church; John Kennedy was in the White House. Times were good.

In 1965 Albert Cardinal Meyer died of a brain tumor after returning from the last session of the Vatican Council. Three months later John Patrick Cardinal Cody was appointed head of the Church in Chicago. It was August 1965. One of his first acts was to call his old classmate from Rome. He said to Monsignor Burke, "Ed, I'm glad you're in the diocese. We will be able to work together at last." Ed called Father Jack Egan immediately. He was excited about Cody and felt that he might be in again. "It's a new day in Chicago!" It was a new day in Chicago, but in a way no one could have predicted.

Confrontations with the cardinal, from the right and from the left, became the norm. Monsignor George Kelly states that Cody's "personality and leadership style may have brought matters to a head . . . [but] the seeds of confrontation were already planted," and the cruel irony is that John Patrick Cody came to Chicago from New Orleans with the reputation of an integrationist.

Prior to that he had been bishop of Kansas City, where he had built many Catholic schools; in Chicago, he closed schools, especially those in the inner city that were not financially viable.

In 1954, the Supreme Court said that separate was not equal. Three years later Eisenhower sent troops to a high school in

Little Rock, Arkansas. Rosa Parks refused to move to the back of a bus; buses were boycotted in Montgomery, Alabama. The civil rights movement had taken off. Within a short time, there would not be a person or an institution in this country left untouched by the force of the civil rights movement. And in Chicago, the home of the Catholic Interracial Council, the archdiocesan pot was boiling.

When Benjamin Willis an anti-integrationist was rehired as superintendent of the Chicago public schools, twenty thousand people, led by Martin Luther King, marched on City Hall.

In response to pressures from integrationists, Monsignor William McNanus, superintendent of Catholic schools in the archdiocese of Chicago, established a program of voluntary busing called Operation Hospitality. An inner-city parish was matched with a suburban parish. Black students were bused to the white school, and a white suburban family was assigned to look after a black child during the time he was in their neighborhood. If the school was close, he went there for lunch; if he became sick at school, the family cared for him.

Operation Hospitality spelled integration. Pure, simple integration. Integration—the luxury of the suburbanites who knew that blacks could never afford to move into their suburbs. Integration—the very word meant a $20,000 drop in the property value of a little Chicago bungalow and the demise of the old neighborhood and the old parish. Integration was for those who lived in the city—ethnics, white ethnics, white Catholic ethnics, like the white Catholic ethnics who lived in St. Bartholomew Parish.

On January 15, 1967, a famous letter was distributed at Sunday Mass at St. Bartholomew. In his typical nonideological fashion, Ed Burke went along with his people. He had listened to their fears and felt their anxieties long enough. He felt it was time to speak:

> Anyone with enough temerity to challenge integration was accused of being unchristian. I am numbered in that category.

My reasons for opposing integration are based on the conviction that the proponents of civil rights possess a superficial viewpoint of what integration really is.

If one does not buy this physical proximity, he is not Christian. I, however, profess to be a Christian, love my neighbor, and would do anything to help him out because I see Christ in him.

When we fight for the rights of the Negro we cannot overlook the rights of the white person. He has been forced to support, unaided, himself and his family. If he owns property, he purchased it by the sweat of his brow and is a true Christian when he asks that his possessions be not disturbed.

The Negro has God-given rights equal to the rights of the white. He has a God-given right to a living wage and a proper place to live. He has obligations equal to the obligations of the white. He must obey the laws of the area in which he lives. He must have a respect for the upkeep of property. He, too, must have a respect for his neighbor.

[Regarding Puerto Ricans]: When these poor people realized we were going to help them, they were so grateful they would do anything for us.

[As for Negroes:] They will never make progress until they learn to accept obligations. I'll help them in any way that does not damage the rights of the whites.

I pledged, under oath, to safeguard the well-being of those committed to my care, both spiritually and materially. That pledge I intend to keep—with God's help—even if it means resigning as pastor.

This was to be the final undoing of Ed Burke. Cody, already under fire, pulled out his big guns to shoot Ed Burke down. Monsignor Daniel M. Cantwell, head of the Catholic Interracial Council, refuted Burke's remarks:

[Monsignor Burke's remarks would serve to] entrench a very important area—the northwest side—in its white ghetto mentality.

Over the years, one of the great difficulties in making progress has been the people who wanted arguments to bolster their prejudices—especially moral arguments—and they have found it convenient to quote a clergyman, especially a prominent one.

No one came to Ed Burke's defense. He was as out as out could be. Even many of his parishioners turned their backs on their "racist" pastor. His liberal friends kicked him in the teeth.

Times had changed. Vatican II had changed all the rules. Ed Burke told his assistants that they would turn the altar around over his dead body. The old Church was his Church. His assistants didn't like him. They didn't understand his rules. He wanted a monologue; they wanted a dialogue. He wanted to call the shots; they wanted collective decision-making. A young priest stated it was not until he was assigned to another parish that he discovered the rules of loyalty and honor that Ed played by. If a parishioner or another pastor went to Ed about one of his priests, Ed would not deal with them. He was loyal to his priests. He did not attack them and would not allow others to do so. In return he expected utter loyalty from them.

As Ed aged, his health deteriorated. In 1948, Ed was on his way to a hunting lodge in Canada with two priest friends when a heavy fog set in. The pilot, who was not licensed to fly with instruments, brought the plane down in a rocky Canadian lake. The three priests thought they were going to die and gave each other absolution, opened a can of peaches and a bottle of Scotch, and prepared for the worst. They were rescued by a Canadian forest ranger.

Ed's right leg was never right after the crash. The ankle had broken in three parts. He was forced to have surgery to strip the veins and had to wear an elastic stocking, but the bones still pressed against the veins and caused circulation problems. Later, while in Germany with his niece Carol, he tore all the ligaments, aggravating the old injury. Phlebitis developed. He was in and out of the hospital with water retention.

Ed had other serious physical problems. His liver did not function properly. He developed a heart murmur. He had brain surgery for a blood clot. The phlebitis flared up again and again. He had cataract surgery.

Ed's latter days were spent in pain and disillusionment. The Church of 1975 was not his Church. The people—all the people he had ever gone to bat for—the priests with big ideas, parishioners who were afraid of losing their homes, people who had pretended to be friends but had only wanted his power—were no longer around. His friends at the chancery seldom called. They said they were busy; he said they didn't need him.

He hated the new parish committees and nuns who ran around like college girls. He hated how they were changing the Sacraments, the Mass, and the beautiful old prayers that had been good enough for Catholics for two thousand years. He hated all those damn Protestant songs they were bringing in.

Ed Burke, despite all his pain and all his disillusions, was not a broken man. He was still digging into his pockets for money for a family who couldn't make their gas payments, for some inner-city nuns who couldn't make ends meet, or for a priest who needed to get away.

Always religious, Ed's spirituality deepened. His parishioners would see him walking in the alley behind the church with his rosary. He took the early Mass, arriving an hour before to begin his meditation. Some of the altar boys were frightened of him because of the stories they had heard about how important he had been. They were also frightened because he moved so slowly around the altar—when he genuflected he had to struggle to get up and they didn't know whether they should help him or not.

In January 1975 the phlebitis returned. Gangrene set into the bad leg. His body had been through too much to undergo surgery again; there was nothing to do but wait. Ed, the big old warrior, knew when he was licked. With the same style and intelligence that had characterized his whole life, Ed Burke recognized that his time was running out; that, although he had never become Bishop Edward M. Burke, what was meant to be for him had been; and that there was no sense in questioning it. He knew that to sit and stare at that grieving river of history and memories was only a waste of time.

Ed Burke died on February 5, 1975, at Resurrection Hospital. That evening his body was brought to St. Bartholomew's Church. Three priests came to pay their respects and stood, speaking loudly at the foot of the casket. A niece of Ed's, kneeling in the front pew, heard one priest say that Cody would be there the next morning for Mass—he wanted to be sure Ed was dead. Rumor had it that Ed had put out $10,000 for Cody's neck.

Ed Burke was not about to go out without a bang. A solemn Requiem High Mass was held on February 8, 1975. The church was packed—family, priests, friends, parishioners. The big and important—the small and insignificant. All those whom Ed had touched during his life.

Katharine Burke, Ed's sister-in-law, had died the previous year. Katharine and Ed were never close. As the years passed, the antagonism between these two strong-willed person increased. Before the funeral, Katharine's sister, Mary, filed into one of the front pews reserved for the family. Before Father Joe Burke began the Mass, she was stricken with a heart attack and died before an ambulance arrived. Her only daughter had not yet arrived at the church. Nieces and nephews drove up, saw all the commotion, and thought it was just part of the cardinal's entourage.

As the Mass began, a deranged woman leaped over the communion rail and charged the cardinal. It appeared that she was attacking him with a knife. None of the priests moved to protect the cardinal. The woman was restrained by the police. No knife was found.

Father John Merron, a friend, delivered Ed's eulogy. He said that Ed was a gambler—he loved pitting himself against the horses, against the odds. Ed never bet to place; Ed never bet to show; Ed Burke always bet to win.

In Ed Burke's own way, by his own rules, he did not come in second or third. He came in first: he was true to himself, to his church, to the traditions and values of his people, to that grieving river of memory that never for one moment let him forget who he was.

5

A Sacred Heart Education

After graduating from St. Scholastica in 1951, Jane went to St. Mary-of-the-Woods in Terre Haute, Indiana, for her freshman year of college. Wanting to be closer to her family and bored with the sleepy hills of Indiana, she left Terre Haute after one year and enrolled in Barat College of the Sacred Heart in Lake Forest, Illinois.

On the surface Barat College was an anomaly—a Roman Catholic institution of higher education situated in the midst of Chicago's Protestant elite. Lake Foresters, returning home from Chicago on the old Norshore line, probably chuckled to themselves as the train halted and the conductor called out Barat's own little station a half mile before the Lake Forest stop: "Winnetka, Glencoe, Braeside, Ravinia, Highland Park, Fort Sheridan, Sacred Heart, Lake Forest."

Lake Forest lies thirty-three miles and four generations to the north of Chicago's Loop. It was founded in 1861 before the state of Illinois chartered towns and villages. At that time a group of Presbyterian elders from Chicago purchased three square miles of lakefront property and established an academy to ensure the religious education of their children. (This is now the site of Lake Forest College.) As leaders of the young Chicago business community, they began buying up the lakefront property and building summer homes among the thick, winding ravines and graceful slopes of the Lake Michigan shoreline.

Chicago was hog butchering to the world, and the Armours and Dicks and Swifts and McCormicks and Farwells and Ryersons and Donnelleys were tastefully ensconcing themselves in baronial estates far from the hot crowded city. These homes were designed to be virtually invisible for most of the year; when the oaks and elms shed their protecting leaves, brick walls and iron and stone gates inhibited the curious.

Benjamin Disraeli observed that increased means and increased leisure were the two civilizers of man. By his standards Lake Forest is truly a most civilized place. Perhaps more than being a town or village circumscribed by specific geographic and legal boundaries, Lake Forest is a state of mind, an orientation to life that bespeaks elegance, good taste, social responsibility, good judgment, stability, security, and wealth. Lake Forest is a belief that certain values, like Brooks Brothers suits, never change.

Locating Barat College in Lake Forest was as much a political decision as a decision dictated by aesthetics or economics. The same political principle may be applied to what has become known as "busing," or that particular process of social engineering by which a minority group is exposed to the next rung on the economic ladder by geographic movement for educational purposes. At the time Barat was founded in Lake Forest in 1904 and even as late as the 1950s, when Jane Burke attended Barat, Catholics were a minority group, denied full status in American society. The police department, the unions, and the Church were appropriate places for Catholics; for Irish Catholics, the boardrooms, the prestigious law firms, the tenured faculty positions at first-rate universities were, for the most part, out of bounds.

However, Catholics were on their way up. Thus it was essential that daughters of the emerging Catholic power elite—

the lawyers, judges, industrialists, and executives—receive an elite education in the best of surroundings. Jane Burke's father was one of the upwardly mobile Irish Catholics. The son of an Irish blacksmith, Bill Burke was a clerk at Inland Steel when Jane was born; shortly thereafter, he became a vice-president. He left Inland Steel to form the Gordon-Burke Steel Company in 1949 and served as national president of the Steel Warehousemen Association until after Jane finished college. There was no better, more appropriate place for the Burke girls than Barat. Barat would teach them things they must know, do, see, and learn to take their proper place in society.

Although most of the students were boarders, Jane was a day-hop, daily driving north from Sauganash, up the Edens Expressway to Lake Forest and the elegant Gothic red brick building that sits proudly above the tree line on twenty-nine acres of trees, ravines, and meadows.

Each day Jane drove up the sloped drive, circling Barat's front lawn, where a massive iron statue of the Sacred Heart of Jesus stood, facing the main entrance, a traditional French, white-pillared *porte cochere*. To attend her classes, Jane and the other Barat girls walked through the entranceway, up the gray stone steps, through the arched oak doors, up the inner terrazzo steps and into the dark walnut-panneled foyer, with oversized eighteenth-century walnut and brass chests, brocade chairs, and dark, rich oil paintings.

Barat's resemblance to a nineteenth-century French estate poised between the trees and ravines of Amiens rather than to a contemporary midwestern college amid the trees and ravines of Lake Forest is no mistake. The Sacred Heart order that founded Barat College in Lake Forest in 1904 has its roots and traditions in nineteenth-century France. The founder of the order, Madeleine Sophie Barat, was born in Joigny, Burgundy, to a family of farmers in 1779. Her brother, a Jesuit priest, exposed her to the classical and the romance languages—Greek, Latin, Spanish, Italian—and to the worlds of history, philosophy, and theology. He encouraged her to start an order to educate upper-class women, as the Jesuits were educating upper-class men.

Madeleine Sophie intuitively saw the power that would come

to women with an education, a strong, sophisticated Catholic
education that was "not only truth for the intellect, but love
for the will; not only information for the mind, but formation
for the character." A smart politician as well as an aggressive
educator, Madeleine Sophie did not allow her order to be too
closely associated with the Jesuits so they would not be overshadowed by their big brothers in the way the Dominican and
Franciscan nuns had been overshadowed by the Dominican and
Franciscan priests. This fiercely independent spirit was to characterize her nuns a hundred years later; when Cardinal Mundelein asked the Religious of the Sacred Heart to staff a new
college for women on the north side of Chicago, they refused.
They did not want to be under his control; another community
of nuns went to Mundelein College.

Madeleine Sophie, the politician, knew she and her nuns must
keep a low profile, for what she purported to do was going to
make waves and rock boats, since women, even wealthy
women, were not considered proper recipients of education. To
avoid attracting attention, her nuns dressed as the women of
her native Burgundy: a pleated white cap tied under the chin, a
short cape, and several layers of heavy black skirts. She added a
long black veil to pull over the face, a silver cross hanging
around the neck, and a long black rosary hanging from the belt.
Christine de Rivoyre, a French novelist, wrote that the sisters
resembled "queens of spades from the front and great black
birds from the back." Low profile in nineteenth-century Burgundy became high visibility in twentieth-century America, but
their anachronistic dress served well to remind them and their
students of their religious origins in France and of the French
culture that permeated their lives.

De Rivoyre wrote that her Sacred Heart education was
marked by "poetry, spirituality, and family feeling." She used
the term *poetry* to mean *visual delights*, or what Americans call
beauty and peace: "The nuns of the Sacred Heart hold to the
principle that ugliness is noxious to the spirit and that a child
need not be destructive in order to be happy."

The girls who attended Barat walked and studied in this

atmosphere of poetry. Daily the girls walked down the high, airy corridors on freshly waxed floors where the richly framed reproductions of great masterpieces hung on the paneled walls. Daily they ascended the wide oak staircase that curved beneath the muted blue stained-glass windows inscribed in English with the litany of the Blessed Virgin Mary. Daily they could attend Mass in a long dark chapel with varnished oak choir stalls and gaze at fourteen Munich stained-glass windows and fourteen milk-glass and brass lamps suspended from the high ceiling. The girls knelt before a white Carrara marble altar and communion rail, the gold leaf dome of the altar shining down on them, painted with gold leaf made from jewelry donated by alumnae.

They studied in a rich library on long oak tables lighted by stationary brass lamps. They sat on red leather chairs backed with large brass knobs and climbed an ornate narrow iron-worked balcony to find their books. The oblong paneled ceiling in the library was painted in green, blue, and blue-green and stenciled with gold symbols—the ship, the flaming heart, the hatchet, the cross. Discipline, discretion, taste, elegance and understatement.

The external poetry and ambience of Barat College could be seen, touched, and tasted. The internal world of Barat College was that of Catholicity—"a creed, a culture, a way of life"—intangible, elusive. De Rivoyre called this—*spirituality*—the life of the spirit nurtured, strengthened, and formed by and within the distinct world of Catholicism, especially French Catholicism, with its emphasis on theology, philosophy, poetry, art, and literature. Added to the development of a personal life of prayer was the responsibility "to honor the Church and benefit society by exemplifying the ideals of Christian womanhood: purity, truth, service."

Barat College was serious about Catholicism. Its students were to have a "reasoned foundation for their faith," rather than blind faith. Four years of intensive study of the *Summa Theologiae* of St. Thomas Aquinas, the Angelic Doctor, were required for graduation. St. Thomas synthesized all the theology and philosophy of the Church in this comprehensive work.

Abstract and esoteric concepts such as the nature and attributes of God, the history of doctrine, the history of theology, the angels, the governance of the world, habits, law, grace, diversity of gratuitous graces and of life and of states of life, as well as the Liturgy, the Seven Sacraments, the dogmas of the Incarnation and Resurrection were explicated. From the *Baltimore Catechism* to the *Summa Theologiae*, Jane Burke received a thorough, pervasive, and sharply articulated religious education. There was no room for doubt. It was all there, in black and white—the pillars and posts, the balustrades and abutments of Catholicism.

To understand the manner by which Jane Byrne was to exercise the office of mayor of the city of Chicago twenty-five years later, one must understand the effect of her exposure to and assimilation of Catholic theological and philosophical absolutes. It left no areas for speculation, no dusty corners of confusion. It wanted no scratching of the head or furrowing of the brow. Every question had been asked, and every answer had been given. Psychologists call this a *closed belief system*—the locking of the doors of the mind to extraneous information, to new thoughts, thereby warding off threats and anxieties from the outside. Not only did Jane learn a particular body of information, but more important, she also learned about the nature of the authority that taught these facts and these absolutes.

The nature of authority, as perceived by Catholics educated prior to Vatican II, was derived from the very authority of God Himself. It shared in His majesty, His wisdom, and His righteousness. The Church even declared that the Pope was infallible—he *couldn't* (not wouldn't) make an error when speaking officially on faith or morals.

St. Thomas wrote that people in positions of authority are endowed with "the grace of office." If God places a person in a position of authority—a king, bishop, mayor, teacher, mother or father—He does not abandon him or her, but gives that person a special grace or protection. Therefore, the most inept, ignorant, and untalented who are called to rule and make decisions over the lives of others are not alone in their offices and somehow share in the power of God Himself. The obvious corollary is that those in positions of authority are to be obeyed, for they are infused with Divine authority; to obey them, even if they are inept, ignorant, and unworthy, is to obey God Himself.

In 1954, the Rokeach Value Survey that measures open- and close-mindedness were administered to various religious groups. Catholics scored higher than any other in the area of dogmatism, close-mindedness, and in the rigidity of their beliefs about authority. Obedience was a high priority for Catholics; the entire authority structure of the Church depended on it. The Catholic model of the world was the shape of a pyramid. Most people were on the bottom, and they were to respect and obey those few on top.

Jane was interviewed in 1976 when she was Commissioner of Consumer Affairs. The reporter described her "looking like a cool and disciplined Doris Day in her ultrasuede suit, sitting behind the kind of formidable desk that makes a power statement all its own."

She stated to the interviewer: "Power in this place is going by the law. When you find abuse, you create a new law."

During her first year as mayor, reporters were questioning her about her ill-fated support of Ted Kennedy for President. She brought the entire interview to a halt by attacking one of the reporters: "You're off base. You're in the mayor's office, and I will discuss any political business with you outside this office." She maintained the purity of her authority, not despoiling the sacred ground of her mayoral office with the unholy talk of politics.

During the spring of 1980, Jane carefully selected and appointed eleven new people from varying racial, ethnic, professional, and geographic regions to the School Board. Prior to their ratification by the City Council, they coalesced behind a leader and made their choice for School Board president. As they were ratified by the council, they announced their new president. Jane immediately called off the swearing-in ceremony, declared their election of a president an illegal act (for they were not duly seated) and refused to sign their official papers. Her authority had been directly challenged (her own choice was elected as vice-president). Her anger was swift; her reach for control (not signing papers, calling off the swearing-in) was instinctive. Her grace of office collided with the board's grace of office, and Jane could only see their act in terms of insubordination and rebellion. She was psychologically unable to see that the credit for the board's early act of leadership was hers; she had mixed the right formula of individuals and had brilliantly designed a coalition that, under normal circumstances, would have taken months to formulate. Jane's model is the pyramid, not the circle of shared decision making.

The top of the pyramid. The grace of office. Obedience, authority, law. The synthesis of years and years of intensive Catholic training, Catholic reading, and Catholic obedience is so deep within Jane that any challenge or questioning of her behavior or motivations is immediately defended: a chip in her voice, a glare in her eye, an elevation of her shoulder. And any person or institution, from city department head to the *Chicago Tribune*, is instinctively and aggressively attacked if they question her motives, ability, behavior. The balance of power, the system of checks and balances, is not a part of her Catholic heritage.

Apart from the French ambience and pervasive Catholicism, Barat College enjoyed a relationship between faculty and students shared by few other institutions. While the Benedictine sisters saw themselves praying and working and the Dominican sisters saw themselves as a great white army marching for Christ, the Religious of the Sacred Heart saw themselves as mothers in a family. Madeleine Sophie Barat wrote that a mother's love is the only love that can and should be trusted with the education of a child. Her nuns were not called Sister, but Mother. They did not take contrived names like Sister Ralph Ann or Sister Contralta, but kept their own; they were Mother Marguerite Green or Mother Mary Keegan or Mother

Margaret Burke. Their students were their children to love, to nourish, to teach, and to discipline.

The life model taught at Barat was not only the pyramid, but also the family. Their 197 Sacred Heart houses, not convents, were established throughout the world. Wherever a Sacred Heart girl traveled, she was always a part of the Sacred Heart family. At graduation, she received a Sacred Heart "passport" to introduce her if she were traveling or needed a home. Lyons, Antwerp Oxford, Dublin, Seville, Vienna, Tokyo, Shanghai, Bombay, Cairo, Buenos Aires, Melbourne—a Sacred Heart girl, to the second or third generation, was never far from home.

With the changes felt throughout the Church, a Religious of the Sacred Heart is no longer called Mother, but Sister. She no longer wears her habit, but ordinary clothes. She is no longer cloistered, but free to come and go.

In the fall of 1979 a Sister from the Humanities Department at Barat College was studying in Athens. She had spent the day at the port of Athens, was hot, tired, her hair was blown, and she was wearing a simple cotton pantsuit. As she began to get into a taxi a distinguished gentleman opened the other door for his well-dressed wife. They agreed to share the cab. As they began to talk, the nun detected an accent. She asked the woman where she and her husband were from. The woman stated that they were from Mexico City.

The nun said, "I imagine you attended Sacre Coeur."

The woman instinctively knew she was home—"Ma Mere, Ma Mere." Tears rolled down their cheeks as they embraced in the back seat of the cab. The Sacred Heart Family—mothers and daughters—never far from home.

The sense of family was perhaps the most important value of the Burke home, and the powerful role model Katharine Burke provided to her children was complemented by the Mothers who taught Jane and her three sisters at Barat. When Jane Burke and Bill Byrne were married, they followed the Sacred Heart tradition of going out to Barat before going to the wedding reception; at that time, the nuns were cloistered and could not leave to attend the wedding. When Bill Byrne was killed, it was to the Mothers at Barat that Jane went for solace, consolation, and support to help her understand why it happened.

Culture, tradition, and religion were strong influences on Barat girls, but the bottom line, the nuts and bolts concern of the students, was getting a husband—not just any old run-of-the-mill husband, but an upwardly mobile, preferably Irish Catholic, young man. If a Barat girl really hit the jackpot, he would be a Notre Dame man.

On Friday afternoons, especially during football season, caravans of Barat girls would pour onto the South Bend campus for football games, for the parties before and after the games, and for the prospect of meeting a future husband. Upwardly mobiles could not afford to stay back in Lake Forest and study—there was work to be done in South Bend and really very little time in which to do it.

Sister Margaret Burke (no relation to Jane), president of Barat College from 1954 to 1974, classified the progressive anxieties aroused by the marriage-mania expectations of the fifties: "If they were freshmen and not involved, they were nervous; as sophomores, they would be worried; as juniors, they panicked; by the time they were seniors and if they were not involved, they had abandoned hope."

The social life at Barat College was designed so the girls did not have to abandon hope. Their social calendar included dinners, teas, and dances at the best clubs and hotels in Chicago.

Twenty-five years later, after Jane was elected mayor, she reflected on her college years.

> I grew up soft. . . . I never had to worry about anything. . . . I was a very spoiled girl. . . . I just didn't think practically, I guess. I don't think people who are products of the '50s did. We just went along in college, when the thing to do was to get good grades if you felt like and date and go to the Notre Dame

football games, the proms. And I think the generation that came later—in the '60s—while they shook everybody, in a lot of ways they were right. We didn't get involved.*

At Barat Jane's public self was very much as it was at St. Scholastica—quiet, aloof, private, with a steely reserve. She still aspired to be a doctor and majored in biology. Although she served on the student council in her senior year, she was not terribly involved with the school. Cutting classes, she and her mother lunched together downtown on Fridays. Jane's world was the Burke family, and those few classmates who went home with her never felt quite at ease; the strength and exclusiveness of the family was hard to crack.

A friend who was a bridesmaid at her wedding stated that she was as close as anyone got to Jane and they really were not close, not intimate. "Anyone who wanted to be her friend had to do all the work, for there was nothing like her family."

A curious, rather inconsistent aspect of Jane's personality began to emerge with greater clarity during her Barat years. Private, aloof, reserved Jane loved a show, pomp and circumstance, bright lights, the smell of the greasepaint, and the roar of the crowd. When her mother was in charge of a women's luncheon and style show at Queen of All Saints Parish in which the models were to wear fur coats, Jane, with an instinct for the spectacular, suggested they get pillars sculpted from ice and have the women walk through the ice pillars in their mink coats. To add that special dash, Jane got Coach Frank Leahy to permit the Notre Dame football squad to escort the women through the pillars.

Students of the '50s have been called the silent generation, the lost generation, the sleepy generation, with professors pounding on their lecturns, "Somebody, please ask a question." Even within the sleepy, lockstep times, Jane was different. She was very much a student of the '50s, yet was able to maintain

---

*Paul McGrath, "How I Got Involved," *Chicago Magazine*, April 1979, pp 126-130, 164-171. © 1979 by WFMT, Inc. Subsequent quotations from this article are marked with this symbol.

her personage by being a loner. Following a "different drummer," as a classmate noted. Frank, honest, outspoken, able to control people and events. Another classmate remembers Jane as "bright, competent, mature, always serious, even then." "She didn't show any signs of leadership then, but she did show signs of determination," remarked another.

During a college Christmas recess Jane wanted to sell Christmas trees and approached Mr. Koesler, who ran a service station at the corner of Peterson and Kostner avenues in Sauganash, with a request. Jane's younger sisters, Donna and Mary Jill, would take their bicycles in to put air in their tires and he would shout at them, "You kids get the hell out of here. I'm not running a goddamn bicycle shop," and the kids would run. He was notorious in the neighborhood for his ill humor. Jane got her request. She talked Mr. Koesler into giving her a corner of his lots to sell Christmas trees; she could not be intimidated. Jane was determined and had begun to see herself as someone who could control people and events.

One weekend she visited a friend who lived out of town. The following week she wrote her friend's mother a letter thanking her for a lovely time and commenting on her tastefully decorated home, the delicious food and congenial atmosphere. Fooling around with her sisters and mother at home, Jane wrote another letter telling her friend's mother the house looked like a barn, the food was indigestible, and that she hoped she never laid eyes on them again. Jane went out and mailed the thank-you letter.

The next morning Katharine Burke came down to the kitchen and found the proper letter on the kitchen table. The other was on its way. She shouted for Janie. Jane and the girls jumped into the car, sped down the Edens, and flew into the main post office on the old Congress Expressway. She went right to the head postmaster and told him that she absolutely had to have that letter. He said it was not possible. She demanded the letter as her private property. He consented, and the four Burke girls went through the thousands and thousands of letters going out that day. Donna found the little white envelope with Jane's familiar handwriting and shouted across the room, "I found it! I found it!" They grabbed the letter and quickly got out of the post office. Jane got what she wanted.

In the fall of her junior year she was introduced by an old pal, Jim Griffin, to one of his classmates from Notre Dame, a tall, good-looking Irishman from Cleveland, Bill Byrne. Bill invited Jane to a football game in South Bend the following Saturday.

Bill's parents, Bill, Sr., and Aileen Byrne, attended the game, and Bill introduced Jane to them. "I want you to meet Jane Burke."

Aileen turned to her husband, out of earshot of the young couple, and said, "That's your daughter-in-law, Bill."

Bill, Sr., asked, "How do you know? You've never said that before of all the girls Billy has known."

Aileen said, "I just know. I know everything about Billy."

6

A Favorite Son

$\mathbf{I}$t had been a long Saturday morning, early in May before the peonies had bloomed. The Byrnes' yard was bright with forsythia, and the tired brown grass had somehow survived that cold Cleveland winter of 1951 and was greener than Aileen remembered it ever being. On this Saturday morning Bill was up early, although he had been out late the night before. He and his buddies from Cathedral Latin High School had gone down to Little Italy for pizza and beer. They knew that the old gang was breaking up, although many were staying in Cleveland and attending John Carroll University. However, Bill Byrne and George Vosmik, a close friend, had their hearts set on attending Notre Dame on a Naval Reserve Officers' Training Corps (NROTC) scholarship.

Eighteen months earlier, UN forces had landed at Inchon in South Korea and recaptured Seoul from the Communists. General MacArthur had been in Korea since July; the country was gearing up for another war. Mothers were getting nervous, and young men were dreaming of glory in faraway battlefields.

Bill had been in and out looking for the mailman. Today he

was to hear from Notre Dame. Into the backyard, shooting baskets against the garage, into the kitchen for another Coke, out the front door, back into the front room. At 11:42, the mailman rounded the corner and Billy took off. The mailman knew Bill would be waiting for him and had the long white envelope with the Notre Dame postmark ready.

Bill grabbed the envelope, tore it open, and let out a roar.

"I made it!! I made it!!"

Notre Dame had accepted him on full scholarship from the Navy. More than 20,000 high school seniors had applied; only 1,670 won. Decisions were based on mental and physical tests and extensive interviews with naval staff.

Since he was a child, Bill had loved the Marine Corps. They had more style, class, heartier nerves, bigger hearts; they were tougher and demanded more discipline. Although separate from the Navy, the Marines had always been identified with the Navy for they were founded four days after the Navy for the specific purpose of protecting naval ships. It was Bill's dream to be a Marine flier, a "jet ace," the toughest job in the toughest branch of the service.

The drama and flair of the Marines suited him well. He loved the dramatic and the theatrical. When he was at Cathedral Latin he worked as a curtain puller at the Play House and memorized many lines that he used to flavor his own writings and debate work. During his senior year the Latin debate team won twelve trophies, ten medals, and six ribbons for excellence in speech competition throughout the state of Ohio. Bill was the treasurer of the team as well as sports editor of the *Latineer*, the school newspaper. Although he was athletic, his father discouraged him from joining the teams, for he would only end up with a broken shoulder or a trick knee. He won a Kent State award for journalism and managed to be in every play that Latin produced while he was there.

Bill's interest in journalism can be traced to his grandfather, Patrick Dwyer, an Irish immigrant who, as a foundry worker, was fascinated with castings and metals. As a young man with a large family, he had been close to death during the flu epidemic of 1919. During his recovery he began thinking about the pillars of Solomon's temple and how they would have been cast, considering the limitations of technology and the materials of four thousand years ago. He hypothesized the process, wrote it as an article, and sent it to a trade journal as a lark. He forgot about it until he received a payment for his work and was offered the position of editor of the journal. This was a chance to work with his mind. He moved his large family from Canada, where he and his wife, Maggie, had originally settled, to Cleveland. A prominent Cleveland attorney, John Patrick Hyland, stated, "The Dwyers were not any run-of-the-mill Irish. They were real class Irish—real class from Tipperary."

His grandson, William Patrick Byrne, Jr., was born on February 3, 1934. A young priest, Father Edward Ahern, had come to the hospital to bless throats for St. Blaise Day. Aileen held out the little blond baby, and Father Ahern placed two ivory candles, tied together in the form of a cross, on his little shoulders and asked God's blessing and protection from diseases of the throat. Twenty-five years later, Father Ahern became a monsignor and attended a wedding reception for Terry and Mary Conway. Bill, a Marine flier by then, flew into Cleveland to congratulate his friend, Terry. There was noise, partying, and music in the beautiful Westlake Country Club. Everyone grew quiet as the big handsome Marine, in full dress, unexpectedly walked into the room. Bill spoke to Monsignor Ahern and told him that he was flying into Chicago that evening to see his wife and child. Monsignor Ahern, who saw Bill on the day he was born, was the last priest to see him alive.

Billy started school a year earlier than most children. Father Kelly at St. Gregory's in South Euclid questioned him and found no reason to keep the bright, verbal, happy boy at home any longer. Billy loved school and did exceptionally well in religion, history, reading, and English, despite the fact that he was younger than his classmates. He loved to read, write and, mostly, talk. He came home from school one afternoon, when in the third grade, and said to his mother, "Sister Dolorosa likes me. She moved me right up in front of her." Billy was also an altar boy who took his responsibilities seriously and, as many other Catholics, went to CYO camp each summer.

While Billy was in grade school his uncle, Michael Dwyer, was in the South Pacific serving in the Army. Billy received the following letter, dated November 11, 1942:

Dear Billy,

Your fine letter of October 17th just arrived last night. My goodness, your writing is getting better all the time, and it is very neat.

I still have your lucky piece, Bill. Indeed, I wouldn't be without it, because it represents a little boy's faith in the future— something we cannot do without. I don't have the comic book anymore, though. After I read it, I gave it to another soldier, so he could read it.

We went for a ride on the horses, a few weeks ago, down to a native village. We were talking with a little dark boy about 8 years old. He told us his name was Bill. How would you like to be running around on an island in the south seas, eating coconuts and sugar cane instead of candy? This little gent seemed to be pretty happy about the whole thing.

Don't forget to write, Billy, and say "hello" to mommy and daddy for me.

Keep the Faith,

Michael

When Billy was 11½ years old, his sister, Maureen, was born with a congenitally displaced hip. Surgery, traction, wheelchairs, crutches, and hospitals marked her young life. Although Billy had always been a kind and gentle child, he became kinder and more gentle as he saw all that his little sister endured. Rainbow Hospital in Cleveland became Maureen's second home, and every child there knew Bill Byrne. They knew the Notre Dame schedule and would wait for Billy to come home on vacation. George Vosmik called Bill "the knight with the joyful countenance." To the sick children at Rainbow

Hospital, he was larger than life, a handsome big brother who made them laugh.

Bill wrote the following letter to Maureen when he was at Notre Dame. Maureen was eight.

March 17, 1953

Dear Maureen,

I was certainly amazed to receive a letter from you the other day and likewise I didn't realize what a really fine little writer you are.

You got your report card already I suppose and I hope that at least you got some good grades. Perhaps if we pool our two averages I might have a passing mark. Seriously though, I just know that you got your usual straight A's and if you didn't you had better watch out for me when I'm home because I'll have you studying during your vacation.

Speaking of this summer, my cruise is shorter and so I will have quite a bit of time both before and after I spend my time with the government. So . . . maybe we will be doing a little swimming and other things together.

I doubt if I have to tell you to be a good girl, but with Bampy [their grandfather] staying at the house and all of the other things that are on Mommy's mind, she could hardly find time to think. I suppose that you are helping her out all that you can for I know that you are very considerate. Just see if you can do anything to help and I know that Mommy will really appreciate you for everything.

In a little bit less than two weeks I will be home and it certainly will be good to be there. It has been almost eight weeks since I have been there and the longest time before that was this past summer on the cruise.

In the meantime, stay good, be good, and keep the faith.

Love,

Billy

To touch the spirit of Bill Byrne is to turn to Notre Dame, in a small northern Indiana town noted for its changeable climate. A Holy Cross priest, David Schlaver, describes the institution:

> . . . a little too far from anywhere, with seemingly little to attract people except what happens in this special place. Many have come and stayed for a lifetime. Few have passed through untouched. The distinctiveness of Notre Dame has made its mark and in this way has spread throughout the land . . . a place with a sense of place, a place that cares, a place where the motto could well be written, "please touch."

Notre Dame has been touched by and has touched the lives of not only those young men who formed the Notre Dame elite, but also the lives of all American Catholics, who constituted one of the largest self-absorbed, self-aware, defensive minority groups in this country. When John Kennedy stood with snow falling on his hair that magnificent January afternoon and his voice rang out across the country, "Let us begin." Catholics knew that he was talking to them and that they had entered a whole new era. Catholics had arrived. Irish Catholics had arrived.

Before that afternoon, Catholics had not arrived. They were locked in steerage, citizenship papers tied up. Catholics were dark, sinister, and foreign. Catholics had names that ended with vowels or *ski*, that began with *O*, *Mc*, and *Fitz*. They couldn't eat meat on Fridays and fasted on certain days. Their priests wore long black dresses, spoke Latin, and had great power over the lives of their people. And the darkest, deepest, most threatening part of the Catholic religion was the confessional—a dark wooden cubicle into which Catholics entered to tell the priests their sins.

Defensive, subjugated minorities have always needed symbolic events, symbolic places and people to represent their strength and dignity; to remind them that, regardless of others' opinions, they know the truth about themselves and in time they will show others their strength and their dignity. If the civil rights movement had not had Rosa Parks, Martin Luther

King, Selma, Little Rock, and Montgomery, there would have been other people and places to symbolize the strength and energy of black Americans.

Edward Sorin, a brilliant young Frenchman who founded the University of Notre Dame in 1842, outsmarted bishops, religious superiors, and government officials with his clever ways. Edward Sorin was the prototype for the Rocknes, Cavanaughs, Leahys, and Hesburghs who were to follow. He finessed the placement of a U.S. government postal station at Notre Dame so Notre Dame would appear on all government maps and not be swallowed up by South Bend. He finessed the placement of Highway 31-33, known as Dixie Highway, which connected Chicago with Toledo, Detroit, and Cleveland, so as to skirt the edges of his campus to provide ready access to Notre Dame. He wanted a women's college adjoined to Notre Dame, but the bishop of Indiana feared Sorin's empire building. Sorin pressured the bishop of Detroit to allow him to begin St. Mary's in Bertrand, Michigan, four miles across the state border. When the Indiana bishop died, he moved St. Mary's back across the state line to Notre Dame where it belonged.

In 1879 the aging Sorin was in Montreal, preparing to embark on his thirty-sixth transatlantic crossing to France, when he received word that Notre Dame had burned to the ground—the main building with the university library, museum, and archives, as well as the infirmary and music hall. He returned immediately. Professor Timothy Howard describes the moment.

> He walked around the ruins and those who followed him were confounded by his attitude. Instead of bending, he stiffened. He signaled all of them to go into the church with him. . . . After looking over the destruction of his life's work, [he] stood at the altar steps and spoke: "If it were *All* gone, I should not give up. . . . The fire was my fault. I came here as a young man and founded a university which I named after the Mother of God. Now she had to burn it to the ground to show me that I dreamed too small a dream. Tomorrow we will begin again and

build it bigger, and when it is built, we will put a gold dome on top with a golden statue of the Mother of God so that everyone who comes this way will know to whom we owe whatever great future this place has."

The City of God with the golden dome was built in the little northern Indiana town. It was the biggest, the best, and the most. It was a symbol that Catholics were number one and that Irish were number one, even though the rest of the country was not aware of such excellence. In 1977 Father Hesburgh, president of Notre Dame, stated:

> Many people have given their blood, sweat, tears, and lives for this place. I happen to think that this is the greatest place on earth, but it can still be better. . . . A lot depends on our own vision. . . . We can do it. We have the faculty, the students, and committed alumni and friends to help us do it. You'll see. We'll do it and do it with style.

As the Seven Sacraments of the Church are outward signs of inner grace, the symbol of Notre Dame, the blue and gold *N* and *D* sprinkled throughout the country on jackets, sweat suits, ski caps, glasses, toothbrushes, car decals, notebooks and pencils were outward signs to the Catholic community of its inner strength and worth. Catholics were not impotent. They could win.

Catholics have always reveled in symbols and signs, as if revealing too much about themselves would somehow place their very existence in jeopardy. Catholics intuitively understood the scene from Quo Vadis in which the two Christians, hiding in fear of the Romans and cautious about revealing their identity to each other, drew a small fish in the sand with a stick; when they recognized each other as fellow Christians, they quickly rubbed the sign out with their feet so as not to be discovered.

No better, more appropriate sign of hidden strength, smarts, and power could represent what Notre Dame was all about than football. The Notre Dame song, "When Irish Backs Go Marching By," is filled with the blood-soaring echoes of an old Irish war chant that sent young men off to die for the Holy Ground.

John McIntyre, a classmate of Bill's from Cleveland, said, "Notre Dame taught me to win, not to lose. Its motivation was excellence. It taught me not to equivocate, but to win."

Another classmate of Bill's, his best man at his wedding, Captain Jim Ehret, perhaps now grown a bit jaundiced, stated: "We had the wool pulled over our eyes. Football, religion. I've had to learn that the sun no longer rises and sets behind the golden dome."

In the '80s the Notre Dame culture is no longer applicable and may even be an embarrassment for some. But in the 1930s, '40s, and '50s, it was essential to the survival of a people. Daniel Patrick Moynihan, in *Politics as the Art of the Impossible*, reminisced:

> One recalls far more vividly growing up in New York City in the poverty-ridden 1930s and yet possessing in that Notre Dame football team a symbol of tribal might and valor that can stir the blood atingle to this day. O, the golden Saturday afternoons when, in the name of every Irish kid caught in that social wreckage of the Eastern slums, thunder indeed shook down from the skies, and those mighty Polish tackles swamped the Navy!

If the spirit of a people is held together by its symbols, they are nourished by its myths, its stories, and its poetry. Notre Dame has its own mythology, much of which is garbed in the football tradition. What Catholic kid growing up in the '40s and '50s did not thrill when he or she read about the famous George Gipp, who, burning with a fever and on his deathbed, asked The Rock not to let the boys forget him? And Knute Rockne telling the 1928 squad before facing the undefeated Army: "Before George Gipp died, he said to me, 'Rock, some day when the going is real tough, ask the boys to go out and beat Army for me.'" Notre Dame beat Army 12-6, and the chant, "Win one for the Gipper," became immortal.

Grantland Rice wrote these famous words after a 1924 Notre Dame victory over Army; these, too, are part of the Notre Dame apocrypha:

> Outlined against the blue-gray October sky, the Four Horsemen rode again. In dramatic lore they are known as Famine, Pestilence, Destruction, and Death. These are only aliases. Their real names are Stuhldreher, Miller, Crowley, and Layden. They formed the crest of the South Bend cyclone before which another fighting Army team was swept over the precipice of the Polo Grounds Saturday afternoon.

And there was no Catholic kid growing up in Cleveland in the '40s and '50s—especially on the east side, as Bill Byrne did—who did not know that the five Miller girls' father, Judge Don Miller, was one of the Four Horsemen. Many did not know the meaning of the Four Horsemen and thought that perhaps the judge had been a cowboy before he was a judge. But everyone knew that it was important and that it had to do with Notre Dame, being Catholic, and winning.

Bill Byrne fit into Notre Dame as a slender hand fits into a soft doeskin glove. Rather than majoring in a single subject, he was one of the 158 students in the general program of liberal education. The general program was based on the study of the Great Books, which formed the core curriculum for undergraduates at the University of Chicago. Father John J. Cavanaugh, president of Notre Dame until 1952 and long associated with Robert Hutchins at the University of Chicago, wrote that he was attempting to "break Notre Dame out of the monastic mentality." At this time Notre Dame was not known for its intellectual prowess. Yet those in the Great Books program were part of an intensely challenging atmosphere. It was a closely integrated program. While they were reading Descartes in French, they were also studying him in philosophy and math classes. Most students who were part of the NROTC and the general program majored in math, English, and philosophy and minored in chemistry, military science, and physics. The extensive reading, the many seminars, and the writing demanded by this program suited the talents and curiosity of Bill Byrne.

Twenty-five years after he graduated, Bill is remembered with the same clarity as when he was there, walking across the quad in his orange V-necked cashmere sweater that he wore for four years as a good luck omen; taking the screen off his window in the subterranean level of Lyons Hall and letting in those who had been locked out; lying on his bed as people sat next to him and talked with him, looking as if he was awake when he was asleep, for he had an inimitable ability to sleep with his eyes half open.

On his first day at Notre Dame Bill knocked on Ed Fox's door, dressed like the emperor with new clothes, a beer can in one hand, extended his other hand, and said, "I'm Bill Byrne, and I'm running for class president." Bill was elected vice-president of the twelve hundred some freshmen. He is remembered for his wit, intelligence, his very quick mind. Perhaps the only quality that would match, or perhaps complement, his intelligence was his humor, which, as a classmate said, was "serious and outrageous at the same time, upbeat and irreverent." Bill was elected to the Blue Circle, which was the most prestigious organization at Notre Dame. It was a service society of honors and achievers elected by upperclassmen.

He loved language. He loved to write and talk, and many still remember the brilliant paper he did during his senior year on humor, with emphasis on Falstaff. He was a regular announcer on the Notre Dame radio station, WNDU. One of his talks was entitled, "Little Red Hooding Ride." Bill was warm, bright, expansive. He loved people and people loved him. Bill Reale, another Notre Dame classmate from Cleveland, stated:

> Bill was the most popular guy in the class. He was so bright, always with a smile and a quip. Everyone liked him. He was a

Margaret and Michael Burke, Jane's paternal grandparents.

John Francis Nolan, Jane's maternal grandfather.

Katharine Burke.

Katharine and Bill Burke, Jane's parents.

Bill Burke with granddaughter Leal on lap.
Mary Jill and Donna are at right.

On board R.M.S. *Queen Elizabeth*, 1950. Jane at far left; Monsignor Edward Burke in center.

Audience with Pope Pius XII. Monsignor Burke to left of Pope; Jane to left of Monsignor Burke.

Right Reverend Monsignor Edward M. Burke, Jane's uncle.

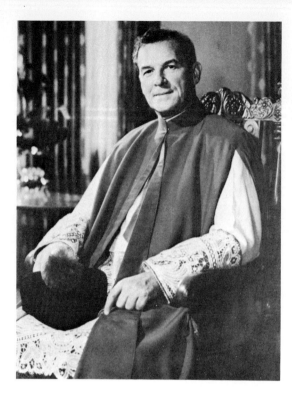

Right Reverend
Monsignor Francis J.
Dolan, pastor.

Queen of All Saints Basilica.

Senior Skiagrams

Notre Dame Victory March, A Tree in the Meadow, The Spider and The Fly, My Funny Valentine, Green Eyes, Going My Way.

LIKES—coffee, letters from Spain, bugs, phone calls to Russia, Mr. Koestler, potato salad, football games, people from Cleveland.

DISLIKES—toothless judges, plastic school buses, five o'clock classes, bridge, second line of songs, her car, certain type of birds.

KNOWN TO SOME FOR—rabbits in the seminary, all night beauty salons, darling of Eden's, white leather jacket, Bonwit's best advertizer, Saturday morning jaunts to Notre Dame. *When Irish Eyes are Smiling, The Typewriter Song, Fishtail Boogie.*

(Top) Graduation, St. Scholastica High School, 1951. "Janie Burke: Neat and nice . . . doctor to be . . . success assured . . . cool poise." (Right) *Barat News*. (Bottom) Notre Dame Cleveland Club dance, Christmas 1954. Bill and Jane are the second couple from left.

Billy, three years old, with his father, Bill, Sr.

Billy Byrne, two years old.

Billy Byrne, four years old.

William Patrick Byrne, Notre Dame graduation, June 1955.

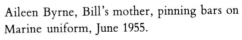

Lieutenant Byrne after first cross-country flight.

Aileen Byrne, Bill's mother, pinning bars on Marine uniform, June 1955.

Mrs. William Patrick Byrne
December 31, 1956.

Bill Byrne with daughter, Kathy,
born December 31, 1957.

Baptism of Kathy; Bill holding baby,
Jane in foreground, Maureen Byrne,
godmother, in background.

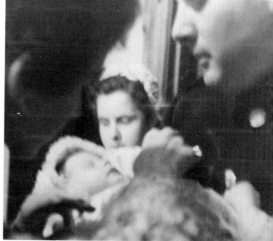

Jane sworn in by Mayor Daley as co-chairman of the Democratic party in Chicago. Daughter Kathy in background.

Commissioner Byrne and Mayor Daley at groundbreaking.

Elena Martinez with candidate Byrne during campaign. *Courtesy of Martha Leonard*

Primary election night;
Latinos for Byrne.
*Courtesy of La Raza
Publications*

Night of primary victor
Elena Martinez with
Kathy Byrne. *Courtesy o
La Raza Publications*

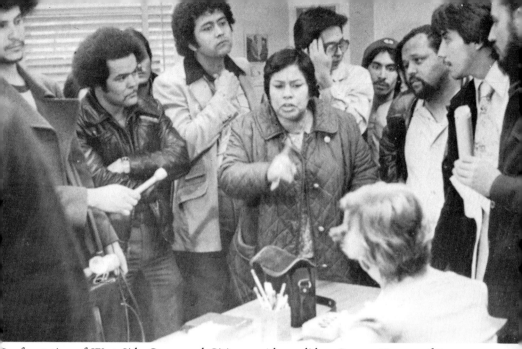

Confrontation of West Side Concerned Citizens with candidate Byrne. *Courtesy of La Raza Publications*

Elena Martinez behind Byrne.
Courtesy of La Raza Publications

Swearing in as mayor of Chicago by Judge John Powers Crowley. Former
Mayor Michael Bilandic in background. *Courtesy of Martha Leonard*

Mayor Byrne with Mrs. Richard J. Daley. *Courtesy of Martha Leonard*

Chicago Fest, 1979. Mayor Byrne and Jay McMullen with Blues Brothers.
Courtesy of Martha Leonard

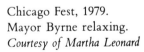

Chicago Fest, 1979.
Mayor Byrne relaxing.
Courtesy of Martha Leonard

Celebrating her forty-sixth birthday as mayor of Chicago. Alderman Vito Marzullo looks on. *Courtesy of Martha Leonard*

Preparation for the Donahue segment of the *Today* Show, May 1979. *Courtesy of Martha Leonard*

Conferring with Democratic congressional leader Tip O'Neill. (Below) With President Carter at a fund-raiser, October 1979, immediately after stating that if the election were held that evening, she would vote for him. She endorsed Senator Edward Kennedy two weeks later. *Photos courtesy of Martha Leonard*

Summer in the city, 1979. *Courtesy of Martha Leonard*

A citizen of Chicago paying respect to the mayor. *Courtesy of Martha Leonard*

good student. He might have gone into politics; he liked being on stage and was sensitive to people's problems. Politics would have been a natural for him.

He was bright, dramatic, loved an audience. On Saturday mornings during football season, he stood on the roof of Walsh Hall, beer in hand, and recited poetry to the incoming crowd. Bill was a "guy's guy," loved to drink beer, loved a party and the excitement of just being a part of Notre Dame. For all his humor and clowning, he was not frivolous, flighty, or a light-weight. Bill was not overtly religious but frequently slipped into daily Mass.

For all the football and beer-drinking fun, Notre Dame in the '50s was a serious disciplined place, with an environment somewhere between that of West Point and a monastery. George Vosmik described the constraints:

> Anytime you'd get out of bed during the day, somebody would be saying Mass. You'd go to Mass out of rote and habit. You had to make bed checks at 7:30 A.M. three days a week. The house rules said that one weekend a month, you were allowed to stay away. You had one midnight privilege a week. At 11:00, the lights went out. They were turned off. If you wanted to study, you had to use the forty-watt bulbs in the hall.

University regulations, specified in the undergraduate manual, "require no more of the student on campus than is required in devout Catholic homes." Schlaver writes that "it was like a large Catholic family, with faculty, students, and administrators living together in the same quarters, in daily contact, with unlimited time for each other and mutual respect." In speaking about the Holy Cross priests who staffed Notre Dame, he states, "Notre Dame has always been centered upon Holy Cross personalities. They recruited students, they taught them, they lived with them, they prayed with them, they recreated with them, they graduated with them, they asked them for money, they married them and buried them."

Bill loved Notre Dame and Notre Dame loved him. The soft spot in his personality was that he was not aware of his many talents. Perhaps that is what made him humble, friendly, anxious to be liked. Tom Raia said that Bill never looked down on people; he respected them and didn't have an enemy in the world. Ed Fox stated that Bill doubted his own merits and would cover this up with jokes. He called himself "Jaybolt"; a bolt that was bent in the shape of a *J* and was worthless had been advertised in *Time* magazine. Perhaps Bill deliberately sought out the Marines—flying for the Marines, landing on carrier ships, coming in low without any cover—to prove his own mettle to himself. Friends also called him "Byrne-Aye," because that was the way he answered drill call.

Bill was six feet tall, weighed 190 pounds, had broad, athletic shoulders, and walked on the balls of his feet as if he were getting ready to box or dance. Yet, within this handsome, bright, expansive young man were haunting painful thoughts doubting his worth and his ability to make something of himself. He never revealed his uncertainties to anyone, but those closest to him knew that more than his share of self-doubt smoldered within him.

When the big, handsome junior from Notre Dame walked into Jim Griffin's house in Sauganash that October evening in 1953 and was introduced to the reserved, somewhat aloof and very small junior from Barat, Jane Burke, a certain chemistry was set off that both felt, perhaps unconsciously at first for it would have been out of character for either of them to acknowledge that chemistry.

Years later, Jane reflected on that chemistry.

> Basically, what attracted me most is that I recognized he was smarter than me. He was a handsome guy. But there are lots of handsome guys. I liked that he was very smart. It made me very calm. He was far more imaginative and romantic than I. He was a reader. He loved the Great Books series. He was in prelaw.
>
> He never dated anyone else after he met me. We met in

October. Since he was from out of town, I visited his family at Christmas. We were in the kitchen and he said, very casually, "You won't believe this, but I'm gonna marry you someday." He never changed his mind. It wasn't anything we really talked about much. We'd only been going out three months.†

Bill was smart and made her feel calm, but Jane was tough. When she became a politician, people called her a "tough cookie," not a "cream puff." She was tough, and Bill sensed her soul of steel, the mettle, the iron will, the determination that swept away every little crumb of doubt. Jane was intense, private; Bill was expansive, loved people and fun. Externally, they were a classic example of "opposites attract"; yet Bill Byrne and Jane Burke complemented each other at a depth that can only be surmised. Jane was a realist. She knew where the relationship was going; it was unrealistic for her to continue thinking about being a doctor. It was virtually impossible for a woman in the '50s, a Catholic woman in the '50s, to imagine combining a family with a career as demanding as medicine. She dropped her medical ambitions and focused her efforts on being Mrs. William Byrne.

Bill's classmates remember Jane as quiet, assertive, knowing what she wanted. Ed Fox recalls Bill being very protective and very proud of her, yet George Vosmik remembers Bill characteristically downplaying their relationship. Bill said to George, "I can't seem to do the right thing with her."

George felt that Bill needed lots of people around him and thrived in their presence; Jane liked to be alone with one person and disliked a crowd. Consequently, she tended to feel neglected. She was "dominant in a quiet way and wanted Bill's attention to herself."

Terry Conway remembers Jane as " . . . so intelligent. She dearly loved Bill. They were extremely close, on the same wavelength. Bill was an avid reader and loved philosophical

---

†Elaine Markoutsas, "105 Minutes with Jane Byrne," *Chicago Faces*, June, 1979, pp 24-27. Subsequent quotations from this article are marked with this symbol.

debates." On trips from Cleveland to Notre Dame with Jane and Bill, they drank beer, told stories, and got into heavy conversations. Terry recalled, "I was a bit apprehensive in her company. I didn't feel that I could converse with anyone who was that intelligent. She was quick and had a dry wit. She had a bit of a facade, stern. At all times, she was in control. Bill had to toe the mark. She had an ability to hide her feelings. If she didn't like what you were doing, you got *the look*."

Chuck Collins, whose family lived in Oak Park while he attended Notre Dame, considered Bill the best liked man he could remember and stated that "Bill had a droll, incisive wit, [he was] a humble person, not aware of his own talents." Chuck and his girl double-dated with Bill and Jane many times through the Notre Dame Club of Chicago. They had big parties at the downtown hotels that, for the '50s, got pretty wild. Chuck had been to the Burke's home many times for dinner prior to the parties. He speculated that:

> Bill might have been a successful politician, but he could not have done what Janie is doing. Janie is made of sterner stuff, far more indomitable than Bill. Bill was tough-minded, but not that highly motivated. I don't believe Bill would have been a survivor like Jane, for he constantly underrated, underestimated himself. Bill was not egocentric. In order to be a survivor, you have to have more egocentricity.

Maureen Byrne recalls Jane coming home to Cleveland with Bill at Christmas. She wore pretty clothes and taught Maureen how to put on makeup, for Maureen had no older sisters to show her. Maureen remembers a lot of kidding back and forth between Bill and Jane. "Billy made her laugh and not take herself so seriously for Janie has a serious face, and even when she is relaxed, she looks mad, when she isn't at all. Janie loved my brother very, very much."

Jim Griffin, who has known Jane since grade school, saw her become more reserved as she got into college and speculated that "perhaps she was overwhelmed by Bill, who was so outgoing. She was private and somehow stayed above the group, where Bill was in the thick of it. Janie was like a German shepherd—she was a one-man dog; she pretty much wanted Bill all to herself, and in a group, they would go off by themselves." Jim recalled a picnic held at an Indiana lake. "It was an overcast, drizzly day and all the other girls had ponchos and jeans on. Janie wore a dress and open-toed shoes. She had a habit of overdressing and always stayed off to the side."

Although a major part of Bill's life was absorbed by studying, partying, and Jane Burke, the reason the Navy was paying his tuition was that he would emerge from his four years at Notre Dame as a commissioned officer. The summer after his freshman year he was assigned to the S.S. *Wisconsin* for cruise duty. He was chosen as aide de camp and when he applied to flight school he was the only one of his group to be accepted.

When they were sophomores, his training group spent three weeks in Little Creek, Virginia, in amphibious training. They flew in on the military boxcars that George Vosmik said looked "like pregnant frogs." One of the planes had trouble, lost an engine, and two of their Notre Dame classmates were killed.

There were 1,670 NROTC students throughout the country who were taking their training at different universities. During that summer, the 1,670 were broken into two groups; half went to Pensacola first and half went to Little Creek first. In the middle of training they switched places so that both groups trained in both places. Forty-one students from the University of Virginia had been assigned to the Pensacola station and were returning from a flight to Corpus Christi, Texas, when the plane crashed, killing all forty-one. Word was received at Little Creek. Bill and George Vosmik, who were at command positions at the time, had to tell the rest of the unit. All they could say was, "Oh, my God," for it could have been any or all of them. The rest of the summer was tense. George and Bill collected $10 from each student and sent the money to the families of the dead students.

After Bill got into flight school, his friend from Cleveland, Terry Conway, told him that he, too, would like to join the

Marines and be a pilot. Although Terry was two years younger than Bill, they were close friends. Terry admired Bill and wanted to be like him. When Terry asked Bill what he thought, Bill said, "For God's sake, no. There are only two of us who are still alive from our original class of twenty-two. The rest are all dead. For God's sake, Terry, stay out of the Marines."

During Bill's senior year the Student Center received forty-three letters nominating Bill to *Who's Who in American Colleges and Universities*. This was the second-highest nomination, trailing only Dan Shannon of football fame. Bill refused what he considered a "false honor," for perhaps he had grown slightly jaded or disillusioned with college life. It had grown too small, too narrow. He had gone out of town with the debate team and had not asked permission. He was punished—they removed him as a class officer. He stepped on someone's toes when he and Terry Conway were planning a dance for the Cleveland Notre Dame Club. He grew tired of the politics and chose to have no part of the *Who's Who* business, despite pressure from his classmates, who felt it was important to his career to be listed in such a prestigious publication. He wanted no part of it and couldn't be budged.

Bill agreed to give the main address at the senior banquet. Actually, he relished the idea; this honor was more his style, something of flesh and blood and not some paper accolade that drew no laughs. The following reflects the humor of the '50s and is excerpted from that talk.

> Perhaps I had better explain why or, better yet, how I happen to be here tonight. Alumni officials have minds that work faster than a bubble dancer doing her act with ping-pong balls. In arranging this bagel bake, they got together with Dick Burke, whose mind works four ways like a cold tablet. . . . the new freshmen take half as long as we did to find out that Mishawaka isn't the name of the Hungarian daily newspaper. . . . Now we're seniors, and the big thing, of course, is jobs. Many I know are going into experimental positions. They are going to test the accuracy of Oriental riflemen. . . . This speech has been very

much like a baby. It was easy to conceive, but it was a helluva labor to deliver it. Thank you. . . .

Four wonderful, glorious, unforgettable years were drawing to an end. In some primitive sense Bill knew that his boyhood would be officially over when he got the sheepskin, and the terrifying world of responsibility and maturity, of marriage, mortgage, tax payments, and children, was all before him. He told his friends he was going to join the French foreign legion. His friends still debate whether or not he ever tried to join, but the French foreign legion would have been a natural outlet for a romantic such as Bill, who wanted to stay young and didn't want to join the rat race too soon.

On the weekend of May 13, 1955, the fiftieth annual Golden Anniversary Ball was held at the South Bend campus. The rambling Navy Drill Hall was transformed into an antebellum Southern mansion. The six hundred couples were greeted by a footman and then walked up a slight rise, where they confronted an elaborate garden of white collonades, white fences, banners, and a myriad of golden roses behind Ralph Materie's Band. Jim Griffin was the chairman of the Senior Ball, and his date, Eileen Hennessy, was crowned queen of the Golden Anniversary Ball.

The entire weekend was filled. At 10:00 Saturday morning, the prefect of discipline, Father McCarragher, celebrated a Mass for the seniors and their dates. That afternoon there were picnics throughout the campus and that evening Don Gels Combo played at the Erskine Country Club in South Bend for an elaborate dinner dance. At 8:00 Sunday morning Father Hesburgh, president of the university, celebrated Mass in Sacred Heart Church on the famous French Gothic altar. After the Mass, Father Hesburgh and Paul Butler, Notre Dame graduate and Democratic National Chairman, spoke at the breakfast held in the dining hall. Sunday afternoon was not scheduled. It was a good time to wind down; there were only three weeks left, and it was the last time that many of the girls would be there before graduation.

It was a good time to be alive, to be young and Irish, and to be a part of the mystique, the spirit and life of Notre Dame. May was always an important month for Jane, for she had been born in May. May was a month of beginnings and of endings, a month of lilacs, peonies, of young green grass and chalky blue skies, of sudden storms and lazy afternoons. It was a month of dances and parties, of Masses and rosaries and May crownings, of friends and priests, of long walks with Bill away from his friends, of time alone with him, of time to be quiet and tranquil.

After breakfast, Bill and Jane walked back past the imposing Sacred Heart Church to the grotto, that spot built into a small hill and so loved by thousands of Notre Dame men. In the high niche to the right is a statue of Our Lady with Bernadette kneeling facing her, as in the famous shrine in Lourdes, France. The shrine faces St. Mary's Lake, which was covered with snow when Father Sorin first saw it. He called it Notre Dame de Lac, for the "lake, with its mantle of resplendent white snow, was to us a symbol of the purity of Our Lady, whose name it bears and also of the purity of soul which should characterize the new inhabitants of these lovely shores."

As the young couple stood before the grotto, with the blue waters of St. Mary's Lake behind them, Bill slipped a ring onto Jane's finger and told her he wanted to spend the rest of his life with her.

7

The Prime of Jane Byrne

Bill graduated and was commissioned as a Marine officer. He applied to and was accepted into flight school. Since the first year of his training was going to be extremely rigorous, the young couple decided to wait to get married and set the date for December 31, 1956.

Jane began teaching fourth grade at St. Juliana Grade School on the northwest side of Chicago, not far from her home, the September after her graduation. St. Juliana had a new principal, Sister Evangelista, who was a Franciscan nun from Rochester, Minnesota. Sister Evangelista was a no-nonsense, strict educator who realized that her first year as principal was important. She intended to run a tight ship—the students, the faculty, especially the lay faculty, had to shape up. This was not a public school. There were certain standards that everyone was going to have to meet, or they could just get out. Sister Evangelista had no time for frivolity or carelessness.

Another young woman, Pat Cassidy, was hired at the same time as Jane. Pat had gone to St. Scholastica High School with Jane. Although she attended Mundelein College rather than

Barat, Pat knew Jane and felt better about beginning her teaching career with someone she knew. During her interview Sister Evangelista questioned Pat about the reasons she wanted to teach at St. Juliana and about her preparedness to take on the awesome responsibility of educating young children. Sister Evangelista did not like hiring lay teachers. She thought Catholic schools should be staffed by nuns but was forced to hire lay teachers because of a shortage of nuns. Sister Evangelista clearly stated her feelings to Pat and told her, "If there is ever any problem between a lay teacher and a nun, I will always support the nun."

Sister Evangelista did not like the other new teacher, Jane Burke. "Miss Burke always gave me a hard time," said Sister Evangelista. "She was spoiled. Her uncle was in the chancery. I didn't like her college transcripts. She was very young and was never really interested in teaching. She was just biding her time until she could get married. I was never satisfied with her teaching. She drove a fancy sports car to school, and she used to smoke in the lavatory. Of all the teachers we had, she was the poorest. She just didn't care."

The fourth grade students at St. Juliana did not share Sister Evangelista's view of Miss Burke. Mrs. Connors, whose daughter, Terry, was in Jane's class, stated, "All the children loved her. She treated the children more like adults than children. She didn't talk down to them, and she made them feel grown up."

The fourth graders did love Miss Burke. She was full of stories about going to see the Pope, about Notre Dame, and about her Uncle Ed who ran the archdiocese for the cardinal. After the class said their morning prayers, they greeted her in unison with, "Good morning, Miss Burke." The boys would bow and the girls would curtsy, staying down for the count of sixteen, as Miss Burke had had to do when she went to see the Pope. Miss Burke brought to her class the black mantilla that she had worn for the Pope; and at the end of the year, she gave it to Terry Connors to thank her for her help in the classroom.

Once a month the fourth graders had to give speeches for history class. They hated to do it until Miss Burke figured out how to make it fun. She told the students that the girls could wear their party dresses and the boys could wear their good suits instead of their uniforms on the day of their speeches. Jane gave pink carnations to the girls after their talks and everyone got ice cream. On that day Miss Burke dressed up for the occasion. Sister Evangelista disapproved, and the kids loved it.

The fourth graders were well mannered that year; it was easy for the boys and girls to behave for a teacher they liked. The students could tell when she was angry, even though she would not lose her temper. She just gave them *the look* and told them, "You're just messing it up for yourself." Miss Burke had order and control, not perhaps the way Sister Evangelista would have done it, but the way Miss Burke wanted it.

When it was time for the fourth graders to learn about their religion, Miss Burke went up to the sixth grade to teach math and science, and the sixth grade nun came down to the fourth grade to teach religion. Jane Burke had received sixteen years of intense sophisticated Catholic education, studying the *Summa* of St. Thomas Aquinas, attending innumerable retreats, days of recollection, hearing lectures by prominent Catholic theologians, reading and studying literature permeated with Catholicism, yet it was not thought wise to entrust the religious education of children to a lay person. Their parents sacrificed to send them to a Catholic school so they could receive their religious education from a nun. To be sure the nuns were on the right track, a priest usually came into the classroom at least twice a month. Frequently, a nun's theological training did not go substantially beyond what she learned in the novitiate, and that usually dealt with the rules, regulations, and traditions of her own religious community. It did not begin to approach the scope and depth to which many Catholic college graduates such as Miss Burke were exposed.

Recess was especially fun with Miss Burke. The girls sat on the steps with her and tried to get some sun. Terry Connors remembers she had "a thing about being tan and blond," perhaps because the handsome Marine she was going to marry was tan and blond. Terry was blond and was in charge of art projects for the class because Miss Burke was not very artistic. Terry was the Blessed Virgin Mary in the Christmas play, another time that the Mother of God was a blond.

Jane had class and style; she was exciting to have as a teacher. For the school Christmas party she wore a green satin dress and a new mink stole. The school secretary remembers Jane as "aloof, snobbish, very intelligent, very poised, very sure of herself." She was sure of herself and of her students, and they were sure of her. On Saturdays her students would ride over to the Burkes' home in Sauganash just to be with her. The boys especially loved her dry, punchy, teasing humor, and they would give it back to her but always knew how far they could go. They liked that, too.

As in high school and college, Jane did not mix with those on her own level. She didn't socialize with the other lay teachers and certainly not with Sister Evangelista. Pat Cassidy was also enagaged, and occasionally they met in the teachers' lounge and compared notes. One day Jane said to Pat, "I don't know what I'm going to do when I get married. I can't cook. I can't even make Jello."

Over Easter vacation Jane went to Florida and didn't return in time for school. Mrs. Burke called Sister Evangelista and told her Jane was sick. Sister Evangelista accepted this until one of the priests at St. Juliana came into the school office and said, "Isn't it nice that Janie is having such a good time in Florida?"; he showed her a postcard he had just received from Jane in Florida. When Jane returned, Sister Evangelista told her that she might not be needed anymore at St. Juliana and that she was probably too sick to teach, anyway. Jane quietly returned to her class to finish off the year.

One of the rules that Sister Evangelista insisted on was that the lay teachers not tell the students the date of their birthdays; it was thought unfair to the poorer children who could not afford to buy their teachers a present. It was May 24, and the fourth graders had planned a big party for Miss Burke's twenty-third birthday. Mrs. Connors brought a large chocolate sheet cake to school at noon; the party was to begin right after lunch. The bell rang and the playground instantly grew silent; another bell, and the children quietly formed their lines. The teachers then led their classes into their rooms. The fourth grade had just finished its afternoon prayers when Sister Evangelista came to the door and called Miss Burke out into the hall. Jane never went back into the classroom. Sister Evangelista said she fired her; Miss Burke said she quit.

Terry Connors is now Terry Connors Murphy and works in City Hall. In the winter of 1979 she went to Democratic headquarters in Edison Park and told them she wanted to work for the candidate. She was the only one on the street passing out literature for her old teacher. Her old teacher won the election and became mayor of Chicago; Terry went to her alderman, Roman Pucinski, and got a job in the planning department. As she sits at her cluttered desk under the official picture of the mayor, blond and tan, Terry acknowledges the strong ties and affection she still feels for her old teacher, repeating what Maggie Smith said in *The Prime of Miss Jean Brodie*: "Give me a girl in her prime, and she will be mine for life."

—◆—●—◆—

Ecclesiastical and worldly splendor marked the Monday wedding of Margaret Jane Burke and Lt. William Patrick Byrne, Jr., which took place in Queen of All Saints Church. The Rt. Rev. Msgr. Edward M. Burke, uncle of the bride, read the marriage service. He was assisted by the Rev. Joseph Burke, and Edward Burke, a theological seminarian, was master of ceremonies.

Chicago Sun-Times
December 31, 1956

Ecclesiastical and worldly splendor had marked much of Jane Burke's young life, and her wedding was the culmination of it all. In the sanctuary were two bishops—the Most Reverend William D. O'Brien and the Most Reverend Raymond Hillinger—four monsignors besides Uncle Ed, and innumerable priests. The Holy Name Cathedral Choristers sang the Mass.

Jane's wedding gown, designed by Sophie of Saks Fifth Avenue, was of white monastery satin with a full-length veil of imported French lace. Katharine Burke chose a Sophie-designed cocktail dress created with pale pink and green leaves on imported lamé; Aileen Byrne wore a *peau de soie* frock of champagne beige accented with copper brown.

The design of the ceremony was the red, white, and blue of the United States Marine Corps. A canopy was set up outside the entrance to Queen of All Saints Chapel, and the official crossed-swords ceremony of the Marine Corps highlighted Bill's Marine status. All six groomsmen were in red jackets and navy blue pants. All six bridesmaids wore navy blue taffeta dresses dyed to match the Marine uniform, accented with scarlet plumes. The surprise of the day was Jane's sister, Carol, the maid of honor, who turned up in a red taffeta dress dyed to match the Marine scarlet and accented with a navy blue plume.

The attendants carried long-stemmed red roses, and Jane carried a crystal rosary. Numerous candles cast soft shadows throughout the church, and the rich tenor voices of Uncle Ed and Uncle Joe contrasted with the soft mellow tones of the Cathedral Choristers. The fragrant smoke of incense curled around the silver candelabra as Bishop O'Brien, looking over the heads of the young couple and nodding to Bill and Katharine, blessed the ring.

As Uncle Joe read the Gospel about the wife leaving her mother and father and clinging to her husband, he saw his brother, Bill, wipe a tear from his eye and he saw Katharine nudge him with her elbow. Bill, clearing his throat, sat up stiffly.

As the Mass was ending, Uncle Ed motioned to Jane and Bill to move to the center before the altar. Carol held Jane's satin dress to one side, and Jane moved gracefully to the middle. Next to her, Bill stood tall and erect, barely touching her. Uncle Ed broke into a big smile as Janie and Bill moved closer together. He looked at Bill, who was biting his lower lip, and said: "William, do you take Margaret Jane as your lawful wedded wife, to have and to hold, in sickness and in health, in poverty and in wealth, 'til death do you part?" Bill solemnly answered, "I do."

Jane then promised to honor and obey. Carol helped Jane fold back her veil, and Jane and Bill kissed. They turned, faced the crossed swords and walked down the long aisle. Bill reached for his mother's hand as they passed the Byrnes. Monsignor Dolan was waiting in the back of the church and was the first to kiss Jane and congratulate the groom. Katharine kissed her daughter and placed a new white fox stole around her shoulders before Jane got into the limousine.

The immediate families went directly out to Barat College. It was a long-standing tradition among Chicago girls to go immediately to Barat to see the nuns, who were cloistered at that time and unable to attend the weddings of their students. The two bridesmaids who were not family were put into another limo and taken directly to the reception. They did not know where the bride and groom had gone.

The reception was as dramatic as the wedding ceremony, held in the Gold Coast Room of the Drake Hotel, with a full orchestra and lavish food and drink. A three-tiered cake was wheeled into the room, and Bill, as the six hundred guests watched, drew his sword and sliced the cake. The guests burst into a great applause and the dancing resumed.

It was after eleven when Bill and Jane were able to get away. They drove in silence, watching the magnificent city disappear as they headed south onto the Drive, past the Field Museum, Soldier Field, past the Museum of Science and Industry, onto the skyway overlooking East Chicago where the steel mills snorted fire into the black January sky, past Hammond and Gary, and into South Bend, where the sight of the golden dome paled the memory of the "ecclesiastical and worldly splendor" of the day.

As Bill turned into the parking lot of the Morris Inn on the Notre Dame campus, they both began to giggle. Bill, as he usually did when nervous, recited some old lines from Shakespeare. Jane never knew if they were really Shakespeare or if

Bill made them up. He fumbled for the key and, chipping ice away from the trunk lock, got their suitcases out of the trunk. While Jane stayed in the car with the heater running, Bill took the suitcases into the lobby and checked in. He went back out and got Jane, holding her precariously to keep her from falling on the ice. Walking past the dry, spindly Christmas tree blinking on and off in the lobby, they could hear the band winding down in the bar and saw the elderly woman staffing the night desk stifle a yawn as she greeted them. She looked at the clock and went back to her crossword puzzle. Bill pushed the button for the elevator, and he and Jane got on.

Before he went to sleep in the strange bed with the strange woman next to him, he thought of these words from *The Prophet*:

> And what of Marriage, master?
> And he answered, saying:
> You were born together, and together you shall be forevermore.
> You shall be together when the white wings of death scatter
>   your days.
> Ay, you shall be together even in the silent memory of God.

— ◆ ● ◆ —

Life was fun and free for Jane and Bill, living in the South where he was stationed. He had 2½ years left in the Marines and planned on law school after he got out. Jane had put to rest forever her own career plans; they would settle in Chicago and have lots of kids. They had the world by a string.

This was the first time Jane had really been away from Chicago, with the exception of her nine months in Terre Haute at St. Mary's. The world was a big, beautiful place—no longer circumscribed by Lake Forest, Sauganash, and South Bend. Jane recalled those wonderful days:

> When we were on our way to Pensacola, Florida, where we were going to be living, what amazed me was the land in between. I was very naive. I found so much of the country

interesting. We were transferred to Kingsville, Texas, and I saw
New Orleans, the whole South. It was all sort of gypsy. We
didn't spend a lot of money on furniture because we were
moving so much. We were living in government housing. But it
was great—we didn't have to keep up with anybody at that
time. We weren't under the scrutiny of anybody. We could
gypsy along the highway. I wouldn't have to have makeup on,
or anything like that. I'd just get up in the morning and get into
the car. I loved it.†

Another gypsy joined them a year after they were married.
A daughter, Kathy, was born on their first wedding anniversary.
A year later, over the Christmas holidays, Jane miscarried.
Friends and relatives who visited the young couple in Florida
remember their happiness together and Jane's total devotion to
Bill.

The household centered around Bill, not around Jane or the
baby. Regardless of who was company, dinner was served at
nine or ten in the evening, when Bill got off duty. Jane grew
calmer, less serious—Bill's easy ways made her relax, feel less
competitive. Ironically, Bill grew more serious. Although there
was no full-scale fighting, he could feel the chill from the Cold
War. There were flare-ups all over the world—the Suez, Syria,
Algeria, Cuba. After he won his wings at Corpus Christi he
was assigned to a helicopter patrol; trouble was brewing in
Lebanon, and American troops were on alert.

Bill and Aileen Byrne were proud of their son. Bill was his
dad's boy, and Bill Byrne hoped that his son and Jane would
settle in Cleveland, take over the business, and even buy a plane
for the company so father and son could fly together on
business trips. Aileen was more realistic. She knew Billy would
never come back to Cleveland. She remembers Jane visiting
Cleveland while she was in college and her nostalgia for home:
"Janie loved Chicago too much. She had a love affair with
Chicago. Even when she was away for a weekend, she couldn't
wait to get back."

Aileen deeply felt that the children should be left to live

their own lives without interference. When Maureen wanted to go into nursing after high school, her family opposed the idea because of her hip problems and her inability to walk. Aileen said to Bill, "Let her do what she wants. You cannot control your children."

Maureen went to nursing school for three years, decided it wasn't for her, and dropped out in her fourth year to attend St. Mary's College at Notre Dame.

Aileen had what she called a "close, instinctive" relationship with her son. He used to call her "good old Mommy." When returning to Notre Dame after a weekend home, Bill, wanting his mother to drive him to the airport, would purposely stall so he would miss the limo from Public Square.

In the front hall of the Byrne home was a small parquet table and on the table was a statue of the Infant of Prague. In front of the Infant, Aileen kept a small vigil light burning to protect Billy. One night she jumped up from a sound sleep, threw on her robe, bolted downstairs, and found the flame of the small candle flickering. Reaching into the drawer, she found another candle, lit it, and went back to bed. The next day Bill called to tell her about the baby and their plans to come to Cleveland soon. She asked if everything was all right. He hesitated for a moment, then told her that the previous evening, when on night maneuvers, the plane had gone into a spin but he had managed to pull it out. From her chair in the kitchen she looked out to the small candle burning steadily in front of the Infant and said, "I know Billy. Are you all right now?"

By the spring of 1959 Jane and Bill were making plans to leave Cherry Point, North Carolina, and return to Chicago. Bill, due to be out of the Marines by the middle of June, had been accepted at the law school at the University of Chicago. They had no place to live but were unconcerned; they would be back in Chicago, near everyone. Tired of government living, they were ready to begin the next phase of their lives.

In the middle of May, Bill had the opportunity to fly to Cleveland. He had to keep up his flying hours—navigational cross-country training—which gave him the chance to get home to see the folks. He left Cherry Point on Saturday morning, May 16, and was in Cleveland by noon. That afternoon, Billy and his father flew west to South Bend and, circling the golden dome, Billy could see small groups of students and their dates picnicking around St. Mary's Lake, as he and Jane had done only four years before. Bill Byrne loved being with his son and asked him about his plans after law school. He hoped Bill and Jane would settle in Cleveland and take over the family business. He and his brother, Tommy Byrne, were getting older and the company would soon need some young blood. Billy told his father that he had no definite plans, that all he wanted was to get out of the Marines, get settled into a little apartment, and get on with law school.

It was a lovely afternoon. Bill was proud as he saw his son, now grown to manhood, confidently and gracefully maneuver the plane. Billy joked with his father about his mother's candlelight vigil before the statue of the Infant. Bill told his son that it was important to his mother and that it probably kept him safe and sound. They were quiet together for long periods of time, enjoying their privacy and observing the flat Ohio countryside that only a few months earlier had been covered with snow. Billy checked his father's seat belt and slowly began his descent.

Back home, Aileen had a beautiful standing rib roast from Heinens in the oven for her two men. Billy and Maureen watched the end of the Indians' game as Aileen set the dinner table with her good linen and crystal. Dinner was ready. They went to the table and Bill said grace.

As usual, they all ate too much. Billy and his father took a short walk before driving to the airport. His mother washed the dinner dishes and packed him roast beef sandwiches on rye for the flight back to Cherry Point. Aileen, Bill, and Maureen drove him to the airport but were not allowed into the military area where Billy checked in. They dropped him off at the curb, kissed him good-bye, and gave him their love for Jane and the baby. His father slipped him a $20 bill to buy something for Kathy.

There was not much to say. It had been a great day, a day without too much commotion, a day like those before he married: Indians' games, a rib roast, good linen, a walk with his father, sandwiches, and a drive to the airport. They watched him walk with his big, bouncy step, into the airport, flight bag in one hand and brown paper bag of sandwiches in the other. Billy turned, waved, and disappeared into the airport.

That evening before she went to bed, Aileen took out a fresh white candle, gently lit it, and asked the Infant to watch over Billy for just one more month. Billy's eight years in the Marines had gone by quickly, had been good for him. He had matured; and although he was getting more serious, he hadn't lost any of his humor, wit, or gentleness. He was just older. She and Bill were older, too. They were thrilled that Billy had a child and a wife. It didn't really matter to Aileen that they would never settle in Cleveland; Billy was happy and that was really all she wanted.

The following weekend of May 23, Jane and the baby flew into Chicago. Katharine and Bill Burke hadn't seen Kathy in three months. She was almost seventeen months old and toddling around the house. Jane was going to look at apartments and get used to being back in Chicago. It was her month—her twenty-sixth birthday was on May 24. A celebration was planned for Memorial Day weekend when Bill could fly in.

Anne Kenny, who lived next door to the Burkes, knew Janie, Bill, and all the Burke kids would be home for the holiday weekend. That Saturday afternoon, May 30, Anne baked two angel food cakes for Janie's birthday to send over to Katharine. It was a hot, muggy Saturday. She decided to wait until Sunday morning to frost the cakes. She and Jim planned to go to 6:30 A.M. Mass to allow her plenty of time to make the fluffy white frosting before the day got too warm. The ancient tradition of neighborliness, her daughter Mary called it.

8

A Rendezvous with Death

But I've a rendezvous with death
At midnight at some flaming town.
When Spring trips north again this year
And I to my pledged word am true
I shall not fail that rendezvous.

Alan Seger, 1916

For three weeks Bill and Eddie Robinson had planned their trip to Cleveland for that last weekend in May. They had gone to Notre Dame together and caught up with each other again in Quantico, Virginia. Eddie was dating Rosemary Kirshner, whose sister, Barb, had been in Jane's class at Barat. The Kirshners lived in Cleveland. Bill wanted to be in Cleveland for Terry Conway's wedding on Saturday, May 30, before going on to Chicago. They planned to leave Cherry Point at about six o'clock Friday night and stay over in Cleveland. After an early dinner on Friday, Bill received the weather report. Cleveland had "completely socked-in weather." They would never get a clearance. They decided to have a few drinks and go to bed early. Bill was tired; he had just returned from a cross-country flight that afternoon. They said goodnight at 9:30 and planned an early start Saturday morning.

At seven the next morning, the weather was still bad in Cleveland. More coffee. By 8:15, the weather had improved somewhat, and the weather report indicated it would continue to improve. Bill filed for his instrumental flight plan for Cleveland, received the plane in good condition, and was in the air by 8:41 A.M. Bill's instruments read 3,000 feet over Rocky Mount, North Carolina; 8,000 feet over Gordonsville, West Virginia; and 8,000 feet over Wheeling.

The relationship between Eddie and Rosemary was becoming serious. Eddie was getting out of the Marines the following March and thought it was time to make a commitment. Studying the blue and green folds of the Virginia mountains dotted with clouds, he turned to Bill and said, "How do you like being married, old boy?"

Laughing, Bill answered, "What's the matter—is Terry Conway putting ideas in your little head?"

Bill turned to Eddie, squinting as the morning sun bounced off the tops of the clouds and into the cockpit. He adjusted his glasses, glanced at the direction indicator, turned back to Eddie, and said, "If you really want to know, it's just great. I love being married. Coming home at night and Jane and Kathy there waiting for me. I feel like a king. I wouldn't trade places with anyone. It's a great life. I don't know, but if you want to do it, do it. You won't regret it. I can't wait to see Conway finally hitched. I talked with him a few weeks ago when I was in Cleveland. Thought he was going to chicken out."

They were laughing when Eddie noticed a frown on Bill's face. The omni receiver wasn't working. The cockpit was dead silent. Bill turned the knobs on and off. Nothing. Neither spoke. The Blue Ridge Mountains faded into the green and black of the West Virginia hills and hollers.

"Damn, damn," muttered Bill.

Eddie shifted in his seat and stared down at the hills. After a long five minutes, the radio came back on.

When they were over Wheeling, the weather report came in from Cleveland.

"Sounds like Cleveland is still socked in," Eddie said.

"Yeah, good old Cleveland," laughed Bill.

Three weeks later, Lt. Edward J. Robinson described the landing in a sworn statement:

> At Wheeling, West Virginia, we received the weather for Cleveland as being bad and low visibility between 900 and 7,000 feet. We were at an assigned altitude of 8,000 feet. Lieutenant Byrne continued his IFR (Instrumental Flight Regulations) flight plan and we made a GCA (ground controlled approach) landing. During the GCA, Lieutenant Byrne was very adept and was always on the position and altitude the controller directed him to be at. We came out of the clouds at about 400 feet, lined up perfectly with the runway and Lieutenant Byrne made a beautiful landing. The time was about 1210, Daylight Saving Time.

A friend of Eddie's was waiting for them. They changed into their dress uniforms, left Cleveland Hopkins Airport at one, and within twenty minutes they were at St. Christopher Church in Rocky River. No one was in sight. Bill went into the rectory to look for a priest to ask about the wedding reception. It was farther west, much farther than they had realized.

As Bill entered the reception—tall, handsome in full Marine dress, making his surprise entrance—the wedding guests stopped talking and turned to see him. Everyone at the wedding knew him, and loved him for his style, which, like his entrance, was dramatic.

After congratulating Terry and Mary, Bill saw Monsignor Ahern standing with a group of people and went to talk with him. Monsignor Ahern, who had known the Byrne family for many years, saw Bill coming, put out his hand, and shook hands with Bill. He asked about his parents and new family, and Bill pulled from his wallet a picture of Kathy and Jane.

After talking for a while, he saw Eddie was getting ready to leave with Rosemary. Eddie pulled Bill aside and suggested that Bill stay in Cleveland for the night and fly to Chicago in the morning. The fog was heavy; it didn't seem to be clearing.

Bill shrugged his shoulders. "It's nothing. I've got 2½ hours of fuel left. I can make it easily into Chicago. I'm anxious to see Janie and Kathy. Nothing to it."

Eddie knew Bill loved to fly "by the seat of his pants," but Bill had flown a lot and wouldn't go up if the weather turned worse. Bill waved good-bye to Eddie, told him to take good care of Rosemary, and said he would see him tomorrow night back at Cherry Point.

Bill excused himself and went to call his mother. He put a nickel into the phone and called the east side; no one answered. No one knew he was coming in. The phone rang for a long time. He hung up and tried again in case he had the wrong number; no answer. The Byrnes were on the west side visiting relatives. Bill hung up the phone, deciding to try again before he left.

Because he was flying, he drank nothing except a few Cokes. At 4:45, he tried to reach his mother again. Still no answer. He had to get going. He located the bride and groom, wished them his best, and at 5:00 headed out to the airport. The couple who drove Bill to Hopkins Airport remember that he was anxious to get to Chicago. They got to the airport at 6:00; Bill thanked them, changed into his summer flight suit, and departed Cleveland Hopkins Airport within a few minutes.

The air was heavy with moisture. What a day to get married—in a fog—Bill thought to himself. The radio was working well, thank God. He wondered what fliers did before radio navigation. Those ground controllers can get you in when the weather is tough. Soon he was through the fog, the haze, and the thick shroud of clouds. In a short time he was over Goshen, Indiana, then South Bend and Notre Dame. No golden dome. Nothing down there, just heavy, thick clouds and fog. As he flew over the grotto, he said a short prayer to the Blessed Mother, asking for her protection for his family and that they soon be settled in Chicago. He had never actually lived in Chicago. Just think of State Street and Michigan Avenue—rooting for the Bears and the Cubs, calling downtown "the Loop." It would be a good life. He looked at his watch.

As he approached Chicago a new weather report came over the radio. There was no way he could land. Glenview Naval Air Station told him he had to go to Chanute. He radioed Chanute Air Force Base in central Illinois, near Champaign, and asked for a clearance to land. It was getting late. If he had known the weather would be so bad, he would have left the wedding sooner.

It took him longer than he had expected. Janie would be waiting for his call by now. He had lost an hour with the time difference. At 9:45, Chicago time, he landed at Chanute. Sergeant Harold Gebhard, USAF, met Bill's plane, an AD 5, in a follow-me truck on the taxiway and directed Bill to the parking area, east of Hangar Number 4. Sergeant Gebhard told Bill that there would be some delay in refueling because of thunderstorms and lightning in the area.

Bill said, "Don't worry. How long does it take to get to Chicago by train or bus?" Gebhard told him three to four hours.

When Bill deplaned, he handed Gebhard the ATC form for fuel. He told him he wanted full fuel service and oil in the aircraft. Gebhard asked how much fuel the plane held, and Bill said that he had 500 pounds of fuel left. He told Gebhard he had tried for Glenview, but weather was below minimums and he was diverted to Chanute, but he had to get to Chicago to see his wife and child. He signed off on the ATC and removed his luggage from the plane.

Private Robert Vaughn, USAF, was also a member of the ground crew that met the AD 5. Vaughn said Bill was in a "good mood and easy to get along with."

He said, "Lieutenant, you really landed her beautiful. Don't you have any landing lights?"

Bill, laughing as he reached for his luggage, said, "I don't really need them with radar. Anyhow, this particular ship is used on carriers where they're of no use, so they just don't bother to put them in. The radar boys bring me in. By the way, where can I get a train or bus schedule? I've got to get to Chicago to see my wife and little girl—I want to go tonight."

Vaugh told him he would check with Sergeant Gebhard

about the schedules. Bill then asked Vaughn where the pay phones were, and Vaughn directed him to the ones in Base Operations. Vaughn and Gebhard then put 539 gallons of fuel and 10 gallons of oil in the aircraft.

Bill headed for Base Operations and immediately went to the weather station. Sergeant Bruce Worley, USAF, was on duty. Bill walked up to his desk and asked, "What's the weather at Navy Glenview?"

Worley picked up the May 31, 1959, 0200 Zebra observation and read: "Two hundred feet overcast/visibility 1½ miles."

"That's about what it was when I got there. Do you think it's going to improve?" Bill asked.

Worley, pointing to the latest surface chart, said, "Not for two or three hours with that northeast wind and this front."

"Cleveland told me the weather would be VFR (visual flight regulations) all the way. I'm going to call my wife. When does the next Navy Glenview report come in?"

Worley said it would be in about forty-five minutes. Bill left the weather station.

Gary Cox, USAF, was on duty in the dispatch section of the Base Operation. He looked up and saw the flier come from Weather, go to the long-distance phone booth just outside the west door of Base Operations, reach into his pocket, pull out a few coins, and dial. Cox watched the flier gesture in the air, as if the person he was talking with could see him. Cox saw him turn toward the weather station, nod to Worley, and look at his watch. The flier shrugged his shoulders to whomever he was speaking. He didn't laugh and appeared slightly disturbed. He looked at his watch again, concluded his conversation, and hung up. He went over to the red Coke machine, dropped in a dime, lifted the green bottle out of the icy water, popped off the top, and gulped it down quickly. He placed the bottle in the wooden crate standing on the floor. A Wrigley spearmint gum wrapper was lying in a small pool of water next to the wooden Coke box. He thought of Chicago—Wrigley Field, the Wrigley Building. Damn, he had to get in.

Slowly he walked down the narrow, cinderblock gray hall.

At the end of the hall was a small seating area. No one was there. The ashtrays were full; the smell of stale smoke annoyed him. He plunked himself down on the cracked red imitation leather chair with the pitted chrome arms. He couldn't get comfortable. He picked up a *Collier's*, thumbed through it, and threw it back onto the table. He closed his eyes, stretched his legs, and folded his hands behind his head. It had been one hell of a day.

He felt he had been born behind the stick of a plane—the long flight yesterday; up early today, only to wait over an hour in Cherry Point with Robinson; the damn radio going out over West Virginia. He wondered if his difficulties were some sort of sign but laughed at himself for still being so superstitious after all his education and training. Guess it was just the Irish in him, looking for signs. He thought of how his mother always threw a pinch of salt over her shoulder whenever she spilled it, and how his father forbade them to put a hat on a bed. He thought of home and of the little candle burning for him in front of the Infant. He wondered about the real difference between faith and superstition. Guess it was a matter of "proper object" of believing, whatever that meant. He was beginning to get tired, and his thoughts were too much for him right now.

Again he reached for his wallet and his picture of Janie and the baby. She didn't want to have it taken but he insisted. He wanted to be with them in the worst way and knew Janie wanted him up there. He looked at his watch and figured the weather report from Glenview should be in by now. At 10:15 he went back to the weather station.

Sergeant Worley looked up as Bill walked in and said, "I got the weather for you," handing him the 31/0300 Zebra weather report. It measured 200 feet broken/800 feet overcast/visibility 2½ miles in fog. (The first 200 feet of altitude were partially open; the next 800 feet were a solid cover; on the ground, visibility was 2½ miles straight ahead.)

Turning to Worley, Bill said, "Wives don't understand about weather. My wife said that the weather looked okay where she was. The same thing happened when I was flying off the Essex. A flight of twenty-four of us was supposed to land at Miami when she was there, and we were diverted to Jacksonville. I called her from Jacksonville and she said the weather looked okay, just a few rain showers."

Sergeant Gebhard came into the weather station and told Bill, "Your plane is refueled. Boy, that thing sure uses oil, doesn't it?"

Bill replied, "It sure does. I was in Korea and they were going to fly some of them back but figured they wouldn't have enough oil. Well, guess I'll give it a try."

Sergeant Worley told Bill that he couldn't sign his clearance after 10:00 P.M. but would call the flight service to get the permission.

Bill said, "No, I haven't made out my flight plan yet and I have my own clearing authority."

Worley shrugged his shoulders and told Bill, "Well, if the weather is still down when you get there, you can always come back here."

Bill smiled, thanked him, and left for Base Operations, the weather report fresh in his mind.

Bill quickly walked into Base Operations, filled out his flight plan for the ground-controlled approach into Glenview, and handed it to Sergeant Cox to check. Cox noticed that Bill had not filled out the weather section of the flight plan and asked him about it.

"I have my weather," Bill said tersely.

Cox then noticed that there was no clearing authority on the clearance, either. Cox asked him if he had his own clearing authority. Bill took the flight plan from Cox and signed his own name quickly without saying a word. Sergeant Cox assumed that Lieutenant Byrne had his own clearing authority since he signed his own clearance. Bill made no phone calls to flight service nor did he use the hot line in the dispatch office.

Sergeant Cox asked Bill if he wanted the driver to take him out to his aircraft, and Bill said no, he was in a hurry because he just had to get to Chicago to see his wife and baby since the train wasn't leaving until the following day. He just wanted to get going. It was eleven o'clock. Dispatch called Gebhard and told him that AD 5, serial #132664, was cleared to go. Sergeant Gebhard was waiting for him outside the door in the follow-me truck, so Bill got in. They headed for the AD 5. The air was still heavy.

Sergeant Gebhard put Bill's flight bag into the aircraft as Bill walked around the plane, giving it one last inspection. Private Vaughn was standing next to the plane and asked Bill if he'd received clearance at Glenview.

Without turning, Bill replied, "It's still weathered in. I think I can stay up long enough to get in later. If not, I'll be back to see you. I've got six hours of fuel, and I'm just going to fly around until they let me in. I'll probably run out of oil before I run out of gas."

Harold Gebhard recalled Bill as "very friendly and seemed to be in very good spirits. He didn't seem fatigued, but very happy and wanting to get to Chicago to see his wife."

Bill started the aircraft and taxied to the runway. The ground crew watched the plane lift off the ground and slowly climb into the heavy black prairie sky.

Vaughn turned to the sergeant and said, "He sure knows that plane. He can sure handle her with the best of them. I wonder if we will see him back tonight?"

The sergeant shook his head as they climbed back into the dark green truck and said to the private, "No way."

9

A Star Up Against the Moon

The AD 5, #132664, flew north. Bill had difficulty with the Naperville omni. The reading was erratic. Joliet radio directed him to call O'Hare. He was indentified by O'Hare, as well as by Glenview, by the last three digits of the serial number 132664, or "664." When he came onto the O'Hare radar scope, his altitude was 5,000 feet after turning to a heading of 190 degrees south. O'Hare directed him to a right turn, heading at 270 degrees for radar identification. (000 or 360 degrees is due north; 90 degrees is east; 180 degrees is south; 270 degrees is west.)

With a right turn to 360 degrees (north), they told him to descend to 2,500 feet. He was nine miles west, southwest of Glenview on a long downwind leg for a GCA (ground-controlled approach) to Runway 17. O'Hare gave him the Glenview weather: "indefinite 100 feet obscured, with ⅜ mile visibility in fog." (Weather conditions were bad and accurate reading of a measurable ceiling was impossible. The real ceiling was not definite. There was fog, limiting vision to ⅜ of a mile straight ahead.) Marine 664 was then given instructions to perform landing cockpit check and to reduce to approach speed. The AD 5 was then vectored to O'Hare at 170 degrees, 2,500 feet, eleven miles from the end of Runway 17, and handed off to Glenview.

Lieutenant Noble Nofsinger, USNR, was the officer on duty at Glenview, GCA Unit 25, on the night of May 30, 1959. Lieutenant Nofsinger had attended the naval GCA operators school and been assigned to Glenview GCA for two years and two months. Lieutenant Nofsinger was also a qualified pilot with twenty-six hundred hours of flight time. The following is excerpted from the taped conversation between Lieutenant Byrne (664) and Lieutenant Nofsinger (GCA).

GCA: 664. Have you in radar contact 9 miles from airfield. Descend to 1,700 feet without delay.
664:     Roger, descend to 1,700 feet.
GCA: Turn right 175 degrees. Perform cockpit check. Present altimeter reading 29.95. Read back.
664:     29.95 altimeter setting.
GCA: Minimum ceiling 200 feet, visibility ½ mile. Current weather indefinite 100 feet obscured, ⅜ mile with fog.
664:     Roger.
GCA: Request pilot's name, rank, serial number, and organization.
664:     Pilot's name BYRNE: Bravo, Yankee, Romeo, November, Echo; initials Whiskey, Papa. First Lieutenant, 067892, Headquarters, Marine Corps Aviation School, Cherry Point.
GCA: Roger. This is final control. If you do not have approach end of runway in sight as precision minimums,* execute a missed approach straight ahead, climb to 2,500 feet, and stand by for further instructions. Over.
664:     Wilco.

---

*The precision minimum at which the pilot must have the end of the runway in sight is 50 feet altitude at Glenview Naval Air Station. If he does not have the runway or runway lights in sight, it is against regulations for him to land, and he must take a wave off and get clearance for another attempt.

GCA: Turn right now, 180 degrees. Maintain 1,700 feet. You
         are 5 miles from touchdown end of runway. Wheels
         down and locked. Acknowledge wheels. Over.
664:     Roger. Wheels down and locked.
GCA: 180 degrees your assigned heading. Do not acknowl-
         edge further transmissions. Now left 175 degrees
         again. You will be approaching glide path shortly. 175
         degrees your assigned heading. Now advised 1,700
         feet your assigned altitude. Tower has cleared you all
         the way on this approach. Approaching glide path 4
         miles from end of runway. Turn right, heading 178
         degrees; 125 feet below good rate of descent. A
         hundred feet below . . . 50 feet below . . . now 40 . . .
         30 . . . 20 . . . 10 . . . coming on glide path. Leaving
         above 10 feet. Now approaching glide path. Turn left,
         175 degrees now. Holding 15 feet below the glide
         path, 2½ miles from end of runway now. 175 degrees
         your assigned heading, left 172 degrees. Coming back
         on glide path. Going below 10 feet. 172 degrees your
         assigned heading. Turn left, 170 degrees. Dropping 30,
         40 feet below the glide path. Adjust rate of descent. 2
         miles from end of runway. 50 feet below the glide
         path. Bring it up, please. Coming up 40 feet below.
         170 degree your assigned heading. A left 163 degrees;
         correction, left to 168 degrees. Going 50 feet above
         glide path. 1½ miles from end of runway. You are
         going off the elevation scale 200 feet above glide path,
         1 mile from the end of runway at precision min-
         imums. 167 degrees is your assigned heading. . . .
         Elevation is dropping rapidly. You are 200 feet above
         the glide path at precision minimums. Now take a
         wave off. Climb out straight ahead. Climb to 2,500
         feet. Stand by this frequency for further instructions.
         Over.
664:     Over.
GCA: I'll call O'Hare Approach Control. Do you desire to
         try another pass and would you like to have us put in
         for it?
664:     Do I have to get clearance?

GCA: That's affirmative. If you desire to try another one, I'll call O'Hare and get clearance for another pass or have them get you a clearance back to your departure point. Over.

664:     Roger. I can hold here for about a couple of hours if I have to. I'd like to try.

GCA: Roger. Make a left turn now, heading 040 degrees, maintain 2,500 feet. Stand by this frequency. Over.

664:     Roger. 2,500 feet.

GCA: O'Hare has cleared you for another approach to Glenview if you desire. 2,500 feet is your assigned altitude; they have no other traffic. Over.

664:     All right.

GCA: Climb out from field 020 degrees, 2,200 feet.

664:     Roger. Climb out 020 degrees, 2,200 feet.

GCA: You're on your downwind leg, 4 miles east of the airport. Over.

664:     Roger.

GCA: Turn left, 340 degrees; maintain 2,200 feet. Over.

664:     Roger. 340 degrees, 2,200 feet.

GCA: Turn left, 280 degrees, descend to and maintain 1,700 feet. Over.

664:     Roger. 280 degrees, 1,700 feet. . . . Do you know I've still got my gear down?

GCA: Negative. I didn't know you had it down. If you want to leave it down, you can. Now you've got about 2 miles before turn to final.

664:     Wilco.

GCA: Your approach will be to Runway 17.

664:     Wilco.

GCA: Turn left 250 degrees, 1,700 feet.

664:     Roger.

GCA: Now turn left 173 degrees and maintain 1,700 feet.

664:     Roger.

GCA: 170 degrees is your assigned heading, 6 miles from end of runway. Turn right, heading 175 degrees. 175 degrees is your new heading. Your turn to final slightly low, 1,700 feet your assigned altitude. Over. . . . Continue right to 180 degrees, maintain

1,700 feet. The tower has cleared you all the way on this approach. . . . For your information, the weather has deteriorated. You have an indefinite zero, with 3/16 of a mile. You are 5 miles from end of runway. Wheels down and locked. Acknowledge wheels. Over.

664:    Wheels down and locked.

GCA: Do not acknowledge further transmissions. 180 degrees your assigned heading, 1,700 feet your assigned altitude. Approaching glide path now, 150 feet below. Adjust your rate of descent, approximately 600 feet per minute. You are 110 feet, coming up. 5 miles from end of runway. 180 degrees the assigned heading. 180 degrees will correct you to the centerline. Holding now 90 feet below the glide path. Adjust rate of descent a little, please. 180 degrees the heading. Right, 183 degrees, about 75 feet below the glide path, coming up slowly. 60 feet below. Right to 187 degrees. 30 feet below the glide path now. 20, 10 feet below, coming on glide path. 3 miles from end of runway. 187 degrees is your assigned heading. On the glide path now. Nice rate on the glide path. 187 degrees the heading. Now left to 185 degrees, 2 miles from end of runway. On the glide path and heading left 180 degrees. 180 degrees the new heading. On the glide path and holding. 180 degrees your new heading. Left to 175 degrees. 1½ miles from end of runway. 175 degrees your heading. Turn left 170 degrees now. On glide path and holding. Excellent rate of descent. 1 mile from end of runway. Approaching precision minimums. Going 10 feet below glide path. Left 170 degrees, 20 feet below the glide path. Now take wave off. Sir, you are too far below the glide path. The centerline of the runway is too far to your left. Pull up straight and climb to 2,500 feet. Stand by on this frequency.

GCA: Over.

GCA: Over.

Lieutenant Nofsinger was waiting for a response to his wave off instructions from Marine 664 when one of the crewmen outside the GCA trailer yelled in to him, "He crashed!!" The entire GCA crew ran in the direction they thought 664 had crashed. They could see nothing.

It was ten minutes after midnight, May 31, 1959. The lights went out early in the two white houses on Old Willow Road in Northbrook. Douglas Cook and his neighbor, Leonard Ambos, were both shaken out of a sound sleep by a series of explosions, "like fireworks," explained Mr. Ambos. "Two loud, a series of smaller ones, one loud, a series of smaller ones, one loud."

Douglas Cook heard an engine roar, "perhaps the pilot revving the engine at first sight of the treetops as he banked to the right." Cook ran to the window as he heard the roar. He saw the AD 5 come low over Holste's pasture land and strike a tree "with an instant explosion and a series of spontaneous and echoing rumbles of tearing debris."

Cook grabbed his bathrobe, Ambos grabbed a raincoat and shoes, and they tore across the road and climbed the northeast fence of Sunset Memorial Cemetery, "tracing the wreckage parts through the illumination of burning debris, trying to locate the fuselage portion to aid the pilot. They located the cockpit, fuselage section and the pilot." The body they located was "scorched and apparently dead." They looked for others but found none.

Douglas Cook and Leonard Ambos stood alone in the heavy, foggy haze with the burning aircraft and the dead pilot. The large monument with the Lord's Prayer was struck, trees were down, bushes were burning, and gravestones and markers were uprooted. The fuselage, still burning, was deep in the ground. Propellers, wings, landing gear, wheels, engine cylinders, pistons, rudders—the AD 5 looked like a child's toy smashed to the ground.

Cook and Ambos walked helplessly among the dead. The two waited, wondering if anyone else knew what had happened. The aircraft continued to burn, small explosions constantly breaking the heavy black and red haze. The acrid smell of burning gas, oil, and heated metal permeated the air. The helmet, shoes, and gloves lay far from the pilot. The parachute popped open after the crash and lay under the engine, burning. Cook climbed on top of a marker and could see Navy fire equipment coming across Shermer Road.

Charles Livingston, USN, was standing on the running board of a truck, facing east, on the approach end of Runway 17 when the AD 5 attempted to land. He watched the AD 5 make its first wave off. He stated at the inquest that he " . . . was able to see the running lights of the plane as he executed his first wave off . . . but could not see the outline of the aircraft due to the dense fog." About its second approach, Livingston said, "From the sound, I knew the aircraft had pulled up to the right. I got back in the truck. I heard the GCA unit call the tower that he was executing missed approach. I put the truck in gear and started to call the tower for clearance back to the unit. I saw a flash. . . . The flash appeared to be behind me or to the west of the runway."

Livingston circled by, picked up the GCA crew, and headed toward Sunset Memorial Cemetery. Ambos and Cook had been keeping vigil in the cemetery for fifteen minutes when the fire equipment finally arrived, approximately twenty minutes after the crash. Lieutenant Nofsinger and his crew returned to the GCA station, removed the tapes from the recorders, and immediately took them to the commanding duty officer. Nofsinger had absolutely "no opinion as to what had happened. The wave off was given prior to the aircraft reaching GCA minimums and outside half a mile from end of runway. The pilot had just taken a wave previously and, from all appearances, correctly."

Marine 664's flight plan, personal effects, and papers correctly established his identity. He had also clearly identified himself to Lieutenant Nofsinger—BYRNE, Bravo, Yankee, Romeo, November, Echo, Lieutenant, Whiskey, Papa. Glenview naval authorities attempted to locate Lieutenant Byrne's wife in Cherry Point, North Carolina. She was not there; they had no information as to her whereabouts.

In Cleveland, Bill and Aileen Byrne were sleeping soundly. They returned from the west side in the evening, unaware that they had missed Bill's call. Aileen's older sister, Mollie, had flown in from Hawaii for the Memorial Day weekend. She was staying with the Byrnes. Aileen's younger sister, Jim (so called because the Dwyers' birth order was boy-girl-boy-girl; when she was born, they were expecting a boy and his name was to be Jim; she got the name anyhow) had a "funny feeling" that something was not right, that something ominous was about to happen. She had been on edge all day and had asked Aileen throughout the day if everything was all right. Aileen assured her that everything was fine. Not to worry.

Naval personnel in Cherry Point had the Byrnes' number in Cleveland on file. The phone rang at approximately 5:00 A.M. Bill got out of bed and went down to answer it. Maureen awoke, turned over, and felt a stab go through her body. She reached for the door, opened it, and saw her father walking heavily up the stairs. Aileen met him on the landing. Bill looked at her, grabbed hold of the railing, and said hoarsely, "The Champ k.o.'d." Maureen heard her father saying something about the Navy, the fog, couldn't find Janie, a cemetery, the Champ k.o.'d. The Champ k.o.'d.

The sun was not yet up. The stair landing was dark; only muted shadows thrown by the little candle burning beneath the Infant lighted the hall. Aileen began crying softly. Her sister, Mollie, got up, put her arm around Maureen, and they went down to the kitchen to make a pot of tea. Maureen was crying. Mollie looked at the soft blue flame curling around the old copper kettle. She thought of that play she had read so many times since she was a girl:

> . . . that wind is raising the sea, and there was a star against the moon, and it raising in the night. . . . He's gone now, God spare us, and we'll not see him again. He's gone now, and when the black night is falling, I'll have no son left me in the world.
>
> *Riders to the Sea*

The black night had fallen across the dark prairies of Illinois, and Aileen had no son left in the world. She had slept deeply, peacefully. She had had no feeling, no premonition, no sense of imminent danger to her son. He had slipped from her arms in a flash of light. Numbness. She went down to the kitchen for a cup of tea. The family sat in silence, broken only by a gasp, a sigh. They went back upstairs and dressed for the early Mass. Bill had called the airport; they were flying to Chicago on the first flight. Maureen, Mollie, and Aileen were still in the kitchen when Bill came down, ready for Mass. His eyes were red.

William Patrick Byrne, Sr. He would never use senior again. There was no junior. Billy would never come back to Cleveland, would never be a part of Basic Aluminum Casting; they would never get a plane for the company, and he would never have a grandson, William Patrick Byrne III. Bill saw the little white statue, standing so confidently, next to Aileen's candle, a symbol of a mother's faith. He struck the statue with his fist, shouting, "You blew it this time!!"

In Sauganash, the Burkes had stayed up late. Jane's older brother, Billy, and his wife, Carol, were over until after midnight. It had been a strange night. Bill Byrne was supposed to be in at around nine. Jane was anxious to see him. Katharine Burke had just come home from the hospital after a minor bladder problem. Jane's sister, Carol Burke, had been out at a party with John Powers Crowley and had called home a number of times. She was positive that there was something wrong with Katharine. They had tried to reassure her that everything was fine, but Carol knew something was wrong. She had a "spooky feeling" all evening and was not enjoying the party. After an hour at the party John brought her home because she was obsessed with the idea that there was something wrong; no one could convince her that everything was all right. The spooky feeling wouldn't go away.

Jane and Kathy were sleeping in Donna's room. They had put up the crib for Kathy in there. Carol and Mary Jill were in the other room. The phone rang about 5:10 A.M. The phone was in Bill and Katharine's room. Bill took the call. He hung up and opened the door of his daughter's room. The light from the hall fell on the end of Kathy's little crib. Bill went in and sat at the end of the bed. He gently roused Janie and softly said to her, "I have some bad news for you. The Navy just called. Bill's plane crashed in Glenview."

Donna rolled over. She heard her father say, "Bad news . . . Bill . . . bad news." She thought something had happened to her brother Billy and his wife on their way home that night and she couldn't figure out why he was just telling Janie.

Jane jumped out of bed and ran into her parents' room. She grabbed the phone and shouted into it, "Hello, hello. What is this? Hello . . . hello. What's going on?"

Her father followed her into the room, gently took the phone from her, and told her again that the Navy had called, that there was no one on the phone. It was true. Bill was dead. He had crashed in Glenview.

In an interview, Jane recalled those moments:

> My first reaction was, "Oh, my God, this is terrible. Where did it happen? How did it happen? How did he look? What happened to the body?" All those things were going through my mind. I was angry, hurt, all those feelings. I asked God, "How dare you do this?" I thought, "This is stupid. Here he was with two weeks to go in the service. He had just been awarded a scholarship. Everything was open. We were re-establishing ourselves. It was senseless."

> I walked into my bedroom to put on my robe and glanced at Kathy, thinking, "She's only 17 months old." I remember looking out that window, thinking to myself, "She will never know her father. She will never know him." It was worse for her. She was so tiny, so helpless. She was asleep and her whole world had changed before she woke up and she didn't even know it.†

Katharine Burke was crying. She later told a friend that she had walked into Donna's bedroom and saw Janie sitting dry-eyed at the end of the bed. She looked up at her mother and said in a flat, factual voice, "He's dead. He's gone. The plane crashed. He's dead."

Katharine was frightened for her daughter, because she

seemed so rational and felt that no one need get excited. She prayed, "Dear God, give me strength for this child."

Jane did not cry. She was too stunned, too numb. She sat and stared.

They called the rectory and Father Jim Dolan arrived at the house in five minutes. He and Janie sat in the front room alone for nearly an hour. The Byrnes called from Cleveland; they would be in on the first plane. The baby was up. The whole house was up. Carol Burke realized that her spooky feeling was about Bill, not her mother. Father Jim left. He had the early Mass at Queen of All Saints.

Jim and Anne Kenny got up early that warm May Sunday. They were going to the early Mass so Anne could get home and frost the angel food cakes for Janie's birthday. She noticed that the Burkes were up. They went to church and Anne was sitting, waiting for Mass to begin, thinking about her frosting. Father Jim Dolan, vested for Mass, came out onto the altar preceded by two sleepy altar boys. He addressed the small congregation, "Please pray for the repose of the soul of Lieutenant William Byrne who died early this morning."

Anne felt as if someone were strangling her. She turned to her husband and said, "Jim, take me out of here. I can't breathe."

By 8:00 A.M. the roads around Sunset Memorial Cemetery were closed. Otis Keller knew that he had to get to work because he heard about the crash on the radio. It was his cemetery, his people, and he wanted to know what happened. He pulled out his union card, Local 106, AFL-CIO Cemetery Workers, and told the state trooper that he had to get through. They let him in.

Sunset Memorial Cemetery was opened in 1925 for the black community in Evanston and Waukegan, the southernmost and northernmost tips of the North Shore. Blacks had traditionally supplied labor for the affluent communities along the lake; when they buried their dead, they went to this small cemetery in an unincorporated area of Cook County, which was later annexed to the village of Northbrook.

Keller walked into the grassy cemetery and through the Garden of Faith, the Garden of Love, and the Garden of Life. Parts of the plane were everywhere. The large monument was in rubble. The propeller was in the southern end, near the Garden of Meditation. The Navy soon brought in heavy machinery to remove the plane, tearing up graves as they moved it in. The machines sank in on the tops of coffins, leveling tombstones that had survived the crash. The evergreens and elms were gone. The peonies and petunias were ashes. The Navy would be there for the next six weeks, picking up parts of the plane. They were there with their notebooks, cameras, yardsticks, slide rules, and manuals.

It took Keller six months to repair the major damage done to Sunset Gardens; for years afterward he came across bolts and washers from the plane. As he cut the grass and trimmed around the stones, the burns and scorches on the markers reminded him of the AD 5 and that May morning in 1959.

By 11:00 A.M., the Burke house was filled with neighbors, friends, and cousins. Jane had dressed and had quietly slipped out of the house. She got into the car and drove the seven miles out to Sunset Memorial Cemetery. She saw the state troopers, Navy trucks and cars, and the Glenview police. She saw the uprooted trees, the bits of wings and tails and wheels, and the scorched fuselage. The cutting smell of burnt oil and gas, of burnt rubber and metal.

She stood far back in the crowd, staring at the ashes of her life, numbly trying to comprehend what had happened to Bill, what had happened to Kathy and herself as she had slept. She walked in a trance, her arms folded protectively about herself so the forces of death and destruction would not have their way with her. She climbed up onto the low brick wall and looked to the east, the bright May sun blinding her. She shielded her eyes, looking to Runway 17 where the plane should have landed. Up on the wall, she could see the top of the willow tree that was shaved off on the plane's straight, seering path, through the monument to its resting place in the Garden of Life. How cruel, cruel, cruel. One of God's bitter, little jokes—making him die in a little colored cemetery, making him die in the Garden of Life. Bill was dead . . . dead . . . dead. The plane had crashed; he was not alive . . . he was dead. She looked again over at Runway 17 and saw a lone pilot starting slowly down the runway and gently lifting off in the bright, cloudless May morning. She got back into the car and headed home. She had to make some plans.

The Byrnes arrived from Cleveland. Jane greeted them. They were all numb. A family friend remembers Janie "sitting like a stone."

Bill Byrne turned to Jane and said, "Janie, where will we bury Billy?"

She looked up and answered him flatly, "In Cleveland, of course." In Cleveland, on the east side, where Billy had grown up, born and bred, as they say. Three hundred fifty miles from Chicago, in Cleveland, the best location in the nation.

When Cleveland was decided on, Bill went to the phone and called Dave Murphy. The Mahon-Murphy Funeral Home had been in Dave's family for years; all the Byrnes and Dwyers were waked at Murphy's. Bill had gone to school with Dave and, only a few months earlier, had proudly introduced his son to Dave. Bill asked Dave to meet them at the train station. They were getting into Cleveland late that night on the train and were bringing Billy's body with them.

They packed and left on the afternoon train. Late that night, the train pulled into East Cleveland. Dave Murphy was there, and Billy was gently lifted off the train and brought back to the big white colonial funeral home on Euclid Avenue. Aileen and Bill watched their son come home for the last time. They took Jane and Kathy to the house with them; the rest of the Burkes went to a motel.

Back at Cherry Point, Eddie Robinson was back from his weekend in Cleveland. He went in to the bar for a beer, hoping to catch up with Bill and find out how things had gone in Chicago. He saw a few fliers sitting silently at a table in a corner. He approached the table and asked if anyone had seen Bill Byrne. One got up quickly and left. Another told Eddie what had happened. Eddie left the room.

Monday, June 1, 1959, Cleveland experienced torrential rains, sending flash floods through most of the east side. Within an hour, four inches of rain fell, bridges were washed out, rivers swelled, buses were submerged, traffic was halted. In Shaker Heights, basements filled with water. The Bridge Creek Dam in Auburn burst. Utility poles, sewers, mailboxes, street signs were all damaged by water.

Torrential rains and storms have frequently marked tragic deaths. When John Kennedy was shot, an Irishwoman said, "Ah, they cried the rain down that night." The tragic, senseless, untimely death of Bill Byrne seemed to move the heavens to grief. If his wife was too hurt, too numb to cry, if his daughter was too young to cry, then nature herself would lament and spill her own tears. The skies opened up and cried, like a Greek chorus lamenting the death of an Agamemnon.

The rains stopped as abruptly as they had begun. In the Byrnes' living room, the family was gathered before going to Mahon-Murphy's. Overhead came the thundering of planes, their engines roaring through the east side skies. Jane looked up and said dryly, "Here come the Marines."

Maureen looked at her sister-in-law's stony face and was frightened by her black, macabre humor. How could she have said that? Maureen was only thirteen and couldn't make any sense of what was happening. Billy was gone. There were Burkes all over the place. Kathy was toddling around as if nothing had happened. Everyone was so concerned about her parents and about Janie, who seemed so twisted and bitter. Didn't anyone know that she had lost her brother, her only brother?

Jane had lived for 2½ years listening to that thunder. She knew the sound of the Marines. It was a squadron of two ranks from Cherry Point, flying in for the funeral.

The casket was closed. Bill's picture was on top. Mahon-Murphy's was filled for two days and two nights with all the people who had been a part of Bill's short life—family and friends from St. Gregory, from Cathedral Latin, from Notre Dame, and from the Marines.

On the morning of the funeral the family met at the funeral

home and proceeded to St. Louis Church in Cleveland Heights in limousines. In front of the new stone church they saw two ranks of Marines waiting at attention, facing inboard at the entrance. As the casket was removed from the hearse the Marines saluted; as it was carried into the church they turned, followed it into the church, and stood in the front of the church on the left side.

The casket was met at the steps of the altar by the priests, all in black. The main altar was stripped of flowers. On the side altar, the altar of the Blessed Mother, were tiers of lilacs and tulips given by grade school children for the crowning of Mary as Queen of the May. The strong sweet smell of spring flowers was mixed with the incense of the funeral Mass. The Mass was long and hot. *Requiescat in pace. Requiescat in pace.* The Resurrection and Life. He who believes in Me shall not die but shall have life everlasting. *Requiescat in pace.* After the Mass the priests moved down from the altar and blessed the casket with holy water and incense, walking around and around the casket, sprinkling the water, shaking the thurible, praying rapidly in Latin and trying to ignore the early June heat.

The thin widow in black held her baby throughout the Mass. The baby reached for the incense, trying to grab the illusive smoke. Her mother, shifting her to the other arm, tried to distract her with a small toy.

As the priest intoned, *"In paradisum, deducat te angeli"* the Marines formed rank around the casket and preceded it out of the church, forming ranks outside the church. As the casket was placed back in the hearse, the Marines rendered a full salute and quietly got into their automobiles. The family followed the casket out of the church and quickly got into the limousines as Dave Murphy solemnly drove to All Souls Cemetery.

Looking in the rearview mirror of the limousine, Dave saw Bill Byrne—gaunt, pinched, an old man at fifty-two. Bill was staring out of the limousine window, almost as if he were hoping to see his son among the Marines, hoping that this had all been one big mistake. Billy was all right; he was standing there with the rest of the Marines. Why was he in the back of

Dave Murphy's limousine with Janie and Kathy? Where was Billy? What was going on?

The baby squirmed. Jane pulled out a bottle of juice. Aileen took Kathy. Jane leaned back, gasped, did not cry, did not break down. No one said anything. The air was hot and heavy. Jane clenched her fist and pounded on her knee over and over again. "How could this happen! How could this happen! I prayed. We prayed. How could this happen!" She breathed deeply and clenched her fists until her knuckles grew white. The large diamond on her slender finger played with the sun and broke it up into purples and blues and yellows on her black dress. She looked at her ring and at her black skirt, at her black shoes and purse, at the black car. She was much, much too young for all this black. She was Janie Byrne, the gypsy, the young mother, the young wife. She dug her nails into the palms of her hands and closed her eyes to shut out all the black.

They arrived at the new All Souls Cemetery. To the right, beyond the main entrance, clustered a group of young people, teenagers. A fifteen-year-old boy had been tragically killed; his family and friends were at All Souls to bury him.

The funeral procession wound its way around the circular drives and halted at a freshly dug grave. The soil, piled behind the opening, was covered with a green carpet. A lowering device, suspended over the open grave, was likewise covered with a thin green carpet. Family and friends, holding on to each other, slowly made their way toward the open grave.

The Marine officer in charge signaled. Six Marine pallbearers lifted the casket out of the hearse and followed the priests to the grave. As the casket passed in front of the two ranks, the Marines saluted, faced the grave, and followed the casket. One rank formed behind the clergy and another formed beside them. The escort officer shouted, "Parade, rest." As the casket was placed on the lowering device, the pallbearers raised the American flag waist-high and held it there for the rest of the ceremony. The two ranks of Marines stood at parade rest, heads lowered.

The priests, in black cassocks and white surplices with purple stoles around their necks, began the prayers and again sprinkled the casket with holy water. Family and friends joined in the prayers, "Eternal rest grant unto him, O Lord, and let the perpetual light shine upon him. May his soul, and all the souls of the faithful departed through the Mercy of God rest in peace, Amen." "Our Father . . . Thy will be done . . . Thy will be done . . . Thy will be done on earth as it is in heaven." They sprinkled the casket again.

The commander ordered, "Escort, attention!" The two ranks snapped to attention.

He then ordered, "Escort, less firing party, present arms." The pallbearers came to attention and saluted the commander. On command, seven Marines marched to the head of the casket.

The commander shouted, "Firing party, fire three volleys." Three times rifles tore through the bright noonday skies.

Each time, Aileen felt them tear into her. The violence, the explosion, the smoke, the fire, the military, the planes and guns. The violence and death in a cemetery, the violent death of her son. He's gone now, God spare us. I'll have no son left me in the world. Her husband was now a shell of a man; her daughter was on crutches; her son was in a coffin.

A lone Marine, hidden from view, sounded the haunting notes of taps—"all is well, safely rest, God is nigh." Tears were rolling down Aileen's cheeks. She closed her eyes and held Bill's cold hand tightly. All is well, God is nigh. How Billy would have loved this. He loved the dramatic. Why did You do this to us? I prayed to You every day for Billy. Why, Dear God, why did You have to take him from me? Why didn't You take me? All is well, safely rest. God is nigh. . . . Why didn't You take me?

The commander, after the last note of taps, ordered the members of the firing squad to lock their rifles. The pallbearers folded the flag and handed it to the commander. He walked solemnly past the clergy and approached the young widow. She handed the baby to her father, took the flag from the commander, and walked quickly past her family to the squad. As she approached each of the young men who had come to bury her husband, she looked him straight in the eye, extended her hand, and graciously thanked him for coming and for being with her.

There was not a dry eye among the Marines. They stood, their rifles still warm, and looked at the young widow whose fiber was tougher than theirs, whose eyes were drier, and whose hurt was so much deeper. After thanking them, Jane reached for the baby, holding the flag under her left arm. She nodded to the families and led the way to the limousine. Dave Murphy reached for the door and held it open until she got in. She held the baby on her lap.

Aileen got into the limo and looked at the little girl on Jane's lap. She knew this was the very, very end. They all would go back to Chicago and she would never see little Kathy again. God help us, she thought, that's the only little bit of Billy that is left in the world, and she will be taken away from me, too. She could feel the stab in her chest again and moved her hand to the baby's knee.

Jane could see the Marines fall out and head toward the cars. All the people. They started to thin out. She looked up the slope and could see the bronze coffin resting over the grave. To the left, beyond the sycamores, she could see two men wearing gray overalls and stained white T-shirts, laughing and talking as they rested against their shovels. She bit her lip and turned away.

10

The Work of Grief

Bill Byrne's death was untimely, sudden, and violent. Jane was only twenty-six years old—a relatively soft, protected, immature woman who had shown great need for order and control. With his death, all order and control were grabbed from her. The strength of her ego was annihilated. She could not cope. She grieved and mourned; she was devastated beyond any point that she had ever thought possible. And the family watched helplessly as Jane struggled just to exist from day to day.

The broken heart, the dashed dreams, the feeble attempts at understanding. She would protect her own vulnerability; she would stagnate and merely exist, just surviving from one moment to the next, wanting only to die with her husband. The grief and insanity and rage and anger and guilt; the numbness and bitterness and total incomprehensibility of it all.

Because of the nature of Bill's death, Jane may well have been robbed of an opportunity to complete the work of her grieving and to make a satisfactory adjustment to her loss. Her limited resources were strained to the maximum. She emerged from her loss as an angry, embittered woman, hurting for the rest of her life.

Grieving is a natural human response to a loss, any loss. A young child—a normally happy, well-adjusted three-year-old—became agitated, irritable, crying. When the mother consulted with the pediatrician, the doctor told the mother, "He is just growing up and is grieving over the loss of his babyhood." The sadness that comes with graduation, the sale of the family home, a break in a friendship, is grieving, for something precious is gone forever. When the loss is a result of a death, and one over which one has asserted no control, the grieving is so much the greater.

Mourning and grieving are not sicknesses but a basic part of human life and human growth. If the child had been thwarted in the grieving over his lost babyhood, it is more than likely that the child would never have resolved the loss and would not have moved comfortably into a new phase of growth. When the loss is relatively minor, the grieving is minor; when the loss is major, as in death, the grieving is profound.

Grieving is not helter-skelter. There is a rhythm, a process, a step-by-step movement that begins with numbness and, if it is allowed to run its course, ends with resolution. It is a healing, not a disease, and if the healing is complete, the grieving person is restored to a level of peace and completeness. This is not to imply that the survivor has been unchanged by the loss; change has come, profoundly, but the survivor emerges from grieving not only deeply changed, but also with a peace, an acceptance, a wholeness. Those who do not complete this grief work have been called *fugitives from grief*, and they spend the rest of their lives with certain painful negative attitudes and behaviors that become a way of life.

Those who fortunately resolve the loss of a spouse, a parent, a child, a friend, do not necessarily love them any less than those who do not. Age, nature, and maturity make it impossible for some to do the work of grief. Added to this are the circumstances surrounding the death. If the survivor is young and the death is sudden and violent, chances are that there will be no resolution; if the survivor is mature and the death is gradual, chances are that there will be a completion of grieving and a restoration to peace. Jane was young and Bill's death was violent. Everything was against her being able to recover fully from his death.

The first phase in the normal process of grief is that of numbness, shock. The entire emotional network immediately shuts off to protect the survivor from the full impact of the death, and the survivor runs on "automatic." Jane said that she did not cry for six months after Bill died:

> I sort of built a wall. They were worried that I couldn't cry. I remember when I finally broke down. It was midnight Mass, Christmas. I walked in, just solid . . . People would look at me, and I resented it. I had been so stoic. They were singing "Silent Night." And when they got to the part, "Sleep in heavenly peace," I thought, "Well, I hope you are." And with that, I don't know where the water came from, it was like someone opened a faucet. It just flooded out.†

Jane was so accustomed to seeing herself in relation to Bill, and her own survival was so intimately bound up with his, that her mind rejected the signals and sounds of reality while struggling to understand the truth. Her mind set up its own defense: if the full impact of Bill's death had hit before she was ready, the risk of her own annihilation would have become greater.

Those who experience a severe grief period have been observed to react to the initial news of the death with disbelief—the mind instinctively rejects the information as false, a lie. Jane ran to the phone, shouted into it, imagining that someone was playing a joke on her. Her father confirmed the news; she grew silent: "Janie sat like a stone."

Jane returned to Glenview and listened over and over again to the tapes of Bill's conversation with the ground controller. Over and over again she heard her husband's last words, and over and over again, she tried to make sense out of what had happened. Jane's numbness had given way to a frantic, bright red rage: Bill was nowhere to be found. She struck out at the source of her grief and the source of her rage—the Navy.

Where was he? Was he hiding? What had happened? He was just a few feet from the ground—why hadn't he been able to put the plane down? They could have brought him in, she thought. He was almost on the ground, and they made him go back up again. She told people that Bill was actually on the ground, he had landed, his wheels had touched down, and the Navy had made him go back up again to be killed. She felt the Navy had killed him.

Jane knew that her husband was an excellent flier. Bill was a professional; he was smart; he had landed on carriers. This wasn't war; it was only fog. She knew he was very close to landing the first time; it was on the tapes. But she didn't know why the ground controller had not brought him in, instead of sending him back up again. Bill hadn't brought his wheels up on the wave off; he had told the ground controller that and the ground controller had said that he didn't know Bill's wheels were still down. Jane wondered if Bill had been trying to tell the ground controller that he was in trouble. Why was he up and down on the glide path? Why was he shifting to the right and to the left on the glide path? Bill was a first lieutenant, a Marine flier. The radar can bring a plane in through the fog—were the instruments working? What happened? Who was to blame? There were no answers. Just big, gaping questions.

Jane's mind still had not experienced the full reality of Bill's death but began to search for him. In doing so, a whole gamut of emotions—anger, rage, and guilt—bubbling just under the surface, were released. She was like an animal who does everything possible to find and recover a lost mate. Jane could not believe that the loss was permanent and continued to act as though it were still possible not only to find and recover Bill, but also to reproach him for his actions. This is similar to the feelings that a parent of a lost child experiences: fear, anguish, the need to reproach, the need to comfort, to hold, to protect, to be reconciled.

Jane searched for Bill through her anger at the Navy and through her anger at Bill himself. She searched for him through the guilt she must have felt for wanting him to be with her on her birthday. Their twenty-one-month-old daughter Kathy also joined in the search for her father:

> Our belongings were finally shipped up from Cherry Point, three months after Bill's death. You know, Kathy called her father Bull, because I called him Bill and she was too little to get it right. When Kathy's big toy box came, I took it into her room. She started going through it, taking everything out, throwing dolls and toys all over. When she got to the bottom of the box and it was empty, she looked up and said, "Where's Bull?"*

Despite searching, her mind struggled not to deceive itself and attempted to encounter reality. When the belongings arrived in Sauganash, Jane took the boxes out to the alley and burned what was left of their life together. She gave away a sugar and creamer to a neighbor child. She wanted nothing to remind her of the past. Almost nothing.

Injustice breeds anger. For the survivor, this anger is frequently directed at the person who is dead, to God, and to themselves, often in the form of guilt. Jane articulated the source of the anger she felt at Bill's death, namely, the gross injustice of it.

> I never had to worry about anything before that first real jolt. And later on I didn't like my reactions to it, thoughts about religion and integrity and justice . . . I was a very spoiled girl, who had even thought that no one could do this to me. It wasn't just the loss of a loved one in a horrible way; it was like—I really felt this—how dare this happen to me? I thought, This child of mine, this doesn't happen. Where was God? Why are these things happening? And I think maybe that was when I finally got a stiff upper lip, because I never would have believed, out of all the pilots that crashed, that Janie Byrne's—that it

would happen to her. I never would have believed that I could have had a little girl who was not going to know her father.*

Jane was betrayed; the right family, the right schools, the right marriage, pray and be a good wife and mother, be honest and try to live a good life—and look what happened. All she had been brought up to believe was suddenly false; she'd been deceived.

C. S. Lewis, after the death of his wife of only four years, wrote, "So this is what God is really like. Deceive yourself no longer. . . . For in the only life we know He hurts us beyond all we can imagine. . . . Sometimes it is hard not to say, 'God forgive God.' "

Jane commented on her relationship with God during this period:

> All my life I believed in God. I did everything I was supposed to do. People came up trying to be nice, extending their sympathy, telling me to accept God's will. What choice did I have? Did He ask me?†

Jane had no choice. God did not consult her, did not ask permission to take her husband from her. She had kept her end of the bargain: "I did everything I was supposed to do." God did not keep His part, but "hurts us beyond all we can imagine." And Jane grew more and more angry, for the only thing Jane had left was her anger.

Jane not only felt tremendous stress from within herself, but society also put additional pressure on her to adjust quickly. Three weeks after Bill's death, Jane and Katharine met Dr. Janet Towne for lunch. Jane wore the black dress that she had worn at Bill's funeral. Pinned to the dress were Bill's Marine Corps wings. After they had ordered lunch, Dr. Towne looked at Jane and said, "What's with the black dress? What's with the wings?" Jane was crushed and angry at Dr. Towne. The wings were the only things of Bill's that she had left.

In America, the land of the gigantic smile, to sustain loss in the natural way is particularly difficult, writes Mary Ellen Reese in *Moving On*. Formerly, mourners wore a sign that distinguished their condition of grief—a black arm band, a black dress to tell the world, "I'm not myself right now. I'm under stress. Handle me gently, make allowances, and, most of all, give me time." The ancient Jewish custom of mourners rending their garments was not unfounded—loss is a tearing away, a tearing out of a part of oneself. You can't apply a bandage and say, "It'll be all right in a few days" to a heart that's been torn in two. Get rid of the black dress, bury the wings, snap out of it, get on with life whether you are ready or not.

Jane could not snap out of it. She became profoundly depressed. She could not sleep; she lost weight; she became listless, bored, vacant. The family could not get her interested in anything of significance. Dr. Towne advised Katharine to let Jane have the full responsibility of caring for the baby in order to keep her busy, to make her deal with reality, to make her snap out of it.

The full realization of her powerlessness began to hit. Jane became a person without power after Bill died. While he was living she was associated with a powerful person—a Marine flier, a bright, beautiful, expansive human being. She was shy, studious, introverted, without many friends. Her marriage to Bill Byrne allowed her to maximize her own qualities through him. Jane lost power when she lost Bill Byrne. She had no social standing—too old to join the singles, too young to join the widows, too alone to join the marrieds. Beyond the doors of Sauganash—beyond Kathy, her family, and her mother—she was a nonentity. A nobody. Nobody's wife. Mrs. Nobody.

For reasons she held within herself, Jane could not let go, give in. She had undergone the numbness, the searching, the depression. Where was the recovery? There was none. She felt no real lessening of the rage and guilt and depression. She just buried it more deeply. She could not stop questioning, pounding on the chest of God. She could not let go; she could not surrender to reality; she could not accept with grace and humility what life had dealt her.

Acceptance is an act of the will that, in its essence, is the healing. With acceptance, with surrender, comes a certain peace, a certain serenity that could have freed her from her anger and depression. She remained caught in a vise, torn between survival and self-destruction, from which she could never escape. Bill's death set her off on a course of anger and hurt, of reaching for power and control so that she would never again suffer as she had. Never, never again would she leave herself so vulnerable, so unprotected, so open to being hurt and tormented. That was all over.

11

A Great Bubble

By the spring of 1960 Janie didn't seem to be coming around, and her family grew worried about her. Unlike many widows who are left suddenly, Jane did not have to work. The Burkes and the Byrnes were financially well off, and Jane received government money from Bill's death. Jane stayed at home, taking care of Kathy. A year had passed since Bill's death.

One evening, she was watching television. The young senator from Massachusetts was trying to get the Democratic nomination for the presidency. Jane heard him speaking about the Cold War—that three boys died daily in jet crashes. He said, "You are just as dead dying for your country in a cold war as you are if you are shot down with live, hot bullets. Those families suffer as much as if the bullet was there." Jane sat speechless, thinking, "That man really knows. At least now I can know in my own mind that what they did is appreciated, that someone knows."

She put her coffee cup down and breathed deeply, the first deep breath she had drawn for a long time. Finally, somewhere, somebody knows. That man really knows. It was a cold, cold war; there were no hot bullets, but Bill is just as dead. Jane poured herself another cup of coffee, warming her hands on the sides of the thin white cup.

At Barat College Helen Tuohy was getting her friends interested in the candidacy of an old family friend, Jack Kennedy. Helen's father, William J. Tuohy, had been elected state's attorney in 1940, and in 1945 Joseph P. Kennedy had purchased the Merchandise Mart. Shortly thereafter, Kennedy phoned Tuohy and said, "Mr. Tuohy, I have heard that you are a person to know in the city." Tuohy responded, "And Mr. Kennedy, I have heard that you are a person to know in the world." And Mr. Tuohy and Mr. Kennedy became friends.

Kennedy's daughter, Eunice, was engaged to Sargent Shriver, who was working at her father's Merchandise Mart. She came to live in Chicago before they were married, and since she did not know many people in Chicago, J. P. Kennedy called the Tuohys and asked them to keep an eye on her. By this time Tuohy was chief justice of the Cook County Circuit Court. He and Mrs. Tuohy frequently socialized with the young couple, and after their wedding in 1953, they spent a week at the Tuohys' summer home in Eagle River, Wisconsin.

In 1956 Joseph P. Kennedy called Judge Tuohy and told him that his son, Jack, might run for Vice-President. Adlai Stevenson was sure to be the party's choice to face Eisenhower. The 1956 Democratic Convention was held in Chicago and opened with a publicity film on the history of the Democratic party, narrated by the thirty-eight-year-old senator from Massachusetts, John Kennedy.

In 1956 television was called television, not the media, and for the first time, people across the country were vicariously attending the convention, sitting in their own living rooms. Accustomed to seeing stodgy old men with shining heads filling the political arena, the country was caught off guard by the handsome Irishman from Boston.

Wives and friends of delegates, watching the proceedings across the country, called the delegates to ask about Kennedy. In Cleveland, a father turned to his teenage daughter and said,

"Keep your eyes on that Irishman from Boston. We haven't seen the last of him."

Joseph P. Kennedy, who was vacationing on the French Riviera at the time of the convention, had warned his son not to take the Vice-Presidential nomination if offered to him. He saw that Stevenson was doomed from the beginning and that Jack would only get hurt. Stevenson's loss would be blamed on Kennedy's Catholicism; Jack would be politically dead. The iron isn't hot; don't strike yet.

But Jack Kennedy sensed that the iron was getting hotter. He threw away the text of the nominating speech for Adlai that the Stevenson people had prepared for him to read and sat up all night with Ted Sorenson, writing his own script, which blasted the Republican team of Eisenhower and Nixon, stating that one took the high road and the other took the low road. The delegates loved it. So did the mayor of Chicago, Richard J. Daley, who then and there decided to back Kennedy.

Helen Tuohy was fourteen in the summer of the 1956 convention but was able, because of her father's connections, to work as a page on the convention floor. Listening to Kennedy's speech, she felt the air charge with the electricity of his words, his voice. He looked beautiful to Helen—tanned skin, auburn hair, dark blue suit. And the delegates at the convention and people around the country felt the current, too. Everywhere people were talking about Jack Kennedy running for Vice-President. In Chicago, at the Touhy's home in the Walton Apartments, crowds gathered to make signs and banners for Jack. Flyers for Jack were mimeographed and distributed to all the delegates who crowded the Chicago Loop hotels. Chicago was for Jack Kennedy.

Abandoning his prior commitment to Estes Kefauver, Stevenson opened up the convention. Pressure to select Kennedy as his running mate was mounting. On the second ballot, Kennedy came within 33½ votes of the needed majority. The electric tote board broke down at a critical point in the vote counting, and delegates were unaware of how close the race was. John Tuohy, Helen's brother, sat with Bobby Kennedy and counted votes by hand. Jack could see that he would not have enough votes for the nomination, so he graciously withdrew, and Estes Kefauver joined Stevenson as his running mate. Both were defeated by the Eisenhower landslide of 1956. But the nation was introduced to John F. Kennedy, who, at the 1956 convention, began his campaign for the 1960 Democratic Presidential nomination. As he addressed the Stevenson delegates, he said, "I ask you, therefore, to think beyond the balloting of tonight and tomorrow—to think beyond the election in November. . . ." And many were thinking of 1960.

In the November election of 1956 Mayor Richard J. Daley saw the utter defeat of all his endorsed candidates. Daley had been elected in 1955, eighteen months before the 1956 Presidential election. In 1952 Eisenhower carried Cook County by 16,000 votes; in 1956 he carried it by 315,000. Republicans won the Illinois Senate seat, the governorship of Illinois, as well as other state offices—secretary of state, state treasurer, and attorney general. An old political rival, former Democrat turned Republican, Ben Adamowski, was elected Cook County State's Attorney by a wide majority over the incumbent Democrat, John Gutknecht, Daley's choice. Daley would one day be known as the King Maker: ambitious and powerful Democrats, aspiring to the White House, would come on bended knee to kiss his fingertips, to wait silently for his blessing, to look humbly for his nod, and to walk solemnly with him in candlelight the night prior to the election. But 1956 brought only defeat, and he faced it saying only, "It isn't the first time we lost."

Twenty-five years later, Jane Byrne, in her first term as mayor of Chicago, endorsed Jack Kennedy's youngest brother, Ted, for the Presidency, and Alderman Edward Burke for state's attorney. During the Democratic primary in March 1980, Ted Kennedy met defeat by Jimmy Carter and Ed Burke met defeat by Senator Richard Daley, Mayor Daley's oldest son. The position of King Maker is not endemic to the office of mayor of Chicago. The title must be earned.

After the 1956 election Jack Kennedy returned to the U. S.

Senate, and the Kennedy machine began serious maneuvers to win the White House in 1960 for Jack. In Chicago, Sargent Shriver, general manager of the Kennedys' Merchandise Mart, president of the Chicago Board of Education, and brother-in-law to Jack, began to lay the groundwork for the Kennedy operation in Chicago. In 1952 Jack Kennedy wrote a memo to his father, requesting Sarge Shriver's assistance in his Senate campaign: "I think Shriver would be ideal if the Mart can spare him, since I am sure he could be most helpful on research, writing speeches, etc., and I think his judgment would be useful. If possible, it would be good to get him as soon as possible. Can the Mart spare him?"

Sarge Shriver became the Kennedy family ombudsman to the city of Chicago. The son-in-law of Joseph P. Kennedy represented the family's economic, social, and political interests in the city. Shriver was at the Mart when, in 1954, County Clerk Richard J. Daley came to ask Joseph P. Kennedy if he thought he should run for mayor of the city. Daley did not need the assurance of Kennedy but knew not to ignore such an influential person. Eugene Kennedy, a psychologist, considered Daley and Kennedy "mystical allies . . . they could appraise other men and know whether they were soft or hard, dependable or risky, controllable or not . . . both built their empires on reading other people correctly."

In addition to his position as general manager of the Merchandise Mart, and his position on the Board of Education, Sargent Shriver was also president of the Catholic Interracial Council and was active in the social affairs of the Chicago Catholic community. He was at the cardinal's New Year's Eve Presentation Ball in 1959, an annual event at which wealthy Catholic debutantes are presented to the cardinal. The ball marks their coming out as members of Catholic society and their eligibility to begin dating. Tables were purchased for $1,000; proceeds went to the cardinal's charity. Bill and Katharine Burke purchased a table because their second daughter, Carol, was making her debut. Jane did not attend since it would have been her third wedding anniversary and the baby's second birthday.

Carol's friend, Helen Tuohy, was also making her debut. She introduced Carol Burke to an old family friend, Sargent Shriver, who asked to dance with her. Carol had heard all about Sarge Shriver and the Kennedys from Helen and, after their dance, she knew that her parents would like to meet someone so important. Sarge greeted the Burkes, shook hands with Bill, and spent a few minutes talking with them, then excused himself and went back to his wife. Never having heard of Sargent Shriver, Bill turned to Katharine and asked, "Who was that policeman that Carol was with?"

The Burkes were not a politically sophisticated family, but Carol Burke was already smitten. At Barat, there was much talk about Jack Kennedy. Carol had heard Helen tell stories of the 1956 convention and of calls from Joseph P. Kennedy to her father, Judge Tuohy. There was no way that Carol Burke was going to sit this one out. Through Helen, Carol got a job as a tour guide at the Merchandise Mart during the summer of 1960. She and Helen planned to attend the Democratic National Convention that August in Los Angeles, but at the last minute Carol was unable to go. The Kennedy headquarters had already opened two floors at 333 N. Michigan Avenue, and the entire staff was to attend the convention. They asked Carol to sit in the Michigan Avenue office in the event that anyone should call. Immediately she was swamped with calls from people who were interested in Kennedy and wanted to be involved in the campaign.

Carol was not the only Burke taken by Jack Kennedy; the entire family mobilized on his behalf. During the week of July 11, 1960, the time of the Democratic National Convention, the *Chicago American* ran the following article:

Burke Family—A Kennedy Team

The Burkes are for Kennedy—all eight of them. Headed by the father, William P. Burke, a steel company executive, they are manning the headquarters of the Illinois Businessmen for Kennedy at 333 N. Michigan Avenue. Their chief job this week will be to explain to visitors that the tremendous demand for

Kennedy buttons has depleted the supply. But there will be a fresh supply by the end of the week.

Burke is a member of the businessmen's committee. Mrs. Burke is active in the women's committee for Kennedy.

Assisting Carol in welcoming visitors to the Michigan Avenue headquarters are her sisters, Donna, 18, and Mary Jill, 16, and a brother, Edward, a law student at Notre Dame.

Another brother, William, 29, who lives in Deerfield, and a sister, Mrs. Jane Byrne, also are active Kennedy workers.

In the background is Kathie, 2½, who wears a Kennedy button and distributes winning smiles.

The Burkes have been Kennedy backers since Kennedy's 1956 campaign for the Democratic Vice-Presidential nomination.

Although the article said Jane was an active Kennedy worker, at this time she was with her young daughter—in the background. It had been just over a year since Bill's death, a year with no answers or explanations. Jane was in a gray twilight zone, ignorant of the facts surrounding Bill's death, comprehending nothing but that he was gone. It was difficult for Jane to leave that uncertainty and nearly impossible for her to get closure on his death and move on to a new life, a life without him. The uncertainty about the facts of his death gnawed away at her, eroding the small bit of self that had survived his death. She asked and asked but was given only snatches of information; the rest she had to invent.‡

The family was rightly concerned about Jane. She just couldn't seem to snap out of it. They did everything they could to make her life easier, but she was simply not the old Janie—spunky, sharp, ready for anything. Nineteen years later she stated in an interview:

> My sister and the rest of the family were really trying to get me going again, and the more they tried, the more I resented it. It

‡This was seven years prior to the Freedom of Information Act wherein the public can petition the government for previously unattainable documents.

was like, "Don't try to steer me that way, because I'll find my way myself."*

Sarge Shriver approached Margaret Zuehlke, executive director of the Illinois Citizens for Kennedy, and asked her if she would have a spot on her staff for Monsignor Burke's niece, Jane Byrne. He told Margaret that Monsignor Burke, whom he had known for a long time through the Catholic Interracial Council, had approached him and told him the family was worried about his niece who had lost her husband the previous year. They wanted to get her out of the house and felt that it would be good for her to get involved with the Kennedy campaign. Margaret said she needed a secretary and wondered if Mrs. Byrne might be interested. Carol Burke and Helen Tuohy had returned to Barat College, and their full-time involvement with the campaign was no longer possible.

Margaret Zuehlke was twenty-seven years old, the same age as Jane Byrne. A graduate of the University of Minnesota with a degree in labor relations, she had come to Chicago for a job with Continental Bank. After a short training period, she was assigned to the commercial lending department and then the trust department—unusual positions for a woman to hold in the late 1950s. Margaret was a member of the Canyon Club of Chicago, a group of young executives. At a Canyon Club luncheon, she introduced the guest speaker, Sargent Shriver. He and Margaret frequently saw each other at social functions, and when he began recruiting workers for Jack Kennedy's campaign, he contacted her. She was getting married the following December and intended to leave her job at the bank at that time. She handed in her resignation six months early and, with four other young executives, went with Shriver to Wisconsin to prepare for the critical Wisconsin primary.

The Kennedy operation knew it was essential to beat Hubert Humphrey in his own territory. As the senator from neighboring Minnesota, Humphrey was affectionately known as "the third senator from Wisconsin." The Kennedy family blitzed the state and began to unnerve Humphrey. He complained,

"They're all over the state, and they look alike and sound alike. Teddy or Eunice talks to a crowd, wearing a raccoon coat and a stocking cap, and people think they are listening to Jack. I get reports that Jack is appearing in three or four different places at the same time." Jack Kennedy won six of the ten congressional districts in Wisconsin, receiving two-thirds of the delegate votes.

Humphrey lost in Wisconsin, yet declared it a moral victory because Kennedy won in predominately Catholic areas of the state. The evening of his victory, Margaret Zuehlke flew with the Shrivers, Bobby Kennedy, Larry O'Brien, and Kenny O'Donnell on the Kennedy family plane, the *Caroline*, to West Virginia, where the question of religion would be answered once and forever. They worked long and hard, moving into the hills and hollers, trying to slay the dragon of bigotry. The Sunday night before the West Virginia primary, Jack Kennedy appeared on television and said:

> . . . so when any man stands on the steps of the Capitol and takes the oath of office as President, he is swearing to support the separation of church and state. He puts one hand on the Bible and raises the other hand to God as he takes the oath. And if he breaks his oath, he is not only committing a crime against the Constitution, for which the Congress can impeach him, and should impeach him, but he is committing a sin against God.

The tide began to turn. On a call-in radio show, an elderly woman screamed at Humphrey, "You git out of West Virginia, Mr. Humphrey. You git out, do you hear?" Mr. Humphrey lost in West Virginia and withdrew from the campaign.

Margaret Zuehlke and Sarge Shriver returned to Chicago to prepare for the eight remaining primaries. To Helen Tuohy, Margaret epitomized the Kennedy people—competent, bright, working long and hard hours. Margaret was tall and thin, with frosted hair, sparkling, intelligent eyes, and a strong face. Margaret was serious, yet smiled easily, a smile that evoked confidence and success. Although she had never been in politics before, she was a professional. She was smart, organized, and knew what she was about and what she believed in.

Margaret hired Jane Byrne as her secretary, although Jane had no secretarial training. Jane impressed Margaret as being very bright, a quick learner, and very, very loyal. From the first day Jane was loyal to Margaret; it was her job to keep the volunteer workers away from Margaret. There were three women who held the position of co-chairman of women for Kennedy: Jane Dick, Protestant; Caroline Wallerstein, Jewish; and Marge Wilde, Catholic. Jane buffered Margaret from them and was not intimidated by these socially prominent women. Jane didn't care what they thought of her; Margaret was her boss and Jane was there to protect her.

Jane did her job well but somberly. Margaret could not get past the wall that surrounded Jane. Margaret saw Jane as "a hurt deer . . . a wounded animal, so private, so somber, so quiet. She must have been incredibly, deeply in love with her husband . . . she was so hurt." Jane was always well dressed, conscious of her appearance; yet despite the lovely clothes, there was a melancholy, a seriousness that prevented people from approaching her. None of the men who came up to the second floor where the serious campaign work was conducted ever made any overtures to her; they never asked her out, never joked or teased her. Jane would go out and buy lunch for herself and Margaret; loan Margaret money if she ever needed it, yet she never opened herself up to Margaret's friendship.

The Kennedy campaign in Chicago was a delicate operation, always careful to respect Richard J. Daley's sizable ego. Daley did not want a separate Kennedy headquarters in the city—he felt the Cook County Democratic Party Headquarters was more than enough. The word went out that under no circumstances was Daley to be upset by the Kennedy staff. Jane, reminiscing to Milton Rakove, quoted Jack Kennedy saying to his staff, "That's Mayor Daley's city. Give Mayor Daley what he wants." Mayor Daley wanted complete and utter control. The Kennedy people were to stay out of the neighborhoods, stay out of the precincts, stay out of the wards, stay out of

Daley's hair. The parades (routes would be changed at the last minute if the mayor didn't like them), buttons, and fund-raising could be handled by the Kennedy headquarters; but the wards and precincts ("presints," as Daley called them) were to be handled by the party.

Matt Danaher, Daley's lieutenant who was later to become clerk of the circuit court, was the liaison between the Kennedy people and Daley. Margaret Zuehlke was the liaison between the Chicago office and Kenny O'Donnell, who dealt mainly with Danaher. The entire upper echelon of Kennedy people were as close to Margaret as the telephone. Those decisions she felt were better left to O'Donnell or O'Brien were quickly assessed and forwarded to Washington. Those decisions she felt were within her domain she handled, frequently consulting with Jane, who was able to assess the political ramifications of a given situation.

Mike Royko called Daley "the Boss"; Eugene Kennedy called Daley "the Chieftan"; Bobby Kennedy called Daley "the Ball Game"; and as far as the presidential election of 1960 is concerned, Richard Daley was the Ball Game. The famous 8,858 plurality that Daley squeezed out of Chicago made the difference between a Kennedy presidency and a Nixon presidency. Daley, a former accountant, knew his numbers, and if the dead had to arise for an hour or so prior to Judgment Day, what harm? Both sides cried, "Fraud," and Mrs. Nixon stated bitterly, "If it weren't for an evil, cigar-smoking man in Chicago . . . my husband would have been President of the United States."

Kennedy knew not to bite the hand that fed him; the Daley family was invited to have their pictures taken with the new President on his first day in office. Even the father of the President, Joseph P. Kennedy, did not have the luxury of attending his own son's inauguration. (He felt it would be politically expedient to stay in the shadows.) The Daleys were invited to dine privately and spend the night with the Kennedys at the White House, a small reward for Daley's feat. Kennedy became President and Daley became King Maker.

The election was held on November 8, 1960. That afternoon Margaret Zuehlke received a call from Larry O'Brien to tell her that the Kennedy family wanted her to come to Hyannisport to watch the election returns with them. Margaret had been working eighteen-hour days since August and had not had time to get her hair done or shop for any new clothes. She had nothing to wear and couldn't get herself together to go to Hyannisport.

When Jane heard of Margaret's invitation, she excused herself, went home, and returned with a chic two-piece black silk dress for Margaret to wear. Margaret told Jane that she didn't want to wear her dress. Jane insisted and Margaret flew to Hyannisport to watch the election returns with the Kennedy family in Jane Byrne's black silk dress.

Margaret returned to Chicago to close up the Michigan Avenue office. Jane stayed on to help Margaret since Margaret was busy preparing for her wedding, which was less than a month away. One morning Jane brought a large white box into the office. She handed it to Margaret. Margaret opened the box to find a lovely new negligee to add to her trousseau. Margaret was speechless because she had no trousseau. Jane looked up at her and said softly, "I haven't worn these, and I won't be needing them." The Burke family gave Margaret and her husband $50 as a wedding gift. The young couple were of extremely modest means at that time and deeply appreciated the Burkes' generosity.

Margaret was offered a position in Washington with the new administration, but she refused since her husband, John Robson, had a bright future ahead of him in corporate law and she wanted to make her life with him. She kept in touch with the Kennedy people, but for the most part, the election of 1960 was all behind her.

Jane had no such a future to look forward to. After the election, it was all over for her.

It was a great bubble, a lot of fun, but it was over, the man was in the White House, and that was what I was looking for. The

Kennedys offered me a job in Washington, or they said they would write a letter of recommendation to Mayor Daley, if I wanted to continue in politics. I had a baby, so I thought I would go back to school and get a Master's and teach.§

Twenty years later Jane Byrne was running for mayor of Chicago. Her former boss, Margaret Zuehlke Robson, now socially active and the wife of a prominent corporate executive, wrote to Jane, offering to work in the campaign on a volunteer basis. She enclosed a generous check to help defray some of the expenses of the campaign. Margaret received no response to her offer to volunteer her time; the check was cashed but never acknowledged.

After the election the Chicago Board of Health requested names of possible candidates to serve on the board from local hospitals. Margaret Zuehlke Robson was one of the directors of Northwestern Hospital, and the board submitted her name as a possible candidate for the Chicago Board of Health. Margaret's name was passed over.

It was all just a bubble.

---

§Milton L. Rakove, *We Don't Want Nobody Nobody Sent* p. 193.

12

We'll Never Laugh Again

In Washington a new era had begun. The first hundred, the first thousand days were filled with excitement, glamour, and style. Even the mistakes and fiascoes held a certain elegance— the Bay of Pigs, the Green Berets. A steady moving stream of culture flowed through the White House: Robert Frost, Pablo Casals, Shakespeare, the Washington Ballet. The President accompanied Jackie to Paris; the President uttered his famous "Ich bin ein Berliner" at the Berlin Wall and arm wrestled with Nikita Krushchev. The White House had come alive. Caroline met reporters wearing her mother's heels and John-John toddled to meet his father at the presidential helicopter. Bobby and Ethel, Hyannisport, Palm Beach, Peter Lawford and the Rat Pack, the best and the brightest—the country could hardly contain its excitement at the energy radiating from Washington.

And in Sauganash, Jane had to begin making plans for the rest of her life. She decided to go back to school, get her Master's degree, make plans to teach, get her tenure, her pension, her two-week vacations at Christmas, and her three-month vacations over the summer. She had to get established. Marriage was totally out of the question. To hitch her wagon to another man, to depend on a man for her security, for her power and identity, would be an act of folly. There was only one person on whom Jane could depend, and that was herself.

Immaculate Conception Grade School in Highland Park needed a fifth grade teacher for the following school year. The teacher who had begun the year quit, so Jane filled in. In great contrast to the spunky young woman who had taught fourth grade at St. Juliana the year before she was married, Jane barely existed for her fifth graders. Sister Evangelista, principal at St. Juliana, remembered Jane's car, her transcript, her birthday, her students, everything about Jane Burke. Sister Eileen Kelly, the principal of Immaculate Conception, did not even remember that Jane Byrne had taught there. Monsignor Murphy, the pastor, did not remember her, either. In contrast to the fourth graders at St. Juliana, the fifth graders at Immaculate Conception either did not remember her or remembered that they did not care for her. She wasn't mean, but she wasn't very friendly; she did not smile. A student, Jean FitzSimon, remembers her as "very slender, wistful, with a badly pock-marked face."

Jane put a picture of John Kennedy on her desk, and told the fifth graders stories of what it had been like to work for his campaign and to meet his sisters and other famous Kennedys. She simply had nothing else to give to the fifth graders. And they were unable to give anything to her.

Was this what she wanted for the rest of her life? The world of an elementary school teacher: chalk and erasers, spelling tests, geography lessons, faculty meetings, lunchroom duty, milk money, bus schedules, lesson plans, record books, petty gossip, and long, windy conversations with parents. When working on the campaign, she could run over to Saks on her lunch hour, meet her father after work at the Lake Shore Club, or walk down Michigan Avenue to the Drake. Here she had playground duty, where kids would splash her and throw stray footballs, from which she would return to the smell of peanut butter and jelly, of banana skins and spilled milk, of sweaty tennis shoes. The dull little kids, the dull nuns, the dull days and even duller nights. The dull, dull life of an elementary school teacher. Is this what she wanted?

What choice did she have? It was 1962 and the hand that rocked the cradle still ruled the world. Women belonged in the home; if they insisted on working, hospitals and schools were appropriate arenas for their maternal instincts. If a woman was serious about teaching, she would have to get a Master's degree. Jane registered for two courses: educational psychology, an extramural course, from December 18, 1962, until November 25, 1963, and mental hygiene in the schools from March 16, 1964, until April 30, 1964, through the University of Illinois, still located at Navy Pier. Two classes hardly resemble the course load of a serious graduate student, but both were requirements for Illinois state teacher certification (requirements she lacked, since her studies at Barat were in the sciences rather than in education).

The Catholic schools were dead ends. They did not pay well. There was no future in them; a lay teacher could never expect to be anything other than a second-class citizen since nuns filled all administrative and supervisory positions. Jane had been in the Catholic schools since she was five years old. She was now twenty-eight and she was still there. Not exactly progress. She began to substitute at Beaubien Public School near their home. She felt there might be some future in the public school system; perhaps she would get back some of her enthusiasm; perhaps it wouldn't be so awful.

A rose is a rose is a rose, and schools are schools, whether a crucifix or a picture of George Washington hangs on the wall. The students at Beaubien saw the same teacher that the students at Immaculate Conception saw: unfriendly, talking to them only about President Kennedy, his campaign, and his sisters. The students did not care for Mrs. Byrne, and in all probability, Mrs. Byrne did not care for the students.

Jane was sitting at her desk, looking at the sea of faces working on their fractions. Two of the boys were giggling about something. A girl at the end of the second row had her head down on her desk. Jane really didn't care. She didn't care what they did. She looked at the stack of papers to be corrected that evening. She thought of Kathy at home with her mother and wondered if she was still taking her nap. Report cards were due next week, and she had to get them ready: count up tardy marks, absentees, evaluate the effort and the behavior. No different from last year. No different from next year or the year after that or the year after that.

As she sat there, the principal turned on the public address system. The kids looked up from their fractions. Jane looked up at the little yellow box on the wall and, hearing the principal's words, thought she must be dreaming. President Kennedy had been shot? She rushed out into the hall toward the main office. She was furious; this was not something to joke about. If this was someone's idea of a joke, it was in poor taste, she thought. She flew into the office, and from the look on the secretary's face, she knew it was not a joke. She slowly walked back to her desk and sat down, staring at the smiling picture of Jack Kennedy in the small gold frame.

With the rest of the country, Jane watched Jackie in her blood-stained pink suit, holding Bobby's hand, as the President's casket was taken off the plane, to the White House, and then to the Capitol. She saw little Caroline reach under the flag to touch her father's coffin and John-John salute the coffin. She watched the caisson pull the flag-covered coffin through the wet streets of Washington, across the Arlington bridge, up to the cemetery. Along with the rest of the nation, she heard the hooves of the black riderless horse break the silence of the gray despondent day as it followed the caisson to the cemetery. The veil, the twenty-one-gun salute, the military, the Marines, the coffin, the beautiful young man who had barely begun. The widow and children, the parents and family, the grief and utter shock, the violence and the utter cruelty. The future stomped out like a rosebud crushed under the big, ugly heels of death, crushing a dream, crushing the life of a person.

Jane knew only too well what this was all about. She

understood the haunting look on the face of Jacqueline Kennedy; she knew how she felt when she took the flag folded up in a nice, neat, tidy little military triangle. She knew how the guns from the salute tore into her, how the eerie notes of taps signaled the finality of Jack Kennedy's life, how she had to go home and take care of her children and thank people and look into the gaping wound in her heart and wonder if it would ever heal. She knew the feeling of reaching out at night for her husband and touching only the cold sheets.

On the day of the funeral Pat Moynihan and his wife, Liz, walked down Macomb Street in Georgetown to the home of a friend, Mary McGrory. They wanted to be together to watch the burial. Mary turned to Pat and said, "We will never laugh again, Pat."

He replied, "Heavens, Mary, we'll laugh again. We'll just never be young again. . . . Politics is a rough game. I don't think there's any point in being Irish, if you don't know that the world is going to break your heart eventually. I guess we thought we had a little more time—so did he."

But Jane had already learned about life and death, and she was younger than they were. The world does break your heart, and despite what Pat Moynihan said, you don't really laugh again. What is there to laugh about? There was nothing for Jane to laugh about. She had been closer than so many people to the spirit of Jack Kennedy, at least in his campaign. She had caught a little glimmer of what he was all about, of the magic of his power, and of the magic of politics. Jane once said to a reporter, "There's that little thing about politics. It bites you, gets in your blood." Jane knew what she wanted to do. She knew she didn't belong in a classroom any longer.

13

Oiling the Machine

In the upper levels of city government, friendship is an extremely precious commodity. The friendship between Richard Daley and Jane Byrne had no precedent in the history of Chicago politics. The mayor had known the Burke family since he attended De Paul University's night school with Bill Burke, Jane's father. He knew Ed and Joe Burke through his dealings with the archdiocese and frequently saw Jane with Monsignor Dolan at Notre Dame football games and at parish functions. Jane saw to it that Daley noticed her.

Daley had heard that her husband had been killed and that she was left with a baby to raise. He remembered that Matt Danaher had told him she was working down at the Kennedy headquarters. The mayor invited her down to his office. He was impressed by her and liked her and asked her if she wanted to be in politics. She said yes. Daley told her that he had the power to give her any job he had but that she had dues to pay and hadn't even begun to pay them. Working for Kennedy in 1960 and not for the city was, in fact, a debit to be erased. She should have come to Daley to begin with.

Jane's first city job was a combination of luck, foresight on the part of the mayor, and being at the right place at the right time. Federal monies were pouring out of Washington in the name of poverty. In August of 1964 Lyndon Johnson signed the Economic Opportunity Act, appointing Sargent Shriver as director. Federal money meant federal jobs, and in Chicago it was critical to the Machine that these jobs stay under its control. Daley could not have afforded to let these slip away from him, for every job, no matter how meager, was a little diamond, a precious chip, to reflect the beauty of the Machine.

In Chicago the War on Poverty became known as the Chicago Commission on Urban Opportunity (CCUO). Thirty Urban Progress Centers opened in one day. Money was pouring in from Washington, and there was no time for theoretical analysis or philosophical speculation. People had to be hired. The War on Poverty had been declared, and troops had to be recruited. Ed Kennedy, as the coordinator of the Performance Review Unit, had to hurriedly put together job descriptions and a payroll. He needed someone who could screen resumes and pigeonhole potential employees. The young widow with a letter from her committeeman from the 39th Ward impressed Kennedy as being decisive and "strong, very strong." She was a professional, well educated and bright. At Daley's behest, Kennedy hired her immediately and sent her over to Head Start.

A large chunk of the Office of Economic Opportunity monies was earmarked for Head Start. Because of the sensitivity of the Head Start Program—it involved the lives of very young children—various citizen groups did not want this department to be politicized. They did not want Head Start to be used to reward political workers; they wanted it to be run professionally. These groups conducted a talent search and recommended an administrator of the Illinois Children and Family Services for the position of director of the CCUO Children's Services, of which Head Start was the major component. The new director had been in a supervisory position with the state for thirteen years in the Day Care Licensing Division and held a

Master's degree in child development from the University of Chicago.

The new director of Head Start did not view Jane Byrne in the same light as Ed Kennedy or Richard Daley did. She saw a very angry, hostile, bitter young woman who would lash out at those she was interviewing and then retreat back into her shell. Within the first week Jane notified the director that she should have had her position as director. As they continued to work together, Jane grew more and more angry with the director, as if her very physical presence was enough to send Jane into a corridor of rage. Jane did not relate to any of her colleagues; she remained isolated, alone, preferring only to do her job—not out of any particular commitment to the ideals or goals of the poverty program, but because it was a job.

Jane had no need and no time for social relationships with her fellow workers. She did not need their approval or their support. She worked for Daley and for him alone. One with Daley was a majority. Jane had never been a mixer, had never socialized with those with whom she worked, but had always retained a modicum of cordiality. This was no longer needed.

She shared an office with a fellow worker, Mitch Butler, a pleasant middle-aged black man, and never once acknowledged his presence. It became the joke of the office that Mitch Butler had become invisible.

The staff saw a woman who was lonely, forlorn, introverted, yet beginning to enjoy the power of her position. She was responsible for hiring and firing, which gave her control over the lives of others. She sensed the vulnerability of an individual who was looking for a job, especially those who were unemployed and, at times, despised the powerlessness of one in that disadvantaged position. She needed to diminish, to hurt those she interviewed, for in many ways they were much like herself—weak, in need, with lives out of control.

During one interview she excused herself and went into the director's office to ask her if she would mind coming out and sitting in on the interview. The man being interviewed appeared to Jane to be disturbed and she was afraid to be alone with him. The director immediately saw that Jane had provoked him into a rage. He stood up and said to her, "I don't want this job. I don't want to be handled this way. I don't need this abuse," and turned on his heels and made his way out. Jane was completely unaware that she had provoked, antagonized, humiliated the interviewee. There was no realization on her part that she had set off the bitter and acrimonious dynamics. The interviewee was not a person to her but just someone to get rid of, just someone Jane felt would not fit into the plan.

The director went back to her office, sat down heavily, and looked through the smoky glass partition at the very angry young woman. She wondered about the pain that caused Jane to lash out at the innocent young man and to hurt him so much. She wondered what was the source of her haunting rage, her consumate anger that needed to hurt, to wound, to torment other human beings. She looked down the long gray hall and saw the young man, shoulders stooped, eyes down, get onto the elevator. The door closed with a slam.

A short time later, a similar incident occurred. A social worker had been hired by the Head Start Program and within two weeks it was obvious that he was unable to function. The person was deeply disturbed and suicidal. The director realized that hiring him had been a mistake and called Jane to tell her he had to go. She apprised Jane of the person's condition and asked her to be gentle with him because the person was clearly self-destructive and the shock of being let go could easily have an adverse effect on him. But Jane cruelly tore into the disturbed social worker, destroying any remnant of self-esteem he had left. The director and another member of the staff were left to pick up the pieces of Jane's attack on the debilitated person.

The director spoke to Jane again. Jane did not understand what was being said to her and could not accept the sentiments of the director. She again told Jane of her hostile and arrogant behavior toward the people she was interviewing and how she baited and provoked these well-educated, well-qualified individuals to the point where they wanted to take a punch at her. But Jane could not understand. It was just business.

Within a short time, Jane left Head Start and returned to the personnel department of CCUO. She again kept to herself. Jane talked only to Katie Murphy, who had worked with her uncle at the chancery office. Ed Burke had sent Katie to Florida one cold, depressing winter, and Katie had always felt close to Monsignor Burke. Katie saw in Ed Burke's niece many of the qualities of her uncle—his quickness, his pragmatism, his tendency always to evaluate things, trying to decide where the power was, who had it, how they held it, and how he could get some of it.

Since she held a strategic position in the personnel department of CCUO, Jane was privy to the workings of the heart of the Machine. Daley saw in her qualities that he knew were invaluable to the perpetuation of his operations. In Daley's mind, the Machine was founded on the simple equation that jobs equal loyalty equal services equal votes, and that was all that counted. Let the jobs go and there goes the city, there go the votes, and you lose. Jane had the opportunity to observe, and to be an intrinsic part of the equation.

She quickly learned how Daley perceived his broad, yet extremely circumscribed, universe. She was taught to administer his system of rewards and punishments: Reward those who delivered the vote; reward that committeeman, that precinct worker, that alderman who got out the votes and who knew what was coming down—to the very decimal point—in his ward. Those who failed to deliver were out. Who they were, what they brought to the job, and how well they did the job were incidental to their performance on election day. If they failed to deliver votes on election day, they were out.

Jane went to Daley's office on a regular basis because she was, in her position at CCUO, the critical link in the equation on the other side of La Salle Street. She knew what was going on over there, and her reports to him were never off target. With the mayor, she gazed into the underbelly of the Machine; where she missed a gear, where she failed to see a subtle relationship, he would point to what she had overlooked and rarely again would she miss it. She wasn't afraid of him and, in a strange way, she was more comfortable with him than with people she had known for years. And the mayor was comfortable with her. He could tell her things he needed to share with someone but which could go no farther than his office.

During those somewhat regular visits, Jane would argue with him. He liked that. Richard Daley was a political animal par excellence and did not pick his people arbitrarily. He could feel in the air if someone would be tough and straight and honest and loyal. He could taste if someone would sell his soul, and he knew in the pit of his stomach who was weak and who was strong, who would be blown over by the winds of politics and who would survive them. Rarely was he wrong.

Jane asked him over and over again to take her out of CCUO and to bring her to City Hall, but the mayor needed her where she was; Jane did what she was told. But she made it clear to him that she did not want to stay there forever.

Daley once was asked by a reporter why a particular person had lost an election. Daley stared at the reporter incredulously. He said with disdain, "He didn't get the votes." Why else would he have lost? Daley was not in the business of losing elections. If people had to be sacrificed, if lives were destroyed, if careers were damaged, it mattered not one iota, for the Machine, like some Mayan deity, exacted this sacrifice of lives and careers.

Jane instinctively understood this. Her entire view of the world had changed dramatically one foggy night in May. There were big patterns, big orbits, a plan larger than her own in the order of things. Her own life got caught up in an orbit bigger than she had planned. She had no choice; she had to go along; she lost control; and she suffered. That was life. Call it Divine Providence, God's will, whatever. That was life—little people who got caught up in a big pattern and were destroyed. She instinctively understood this.

The Machine was a model of life, and Richard J. Daley controlled it. Through him she found the leverage and control she so desperately needed for her own life. As she gained control she grew calmer. Strong, intelligent men made Jane calm. She had said of Bill Byrne, "I liked that he was very smart. It made me very calm."

Jane commented about Jay McMullen, "Jay's got a good brain, and I felt very comfortable." If Bill Byrne and Jay McMullen made Jane feel calm and comfortable, Richard Daley must likewise have made her feel calm and comfortable. Standing in the middle of his expansive power base, Jane felt freer than she had ever felt, no longer cramped, with the walls of her life so narrow that she could hardly breathe, so confining that she could hardly see any patterns or rhythms.

She did not become less angry but was less anxious. Life was more predictable. She was beginning to exercise a power that she had never dreamed possible. She was no longer Mrs. Nobody; she was Mrs. Somebody. The most powerful man in Chicago liked her. She knew that he liked her, for he shared with her secrets about the city, about himself, and asked for her advice, her suggestions, and her views.

Working for Daley, working in government gave Jane an opportunity to begin exercising her talents, to discover the dimensions of her own mind and soul that had never before been exposed. She became highly analytical, judgmental of policy and procedures, and outspoken in areas in which she had little experience. She found herself attracted to government, to the power it held over people's lives, to the colorful characters who inhabited the corridors of power, to the rhetoric and symbolism of power. She found that she was able to exercise control over people, not only by virtue of her personality, but also through the nature of the positions she filled. She found her helplessness decreasing, her overwhelming sense of vulnerability waning. She began to feel protected—she had a title and a paycheck; people were beginning to know who she was and were beginning to fear her. All along she had known that she couldn't trust anyone but herself, and this truth was beginning to bear itself out. As her sense of control grew, some of her anxiety began to dissipate.

Socially, Jane was in a unique, powerful position. If she had never been married, her sexuality could have been questioned.

But she had been married and had a child, so there was never a question of her sexual orientation. Her child was well cared for by her mother, so she had few anxieties about that responsibility. She was financially comfortable. She was uninterested in relationships with men and clearly conveyed this to them. She was unencumbered by friendships with women; her sisters and mother provided all the female companionship she needed. Jane was free to channel her vast reservoir of anxieties and needs into government and politics.

Her evenings were spent in the 39th Ward, doing whatever she was told. Jane had dues to pay to the system, to the Machine, and she was not going to be found remiss. She rang doorbells, worked the precinct, passed out flyers. She went to the Illinois State Fair in Springfield every year with her ward. And at the end of the day, she sat with her mother in their Sauganash kitchen, where Katharine Burke listened to her daughter tell of the strange kinds who inhabited the world of politics, people far removed from the comfortable, protected world of Sauganash.

Katharine was happy that Jane was beginning to find herself again. She could sense the anger, just under the surface, but it seemed to be better controlled. Jane was getting her spark back. The gloom and doom, her listlessness and depression seemed to have dissipated. Jane wasn't the same, she never would be, but at least she was beginning to come out of it, to find herself. Katharine hated to see her daughter act like a doormat.

14

Of Old Cows, Octane, and Watermelon Wine

One day he called her into his office. It was March 4, 1968. The mayor told Jane that he was looking for a "Commissioner of Consumer Credit." (The title actually was Commissioner of Consumer Sales, Weights, and Measures, but Daley referred to it as Consumer Credit.) At that time the city was running a modest operation, but interest in consumer affairs was growing. Chicago was going to have to have a department—one comparable to, even better than, the one in New York. Jane sat, intently writing down a copy of the job that the mayor was describing. She was half-thinking of how she would begin to recruit for this position.

The mayor raised his voice slightly, "Are you opposed?"

"Why would I be opposed?"

He said, "I'm speaking of you. And if I'm not mistaken, you will be the first woman commissioner in any major city in the United States."

The mayor placed her name before the Finance Committee for their *pro forma* approval. There was never any doubt that the committee would do anything but approve the mayor's choice.

160

Independent Alderman Leon Despres of the 5th Ward, which lies in Hyde Park and includes the area around the University of Chicago, stated, "While she is attractive, and there is a place for her in city government, she is not qualified for the job. But she will look good with the mayor in pictures." The committee approved Jane Byrne's appointment as Commissioner of Consumer Sales, Weights, and Measures.

Jane said of Despres' remark:

> I wanted to get up and slap his face. I was furious, but I was being very calm and cool. I was just about to raise my voice. Keane (then Alderman Thomas) was sitting next to me. He could sense what was coming. He kicked me under the table, pushed his paper and whispered, "Just stay calm." I resented the suggestion that some wanted to find out what skeleton I was in Mayor Daley's closet.†

Seven years later Alderman Despres said, "She and the mayor have a natural affinity. They think alike. They talk alike. They move alike. She is Daley's token woman in the party."

Jane's first office was not even in City Hall. She considered it a "cubbyhole, a dump," located in another city office building. Her salary was $15,000. The staff was small, and there was little legislation to regulate their compliance activities. Jane Byrne was smart and could see that consumer affairs was a growing concern. Consumerism became the forum through which Jane Byrne introduced herself to the public. The lack of legislation worked to her advantage, for where there was not a law, she either introduced one to the City Council or sought to mobilize public opinion against the offenders.

One of her first targets for regulation was the meat industry. The Department of Agriculture had upgraded cuts of meat to create a better market for the leaner grass-fed cattle farmers were raising. Cuts of beef that were formerly marked *good* were now labeled *prime*; *prime* was now labeled *choice*. On CBS television Jane railed at the new system: "If you were to take a piece of USDA *good* and cook it on the barbecue the way you would *prime* or *choice*, you'd break your bridge." In an interview with *Chicago Guide*, Jane remarked, "The meat ordinance was the hardest battle, and the thing I'm proudest of. I felt bad that people had been paying good money to get an old cow."

Chicago City Council passed a meat-grading ordinance to assure uniform labeling throughout the Chicago area, but not before Jane was subjected to intense lobbying pressure from the American Meat Institute, from embassies and consulates whose countries sell meat in Chicago, and from the secretary of state, who told her that the meat-labeling law proposed in Chicago might interfere with free trade negotiations throughout the world. Mayor Daley gave Jane his unconditional support, never questioning or second-guessing what she was doing. He knew that she would never embarrass him or the city of Chicago.

Jane transformed a sleepy department into an aggressive organization that regulated the following areas of consumer affairs: condo conversion, phosphates in detergents, bait and switch advertising, octane ratings on gasoline, unit pricing, and toy safety. Before Jane became commissioner, male investigators were called *deputy inspectors* and were paid on a salary range a full scale above women investigators, who were called *women shoppers* and were performing the same job. Jane upgraded the women shoppers to deputies and put women in charge of the department's public information section.

As the new commissioner's confidence grew, her political instincts sharpened. She took what others may have considered a liability, a small department lacking clout, and used it as a strength. Her department was relatively new and was considered trendy. In the 1970s consumerism and ecology replaced the civil rights movement of the '60s as the main areas of public concern. Consumerism was associated with matters traditionally of concern to women: food, children's sleepwear, toys, health services, etc. As a department, it did not have the public or political stature of departments that focused on traditionally male areas of concern: Streets and Sanitation, Corporation Council and Finance. But Commissioner Byrne took the Department of Consumer Sales, Weights and Measures very seriously. She issued more press releases than most other city departments, called press conferences, and issued weekly price lists compiled from local food chains. The skills of promoting herself that Jane had developed as a young girl were used with great acumen in promoting her new department.

Because she was a woman, Jane's political ambitions were limited to a great extent. It was assumed that, as commissioner of a city department, she had gone about as far as she could go within city government. A 1975 *Chicago Sun-Times* article stated: "There is speculation among local Democrats that Mrs. Byrne may go to Congress or go higher in the Democratic party. But Mrs. Byrne says, 'I don't think you can lay plans.' " In a 1975 *Chicago Tribune* article, the assumption that Jane had no goals or identity apart from Daley was spelled out: "The Commissioner serves a man, not a cause, and if Daley were to leave the scene, Byrne would take her departure right along with him." (Even after she had declared her candidacy for mayor in 1978, there were those who felt she was just front-running for more feasible, attractive male candidates, such as Roman Pucinski, Tom Tully, or Neil Hartigan.)

As a woman involved in the political machinery of a male town, Chicago—Big Shoulders, Hog Butcher, City on the Make—she was at the top, the top for a woman, and thus, because of her gender, was no threat in the scramble for the very top, the pinnacle. It was, in fact, her gender that gave her unlimited access to Daley's mind, for it was totally incomprehensible to him, as well as to her and to the rest, that she would ever occupy his position, much less covet it. Jane Byrne could not have played Brutus to Daley's Caesar.

What could have been a potentially scandalous relationship of the powerful older man with the attractive younger widow never suffered the slightest whisper of impropriety. The mayor was totally devoted to his wife and family; any romantic activity outside of his marriage would have been completely out of character. Those in his administration who were guilty of such activity were soon replaced. Likewise, Jane had neither time nor interest for such activity. At this time she was unavailable to men, and she conveyed this with perfect clarity. Their relationship was characterized as: father/daughter; mentor/protege; boss/girl Friday. The relationship of Jane Byrne and Richard Daley flourished by the nature of its limitations. Despite the fact that they were both reputed loners, they both had a need for friendship and for trust and sharing in a deeply personal way.

Ralph Berkowitz, a Republican campaign organizer, speaking to Milton Rakove, described Daley in his early years as mayor as "the most lonesome-looking man in the world. He'd practically sneak into his own meetings. He was not a cheerleader. He had an inferiority complex."

As Jane's friendship with the mayor grew and her political image became more clearly defined, Matt Danaher began his decline. Their careers were curiously intertwined, meshing at certain points, diverging at others.

Matt had been with him since 1950 when Daley left Chicago for Springfield to be Illinois Director of Revenue. Matt was only twenty-three at the time, but he was a Bridgeport boy who lived only a few doors down the street from the mayor. Matt was the mayor's alter ego, closer than a brother, a man privy to the thoughts and aspirations of the mayor. Mike Royko said that Matt "was one of the few people who could walk past the policeman and into the mayor's house . . . he has served as the mayor's emotional whipping boy, so close that he can yell back and slam the door when he leaves."

It has been written that Daley made Matt in his own image, made him a contemporary success story. When Daley became county clerk, Matt was his administrative assistant; when Daley was elected mayor in 1955, Matt became his administrative assistant in charge of patronage and later became deputy mayor.

As patronage chief, before a ward committeeman would come to see the mayor, Matt would brief the mayor on the status of jobs held in that particular ward. Matt knew the dimensions of every slot and cranny in Cook County and in the city and knew all the warm bodies that occupied them. Daley appeared omniscient to the ward committeeman, thanks to the stewardship of Matt. Matt said of his job, "Like a personnel manager, you get the right person for the right job. Patronage assures the loyalty of those around you; nobody hires his enemies to work for him."

Matt was elected alderman of the 11th Ward, Daley's ward, and was quickly elected to the Finance Committee, while retaining his patronage job. He became vice-chairman of the Finance Committee, president pro-tem of the council. His operation was described by Alderman Jack Sperling as "control by hierarchy and anarchy of the political system."

In 1960 Matt was the link between Daley and Kennedy. Any dealings with Daley went through Matt Danaher. Jane was only a secretary to the director of the Kennedy campaign. But in 1968 Jane caught up with Matt. Jane was made a commissioner in Daley's cabinet. At the same time, Matt was appointed Clerk of the Circuit Court of Cook County, replacing the clerk who had died. He won election for the position the following November.

Matt Danaher's political star began to fade quickly. His young son, struck by a car while returning home from the store, died in his arms in front of the Bridgeport police station. Matt began to drink. The responsibilities of clerk of the court were too much for him. He was a behind-the-scenes man; when he had to dance alone, he couldn't dance. Eugene Kennedy described him as having "the look of the fellow who gets killed at the end of the movie, the look of faulted innocence which seems to invite doom on every level."

In 1973 he was accused of using his position as clerk of the court to buy into lucrative real estate ventures, receiving a higher return on his investment than the contractor. A year later, he was indicted by a federal grand jury for taking $400,000 in bribes from builders needing zoning changes and private financing. Daley accused the U.S. Attorney, Big Jim Thompson, of carrying out a vendetta against his friends; Thompson accused Daley of assailing the good faith and integrity of the grand jury. Matt continued to drink. His wife filed for divorce. He moved out of his Bridgeport home. A few weeks before Christmas, 1974, a maid found Matt's body, clad only in his pajama top and shorts, at the Ambassador West Hotel. Matt had died alone, haunted, tortured, alcoholic.

Matt was waked at a Bridgeport funeral home. One of the mourners whispered, "It's a bad thing. Everyone is feeling the same. We forgot him in his time of troubles. And now he can't hear us say we're sorry." At the funeral Mass, the priest said, "I hope you receive from God a fairer and more merciful judgment than you could ever have hoped to receive here with us."

Mayor Daley was one of the pallbearers, carrying the casket of forty-seven-old Matt out of the church, down the cold icy steps, and shoving him into the long black hearse, finally relieved of the troubles that his friend had brought him.

Matt had been on the outs with Daley for a long time. He drank. He couldn't keep his mouth shut. He had his fingers in the cookie jar. He had betrayed Daley. Matt had fizzled out on him like a wet firecracker. Maybe he had just expected too much from Matt, maybe Matt just didn't have the fiber, the strength. Matt was too soft. Daley had to cut him loose.

Jacob Arvey, commenting on Daley's ability to cut out his own people said, "It's not a nice system, but you've got to be made of stern stuff. You've got to forsake compassion. You've got to be insensitive to the feelings of others. You've got to be unmindful of everything except the ultimate goal." Edward Levine, in his study of Irish politicians, quotes a non-Irish politician as saying, "There's a saying that the Irish (politicians) are sentimental. That stuff is nonsense. They're cold-blooded as hell."

Matt was gone, out of Daley's way, and Jane was in—a perfect replacement, but even better because she had the stern stuff that somehow was always missing from Matt. She wasn't soft around the edges. She intuitively understood the system and was never obstructed by feelings. She was cold-blooded as hell.

Daley had control. Subordinates needed clout, but on top you needed control. The Young Turks, a group of young Machine aldermen who occasionally liked to flex their muscles, used to call Daley the Big Bopper. He would bop them into line. A young attorney, Bill Hurley, had served as a Kennedy advance man in Chicago. After the election he was offered a position in Washington with the new administration. Not wanting to relocate his family, he turned down the job. But rewards were still due him, and he was given a sizable legal contract with a federal department. At six o'clock one morning his phone rang. It was the mayor calling to inform Hurley that he was aware of his government contract and that he had Daley's permission to accept it. Pure unadulterated control. Not clout. Not only was Daley in control of the information (the awarding of the contract), not only did he give the permission (although it was not a condition of the contract), but he kept the upper hand in the conversation (by calling at such an early hour). Daley had been awake and alert for hours. It was essential that Daley maintain control and carefully communicate that cold hard fact.

Jane knew all about control, and she knew all about what the absence of it meant. All this time, since her first job, she had been watching him control and watching him communicate the fact that he, and he alone, was in control—clout or no clout.

The communication of control is an art form requiring mastery of the media: newspaper, radio, and television. The ancients had to send their runners from Sparta to Macedonia, from Thebes to Athens, bearing news of the latest political events. As the Greek runners probably embellished and interpreted the facts of a battle or a death to fit their own vision of life, so reporters and correspondents necessarily interject themselves into the purported objective reporting of the news. Therefore, a skillful politician who must communicate his control must also control what the mountain runners see, hear, and feel. If the runners could not be controlled, the politician had to transcend the runners and communicate directly with the people.

Daley mumbled and jumbled his words, and his press secretary told the press to print what Daley meant, not what he said. Daley's malapropisms became favorite dinner party jokes, and smart, articulate correspondents joined in a chorus of laughter at the inarticulate mayor. But while they were laughing at his malapropisms and making fun of his inarticulate speech, the mayor was masterfully projecting himself beyond his words, even in spite of his words. Viewers and readers got the message. Richard J. Daley was in control; he was in charge. The object of his control—be it the hippies, the banks, the schools, or whatever—was incidental. He was the Boss. There was no need for the public to worry. The wonderful city was in safekeeping in his strong fatherly hands. Even if reporters missed the point of his rhetoric, the public knew the meaning of what they saw and what they heard. Daley was so big and strong and the city was so big and strong that they began to fuse into each other, the lines of demarcation fading. They said, "Daley is Chicago; Chicago is Daley."

Jane quickly learned the importance of control and communication. She began to call her own press conferences and release her own statements; she began to project herself as a force to be reckoned with. Jane revealed that one of the biggest lessons in control that Daley ever taught her was that of timing. "Decisions that I thought he was slow on proved to be correct just by virtue of his little game—his timing." The mayor told Jane:

> It's a big checkerboard. You're in a position to sit back and let them all make their moves. They'll push here, they'll push there. Sit back. And when they're all made, you study those moves. You take your chip, and if you've watched it well, and if your timing is right, you go click, click, click . . . king me. It's all a matter of timing, and don't forget that.

Timing was not a foreign concept to her. Jane played classical piano. She frequently rode horses. Holding back, getting the rhythm, pausing, moving in time, moving with the flow. Moving with the flow of interest in consumerism. She knew that she was on to a good thing, one that appealed to the public. "The mayor has said that the human concerns are at the heart of all the city's programs, and that is the ultimate in consumerism," Jane stated in a 1974 *Chicago Sun-Times* article.

An apparent jurisdictional problem arose between the city and the state of Illinois, which immediately became a political skirmish. Unlike the city of Chicago, the state of Illinois did not have a statutory consumer affairs department with regulatory power. Governor Dan Walker had appointed Celia Maloney as the advocate whose major function was to hold press conferences and testify before the State Legislature about consumer-related bills.

Celia Maloney, a native of Colorado and graduate of Colorado State University, had come to Walker's attention through her work in independent Alderman William Singer's unsuccessful campaign in 1975 against Daley. Married to an attorney, she had been employed for five years in the marketing department of Quaker Oats, belonged to the Committee on Illinois Government, and was a member of the Task Force for Consumer Affairs for the Independent Precinct Organization (IPO).

Her testimonies before the State Legislature had little effect on their voting behavior, but her press conferences were getting attention.

Governor Dan Walker was in serious political trouble with the voters and had been feuding with Daley since before he became governor. The bad blood between Daley and Walker spilled over into Byrne and Maloney's battling over jurisdictional matters.

In August 1975 Maloney called a press conference to accuse seventeen Chicago area businesses of deceptive advertising. Four days later Jane called her own press conference and accused Maloney of "fraud against consumers" and of "cheap publicity tricks," presumably because she felt that the city had the prerogative to protect its own people without help from the state. Maloney refused to respond to Jane's accusations, saying that they should concentrate on the issues.

In early September 1975 Maloney called another press conference and announced that the seventeen businesses had changed their advertising tactics to comply with the law and announced that the Better Business Bureau and the Federal Trade Commission were investigating the situation. Mrs. Maloney cleared her throat, brushed her long hair to one side, and stated, "Reaction from City Hall was slightly less than rewarding." She accused Byrne of starting a personal attack against her, and added, "I would hope Mrs. Byrne would join us in the common fight to protect consumers instead of picking a personal fight with me."

As the cameras focused on Maloney in the communications center on the twentieth floor of the State of Illinois Building, Jane Byrne charged through the doors, crashing the press conference. One newspaper account described her as "a petite blond in a blue suede coat"; Tom Alderman, director of communications of Illinois (and later CBS weatherman) called her a "harridan, shrewish, shrill, heavily rouged—like war paint." Commissioner Byrne, accompanied by her daughter and two deputies, brandished a copy of the consumer protection ordinance passed by the City Council in July, which had become effective in August. Jane glared into the cameras, snarling that it was inappropriate for the governor's representative to try to change the ordinance, since she felt it adequately covered deceptive advertising practices.

> Everything you have proposed has been in the code. I do not propose to take any advice from somebody who is not up to date about consumer affairs. I call this shooting from the hip, or ignorance, and I do not like this grandstanding. I am not going to have you make an erroneous statement about the city's program. I am here to answer you.

Commissioner Byrne was indignant at the actions of the state toward the city, indignant at Walker's cross attitude toward the city. She was indignant at Maloney's intrusion on her turf. The city did not belong to Walker and Maloney; Daley and Byrne owned Chicago.

Celia Maloney watched that long finger with the bright red

nail jabbing in her direction, that powerful fist pounding on the Chicago ordinance, heard the cameras and tape recorders, saw the look of excitement on the reporters' faces as they hurried to get it all down. The bright nails, the bright rouge, the bright red lipstick, the bright, brassy wig. Maloney grabbed her notes and hurried into the small room off the communications room, leaving Byrne and the reporters and cameras to Tom Alderman.

Tom attempted to pick up the pieces, to stick with the facts of the state's investigation, to reiterate numbers and the deep concern of the governor and of the state for its citizens. He knew no one was listening. He knew Commissioner Byrne had won. She had skillfully adjusted the focus of the press conference, fading the survey into the background and zeroing in on the political dispute between city and state. It was no longer a consumer story. It was part of the Walker-Daley war, and Daley's general was much, much tougher and much, much smarter than Walker's.

Celia Maloney was shaken up. The confrontation was in the papers and on the television. Chicago politics. She didn't have the stomach for it. Never in her life had she been subjected to such an attack. Celia Maloney was smart, but she knew she couldn't beat Byrne. Walker would just have to find someone else. She got on the La Salle Street bus, Number 156, at La Salle and Randolph. She had to get home. She saw people nudging each other, more fingers pointing at her, whispering, "That's her. That's her."

She couldn't stay on the bus. She grabbed her bag, pushed her way through the crowd, pushed on the back door, sounding the buzzer throughout the bus. The driver opened the door and she got off, shaken. She got into a cab and asked the driver to take her to her near-north home. She opened the door, walked into the front room, and saw the housekeeper and her four-year-old daughter watching the news. She saw the commissioner call her stupid and incompetent. The whole city, but, most of all, her daughter heard that Celia Maloney was stupid and incompetent. Maloney snapped off the television, muttering under her breath, "I could kill that woman."

Five years later Maloney felt that she had been subjected to harassment, that Jane Byrne was a singularly unpleasant person whose sense of reality was distorted. She felt Jane Byrne had to be pathological: "somebody who takes somebody like me with no political ambitions—apolitical—and saw me as a threat." Jane appeared "stupid, unprofessional, incompetent" to Maloney. She stated that she was not afraid of Jane but was afraid of causing a scene; she did not want to be portrayed as "wild and screaming."

Celia Maloney was not apolitical. If she were, she would not have called three press conferences less than four weeks before the gubernatorial election. But she was not as political as her city counterpart. Perhaps she had not learned as much; she was not as seasoned; she did not have as good a teacher as the city commissioner. Perhaps her own innate instincts were not as sharp.

Jane was learning, and learning quickly. Never walk away from a fight, Mayor Daley taught her. And when you fight, you win. He taught her that winning is the name of the game. Politics is like the child's game, King of the Mountain. There is room at the top for only one, and a loser does not stay on the top. The Young Turks called Daley the Big Bopper. He would bop down those who wanted to get to the top, and he was teaching Jane how to bop down those who wanted to get to the top. Jane knew that Walker and Maloney had to go. She knew how to use the press and the television. You get rid of your enemies, for they will only take the power away from you. That turning-the-other-cheek business had no place in the mad scramble for the top. You don't court your enemies, real or potential. You bop them. You destroy them.

15

They'll Cut You Off at the Pass

In an August 13, 1974, *Chicago Today* article, Sue Roll wrote:

> Political circles buzz with speculation about the whys and
> wherefores of her newfound power in the party. Some say she is
> a wise choice as Daley's spokeswoman because she is one of the
> few remaining figures in Daley's fold not tainted by scandal and
> who doesn't want to be mayor.

There were never scandals of any magnitude while Jane ran
the consumer department. It has become a truism that those on
the top, or on their way to the top, must make a relatively
clear choice between money and power. The explanation of
why Daley and Alderman Keane were able to maintain their
friendship for so many years was that Daley liked power and
Keane liked money, and they stayed out of each other's way.
Jane was attracted to the magic of power in the same way that
Daley was attracted to it.

Jane had always been financially comfortable. She liked
flashy sports cars, expensive dresses, furs. She never stinted on

herself or Kathy, and the resources for her expensive taste were always available. Groveling and crawling for money was not part of her character. Running a clean department became a matter of pride.

> I was told that if I had wanted to play ball it would have been worth a million dollars a year to sit in the commissioner's seat. If I wanted to be corrupt, I have the opportunity to do so, but when he appointed me, I took an oath and he trusted me not to go on the take and keep my inspectors clean. If I didn't do this, number one, I would have broken my oath and let him down and two, if the mayor ever learned of it, I know it would take him two minutes to fire me.

She purportedly halted the shakedown of small independent groceries by city inspectors. The store owners were required to pay the city inspectors $350 per month as a protection against city harassment. When the price went up to $450, a grocer complained to Jane. This shakedown was known as the "We had lunch at the Bismarck Club."

Jane's image was that of Alice in Wonderland. The city inspectors thought she was some sort of dreamy lady, naive, unaware of what was going on; and when she began to crack down on the inspectors, they retaliated, attacking the Walgreen drugstores which Alderman Keane's law firm represented. The inspectors would write tickets charging that there were no oysters in their oyster crackers and no lemons in their lemon cookies. (These tickets were similar to those written by a policeman for illegal parking or speeding; the offender would have to show up in court and would be subjected to fines.) Walgreen's managers complained to their aldermen, to Keane. Daley got wind of it, called her in, and asked her what was going on with the inspectors. She told him the story. The mayor supported her and she fired sixteen inspectors.

On one lunch hour Jane was trying on a fur coat at Bonwit's. It needed alterations, so the sales clerk called in the seamstress. The seamstress at Bonwit's was a full-time city inspector with the Department of Consumer Sales, Weights, and Measures. She was fired on the spot.

An executive with a major food chain complained to the mayor that Jane was "picking on him" by citing his food chain for short-weighting meats and vegetables. The mayor asked Jane what the problem was and she told him, "They cheat." Daley asked Jane to meet with the executive so that there would be no hard feelings, to restore harmony, to show them how to abide by the city's regulations. Jane agreed to meet with the executive. The executive told her that he wanted to be cooperative, so cooperative that he would "be happy to put a pretty little mink around [her] pretty little face." The executive never got into Daley's office again.

Bribery, conspiracy, income tax evasion, grand jury indictments—none of these would ever be a part of Jane Byrne's public or private life. She didn't need the money. She didn't want the money. She watched so many of Daley's friends and associates fall out of favor, lose their jobs, their families, go off to jail. That would never happen to her. Daley knew that, and he saw to it that she began her way up in the Democratic party, for Jane Byrne was a politician and she would never be content with being just an administrator.

The opportunity came in August 1972, subsequent to the Democratic National Convention in Miami. Daley and fifty-eight other Machine delegates were not seated at the convention, because their election had not complied with the new rules for a more equitable representation of delegates stipulated by the McGovern Commission on Rules. Independent Alderman William Singer and Reverend Jesse Jackson led the anti-Daley force.

There had been a vote to decide which of the Illinois delegates would be seated. Since McGovern's nomination was assured, the Illinois furor provided the little excitement the convention had to offer. The critical vote came from the Massachusetts delegation. Senator Edward Kennedy had declined offers to run for President, citing family responsibilities. He did not attend the convention but vacationed in Hyannisport. The Massachusetts delegation voted to seat the Singer-Jackson delegation. This was the critical vote, dampening any hopes the Daley people might have had.

Jane was indignant at Senator Kennedy. She felt that he owed it to Mayor Daley to deliver the Massachusetts delegation for him. She immediately wrote him a letter:

> Dear Teddy,
>
> It was a good thing Mayor Daley was not out on his boat in 1960.
>
> Jane Byrne

Daley was humiliated nationally. Political pundits nodded; they thought this marked the end of the Machine, the watershed in Daley's demise as a national political figure. Four months later the new Democratic politics was buried with McGovern in the 1972 Nixon landslide. He carried only one state; Nixon carried forty-nine.

Robert Strauss, newly elected chairman of the Democratic National Committee, aware that the party had been turned over to amateurs, contacted Daley and offered him the position of chairman of the powerful Resolutions Committee of the Democratic National Committee. The Resolutions Committee was the group through which all party rule changes, including that of delegate selection, were funneled. Daley suggested his Commissioner of Sales, Weights, and Measures, Jane Byrne, for the position. "The appointment," wrote Jay McMullen in the *Chicago Daily News*, "signaled the restoration of Mayor Richard J. Daley to the front ranks of policy makers in the party. Mrs. Byrne is a close political confidante of the mayor and a friend of the Daley family."

In addition to the Daley family, Jane had carefully cultivated the Kennedys. However, Jane's relationship with the Kennedys proved to be a double-edged sword. On the one hand, it gave her authority in matters relating to the Kennedy family. When William Singer, campaigning for mayor as an independent against Daley in 1975, ran an ad on television stating that he was in charge of Bobby Kennedy's 1968 Illinois Presidential campaign, Jane blasted him, saying, "That's trading on the dead, and the dead cannot defend themselves. I'm not denying that Singer worked in the Kennedy campaign, but he certainly didn't run it. What he did was travel on a bus down to Indiana to help out in the primary there. My sister went on that bus, too, but she's not claiming she ran any campaign."

If being a Kennedy associate gave Jane stature, it also caused her doubts about her relationship with Daley. She never knew whether he picked her to be a commissioner on her own merits or because of her Kennedy ties. She said:

> I never knew why Mayor Daley appointed me. I would just love to think he did it because he thought that this particular thing was the right time. But I didn't know if he might have appointed me because he knew that Bobby was going to be a candidate . . . and it would be an asset.*

She felt very personally the reservation that Daley had about her and about everyone. He trusted no one completely. This lesson did not escape her.

In February of 1974 Senator Adlai Stevenson expressed his opinion that Daley might not run for mayor in 1975. The mayor said nothing, but Jane Byrne blasted Stevenson, calling him the "disloyal opposition," and promised to vote for his opponent in the March primary. She added:

> I haven't forgotten that he tried to take over as state party chairman in 1971, and I won't forget that everything he said last week was an insult to everyone in the Democratic party. He and his type are responsible for the ills of the Democratic party. And when I get angry, I get really angry.

When Daley was asked about his commissioner's remarks, he smiled, "Janie has a lot of experience in the political field. She's entitled to her observations."

On May 2, 1974, Alderman Thomas Keane was indicted on seventeen counts of mail fraud and one count of conspiracy. Kerner, Barrett, Danaher, Wigoda, Bush had gone down. Now Keane. Four days later, the mayor suffered a stroke. He was seventy-two years old. Who would take his place? City newspapers published lists of possible successors. Jane called a news conference:

> I denounce the political vultures who have been circling over the scene, attempting to exploit the mayor's temporary incapacity. I don't object to anyone aspiring to be mayor of Chicago, but they shouldn't do a minuet of death around the mayor's sick bed. It makes me sick. The same ones who send him get-well cards are downtown scheming to kick him out of his job.

A ward committeeman, expressing his views on the various men in Daley's cabinet who would have to fill in for him, added, "Don't forget Janie Byrne. She's close to Daley. She might stand up and protect him during the in-fighting. She might finesse all those guys."

Daley survived the stroke, underwent surgery, and returned in September 1974. Three months later he buried Matt Danaher. In January 1975, at a Chicago Democratic party rally, Daley casually announced that Commissioner Jane Byrne was appointed co-chairman of the Chicago Democratic party, sharing the position with him. The Executive Committee met and voted unanimously to confirm the appointment. Jane had moved to the top of the mountain, sharing the throne with the king.

Jane had noticed a change in the mayor. He was thinner; there was a slight problem with his speech due to the surgery. He was uncomfortable with the amount of attention being paid to his health, what he called "making a holy show out of yourself." He was on the mend; he was as alert, as sharp, as ever. But he was different. She called it "stately and compassionate"; he became more kindly, more open with the press. Jane told Milton Rakove, "The sting came out of him." Daley told the press, "I'm lucky I'm here. I have none of that left in me. I don't want to hurt, whatever they do."

He knew that his days were numbered. He had suffered three minor strokes prior to the major stroke in May of 1974. As the mayor looked at Jane, he pointed to his heart, tears rolling down his face, "Here's where I'm going when I go. My ticker, my ticker is going to give out. The doctors told me the stroke damaged my heart valves and that's going to be the problem." The doctors had told him that his mind would be fine, for the surgery had increased the flow of blood to his brain. His mental faculties were fine, but he would not live out another term. He could not see himself sitting at home, waiting to die. He could not fathom the city of Chicago without him running it. There was no one else, for Chicago was Daley and Daley was Chicago. The lifeblood of the city was so intertwined with Daley's that it was almost as if the city would be reduced to ashes when he went. If there were any would-be mayors waiting in the wings, they knew better than to show themselves. Ambition of that sort in the kingdom of Daley was tantamount to treason. Jane commented on the absence of any successors: "One thing he didn't have time to do was to adequately groom a successor. Toward the end, he was trying to bring along more and more of the younger men in the party. But he really didn't have enough time."

Daley had twenty-one years to groom a successor—six terms in office. But to groom a successor would be to admit his mortality, to invite competition, to engage in a futile, worthless effort. Shortly before he died, the mayor told the younger men in the party to stick together after he was gone, almost like a father urging his children not to fight, to remain a family. The mayor was wise, and he knew that the rhythm and flow of power was not his to direct after he was gone. The family would fight, like brothers and sisters grabbing the family silver. Power is an existential quality, as elusive as an early morning dream. The mayor once told Jane, "I'm for the things that you really want, but there are things you want that I can't give you. You have to get them yourself."

Did the mayor ever think that Jane Byrne would end up in his chair? Did he ever speak with his wife about Richie, his eldest son, becoming mayor of Chicago? Did he ever see Richie and Jane tearing themselves apart, locked in a sibling rivalry over his father's position? Daley was a man of his time, a man, in many ways, before his time. He knew that women were becoming a real political force, as demanding as the blacks and Latinos. He knew Chicago. He knew Jane—the dimensions of her mind, the force of her drive, the art of her politics. Daley was a man of instinct, of feeling, of knowing how the wind was coming up from the vast Illinois plains. He was also wise, and he knew the limits of his control, of what he could change and what he could not change, of what he could prevent and what had a life of its own. The sting went out of him. He didn't want to hurt people anymore. He had done enough, more than enough. They could carry on. He had given what he could. He was tired. Very tired.

Shorty after 2:00 P.M. on December 20, 1976, Mayor Daley died of a massive coronary in his doctor's office on Michigan Avenue. The city mourned; he was gone. From across the country, the rich and the powerful joined the people of Chicago at his wake and funeral Mass at Nativity of Our Lord Church. While the city was grieving, the City Council was scrambling to see who would take his place.

Michael Bilandic, alderman from Bridgeport's 11th Ward, agreed to serve as mayor. He stated emphatically that he would not run for the office in the forthcoming special election and would serve the city only until it had time to choose a new mayor. Bilandic was head of the powerful Finance Committee of the City Council and brought a knowledge of city finance and city administration to his interim position. Bilandic blinked slowly and spoke thickly, giving the impression of one slow to speak and slow to think. He lived with his mother, Minnie, in a little Bridgeport home, just like the Daleys. She cooked Croatian food for him, wore long black dresses, and looked very ethnic, very Catholic in a non-Irish sort of way. His brother lived next door. Bilandic had never married, and people jokingly called him the "virgin mayor." He gave the impression that if he had heard the joke, he probably would not understand. It was as if the little brick bungalows of Bridgeport held the secrets for Chicago's mayors, and to choose a mayor from any other neighborhood would jinx the city.

Jane Byrne had lost her protector and mentor. She was out—out in the cold Chicago streets, out as out could be. She had no ward, no group, no people. Just Daley, and now he was gone and she was alone. All those people who had had to stand by and watch her ingratiate herself with Daley could finally get their recompense. The tall Christmas tree was still blinking in the Walnut Room at Marshall Field, Michigan Avenue was still aglitter with the little Italian Christmas lights, and Daley had not even been buried a week when Jane was unceremoniously dumped from her position as co-chairman of the Cook County Central Committee.

George Dunne was elected chairman within days after Daley's death. He wanted her out, saying that there would be some modification of the role of women in the party structure, and that there "definitely would be a place for Jane in politics. Perhaps putting on women's card parties, fashion shows, luncheons, dinners, and the like."

Jane said, "That's politics. I can't have it the way I had it because the mayor is gone." She had told people that she would not stay on after the mayor was gone, for working for Daley was "like a walk through history . . . staying on after he left would be anticlimactic."

Jane was still head of the Democratic Women of Chicago and Cook County, a state-chartered organization that was not under Dunne's control. She moved all her files out of the Democratic headquarters at the Bismarck Hotel. Revenge was so sweet, they thought, watching Jane Byrne turn back into a pumpkin, back into a nobody. She came from nowhere, and she was going right back to nowhere, damn fast.

Jane could feel her power ebb. It was going and she knew it. In October 1977 she called for a luncheon meeting of her executive committee to plan for a large Democratic women's luncheon the following November, honoring a prominent Washington politician. George Dunne, as head of the Cook County Democratic party, was invited. Dunne phoned Jane to express his shock that she would carry on such unauthorized activities. Dunne put pressure on the Democratic regulars to boycott Byrne's meeting. Byrne called off her luncheon, stating that the date conflicted with an important City Council meeting. Jane was getting the message. It was only going to be a matter of time before they would really get her.

Mayor Daley had always told her never to walk away from a fight. She never had, and she didn't intend to begin now. The mayor had always told her not to lose her temper, to learn how to control herself, not to reveal her feelings. She didn't show her hand. She'd let them think she was going along, playing the old Alice in Wonderland role. The mayor had always told her to watch her timing. Hold back. Watch the checkerboard. Watch their moves. Wait. Then go click, click, click. King me. And, by God, that was exactly what she would do.

In January of 1976, eleven months before Daley's death, Jane took over the responsibilities of the Department of Public Vehicle Licenses, in addition to her other duties as Commissioner of Consumer Sales, Weights, and Measures. She had begun with meat and vegetables, extended her domain to include the regulation of electric meters, retail advertising, fuel, public garages, housing, and now was regulating taxicabs. The entire range of consumer goods and services was under her critical eye. She began by requiring safety inspections of cabs driven in the city, eye examinations for the drivers, and uniforms (the drivers rebelled; she lifted the uniform requirement). She demanded tighter regulations for taxi registration.

Richard Daley's bequest to Jane Byrne was to put the taxi industry under her review. On the day he died, December 20, 1976, her regulatory powers over the public vehicles were greatly extended. Daley knew that the taxi companies, Checker and Yellow Cabs, were a hornet's nest. He knew his commissioner and her attraction for hornet's nests. He was getting pressure from both sides. The Federal Trade Commission and the Internal Revenue Service were investigating Checker.

In March 1976 three months after Jane assumed responsibility for public vehicles, the *Chicago Independent* wrote:

> The Checker Connection allowed the taxi conglomerate to inflate its costs, above 86% of fare revenues, thus qualifying Checker for a fare hike under a sweetheart city ordinance. Yellow and Checker have for decades been tied to the very heart of institutional Machine politics in this city. Their meat-hooks were deep, unbreakable. Jane Byrne may have a tiger's tail in her grasp.

Tiger's tail or hornet's nest, taxis were hot. When that ordinance giving her more extensive control of cabs passed the City Council on the day of his death, Jane knew that the mayor wanted her to do something with them. Taxis were becoming an embarrassment to the administration. There was too much publicity about the fare increases. Soon the public would start to complain. It wasn't good for business. It wasn't good for the city; taxis were too visible.

Although the ordinance, giving her jurisdiction over leased cabs, passed the City Council, Daley was dead and Jane's days were numbered. She would never go quietly, tiptoeing out before the sun came up over the Drive. She could read the writing on the wall as well as anyone else. Perhaps she could write on the wall herself, big and bright enough for everyone to read, not just for those nearsighted little men who were out to get her.

On July 7, 1977, the City Council voted to give the cab companies a fare increase. Jane wrote a memo to her files and had it notarized. (This is a standard government procedure known as CYA—Cover Your Ass.)

> I am writing this memo to make a record of all events relating to the taxi cab increase. I believe the entire action was fradulent and conspiratorial and should not have been granted. . . .
>
> One year ago, Alderman Vrdolyak came into my office on

behalf of Checker and Yellow taxis. Daley said, "Don't get yourself set up like that. You tell Vrdolyak not to come to your office with them. . . ."

I sincerely believed Mayor Bilandic was going to run things straight. I do not think he did. I knew immediately the increase was greased. . . .

Bilandic looked at everyone and said, "That's how it's done." I said, "You do know that this is totally outside of the law." Bilandic said nothing. . . .

As it ended up, nothing was going to be added to benefit the consumer and nothing has been.

I have dictated this memo as a permanent record of what I perceive the way the rate increase came to be.

Notarized July 27, 1977

The Federal Trade Commission had been looking into the Checker monopoly. Jerry LaMet, assistant regional director of the FTC, was teaching a course on antitrust law at Loyola Law School when a young black man stopped him after class and inquired why the FTC was not investigating the monopoly held by Checker. The student knew a man who wanted to buy five cabs but found it impossible. Checker was the only company who could purchase medallions (cab permits) from the city. The cab company did this for $72 each and sold them to individuals for $15,000. The man would have had to purchase medallions worth $360 for $75,000.

LaMet had begun the investigation of Checker in January 1973. He knew that the city would not do anything about Checker because it was not politically advantageous for the city to crack down on business. On the other hand, Daley did not like Checker. The FTC assigned two other attorneys and an investigator to the case. After a grand jury hearing, the FTC subpoenaed Checker's records. LaMet kept Jane and her assistant, Terry Hocin, informed about the government's findings.

He told her that the FTC might have to sue the city for allowing the Checker monopoly. Jane told LaMet that she had conferred with the city corporation counsel and they advised her to go right ahead but warned him that the FTC would never be able to get it off the ground. "These are very powerful people. You can't touch them."

LaMet had been with the FTC since he graduated from Northwestern Law School in 1955. He thought that this was just another antitrust case and that politics, as such, "just don't mean a damn thing" when you have federal statutory power behind you. The FTC staff testified before the City Council before the rates went up, assuming that once they made the City Council aware of Checker's strong position in the city, the council would act.

The Council passed the increase on July 7, 1977; it went into effect immediately. LaMet called Jane, requesting a meeting with her. Jane said to him, "I'd like to talk with you. Soon. I can't see you in my office. You'll have to come to the house." Jerry and two of his staff went out to the Burke home in Sauganash during the following afternoon. Jane told him not to park in front of the house, that she was sure that they were watching her. They parked two blocks away, circled back, and came into the house.

It was a hot July afternoon. The commissioner was in a white blouse and blue slacks. Her hair was very short. LaMet had never seen her without her wig. She appeared very upset, angry. She sat in a large chair, the three FTC staff members on the flowered chintz couch. The commissioner was restless— smoking, walking to the window, pulling back the curtain, pacing the floor, lighting another cigarette. She told him that a fix was on. She had written a memo, detailing "all the events leading up to and including meetings, secret meetings, and so-called negotiations relating to the taxicab increase."

She went again to the window. Her voice was low and shaking. "Jerry, if the mayor only knew what they were doing to his city, he would roll over in his grave." LaMet said nothing, thinking to himself, "She really loves the city. This whole damn thing is exploiting, hurting the city. She feels it. She's not making this up. She loves the damn city."

Jane told LaMet that she was frightened. She was frightened for herself and for her daughter. He asked her exactly who she was afraid of. She said, "You don't know the taxi people. You don't know any of them." (Eight months later when she was married, a delivery man brought a beautifully wrapped present to the church. It was a container of dog excrement. She told LaMet that she felt it was from the mayor's office and was related to the taxi business.)

She came away from the window and went back to the large chair. She lit another cigarette. LaMet noticed her hands trembling. "Do you really think you can do something about this mess?" LaMet told her emphatically that the FTC was not subject to the political process, that they had the statutory authority, that he personally would see that justice would be done. Jane looked down at the floor and said firmly, "They'll cut you off at the pass. You won't get it through. I trust you personally, but you don't know them." LaMet told her again that the FTC was not political. The right thing would be done.

In August 1977 the FTC regional director Stephanie Kanwit quit to go into private law practice. LaMet was in line for her position, for he had been with them for twenty-two years and had been the assistant regional director for four years. Kanwit recommended LaMet for the job. The Chicago position went to a Paul Turley, the acting regional director from Cleveland who had been with the FTC for four years.

LaMet received a call from a Chicago newsman, telling him that an informant saw the Chicago taxi people give money to the FTC people in Washington. LaMet reported the conversation to the U.S. Attorney's office. A staff member said that they knew about it, that the federal grand jury was investigating the bribes. Sometime later he asked LaMet, "Are you ready to testify?" LaMet said he was ready. He never again heard from the U.S. Attorney's office.

LaMet was excluded from staff meetings. The assistant bureau chief from Washington came to Chicago, but LaMet could not see him. LaMet was assigned to another investigation. Shortly afterward, one of the two staff attorneys left the FTC;

the remaining attorney took over responsibility for the Checker investigation. LaMet did not know the taxi people.‡ He got cut off at the pass.

Jane decided to go public with her memo of July 27. On Thursday, November 10, 1977, the *Chicago Daily News* broke the story. On Friday, November 11, Alderman Edward Burke, known as Pretty Eddie, head of the City Council subcommittee that approved the fare increase, announced that he would move to strip Commissioner Byrne of her authority to supervise the taxi industry. He stated that any city employee who withheld valuable information, which a City Council subcommittee should have received to enable them to do their job properly, should be fired. When he was asked if he were referring to Mrs. Byrne, he said, "Yes, that's true," and that he would move to strip her of her authority "if the mayor doesn't do it first."

Commissioner Byrne said, "Well, they are not going to make a scapegoat out of me, particularly when I testified about this before the subcommittee. I testified under direct questioning from Alderman Burke. He's shooting from the hip." Alderman Burke said that he believed Mayor Daley had made a mistake in transferring control of the cabs from a licensing commission to Commissioner Byrne.

On Tuesday, November 15, on the ten o'clock news, Walter Jacobson asked Mayor Bilandic if he would take a lie detector test. He said that he certainly would. Greasing was a serious charge. The next day, November 16, Irv Kupcinet wrote: "Color Jane's future in City Hall as dismal." Jane said, "I was not going to sit there like a sitting duck. I can't change what I went through. And I'm not going to change what I said." When she walked through her department, the staff stood and clapped.

---

‡In June 1980 the FTC officially announced that it ended its seven-year investigation of Checker and Yellow Cabs because cabs are not engaged in interstate commerce; the FTC stated that a monopoly may exist but that the state of Illinois should look into it.

On November 17 Jane also agreed to take a lie detector test. She said, "I have to live with myself and I can. My mother said a long time ago, 'To thine own self be true.' Mayor Daley ran a tight ship. Wherever he is, he must have laughed." A reporter pulled up in front of her Sauganash home in a Checker cab, and the commissioner hurried over to the curb to check the medallion.

On Sunday morning, November 20, Mayor Michael Bilandic passed all four of the questions on the lie detector test. The test cost $200 and was paid for by the *Chicago Daily News*. Bilandic offered to pay for the test himself.

At 9:00 Monday morning in City Hall, Mayor Bilandic announced that he had passed the lie detector test and that Commissioner Byrne was fired. Sharon Gist would take her place. With that announcement, Gist and two husky male coworkers pushed their way through a crowd of reporters waiting outside the Consumer Sales Department, marched into Jane's office, and slammed the door. Gist had been employed in the city Budget Department under Director Ed Bedore, whom Jane had called a "snake." Wanda Smolinski, Jane's secretary, stood to answer the phone. In the flash of an eye, Sharon Gist's secretary grabbed her chair.

Soon after, Jane walked into her office. On the floor, in cardboard boxes, were the contents of her office, her personal belongings. The pictures of Daley and Kennedy had been thrown in on top of pencils, paperclips, and rubber bands. She reached down, lifted the pictures out of the box, and looked into the eyes of Richard Daley. Her hands were trembling, and she could feel her neck redden. She cleared her throat and said to the reporters in her office:

> We'll see what the public says about Bilandic. He has to face the voters in a year, and I'll tell you, I'm going to work against him. I haven't spent eighteen years of my life working in city government and in the Democratic party to be turned out by someone who greased a fare increase. I'm glad to be out of it— temporarily, as far as I'm concerned—because it is a terrible,

terrible administration. Can you imagine Mayor Daley's picture stuck in a box? This is as cheap as everything else that is going on in this building.

She directed an assistant to ship her belongings to her home. She thanked her staff and said good-bye. She took the elevator from the eighth floor to the first, got off and walked through the bright marble lobby of City Hall, decorated for Christmas. She pushed the revolving door, momentarily seeing herself as she was reflected in the cold brass door frame. A sharp wind caught her on the corner of La Salle and Randolph. She pulled her coat tightly around her. Jane climbed into a cab, the meter already ticking before she slammed the door.

16

It's All Mine

St. Patrick's Day, 1978. For the second year Michael Bilandic led the parade down State Street. The movers and the shakers crowded the streets, trying to get close to the mayor. It was important to be seen near him. It was a great day in Chicago. The Irish Rovers, the Harp and Shamrock Club with the jaunting carts and maypole dancers, St. Rita's Marching Band, the Sons of St. Patrick. The Clancy Brothers and Tommy Makem were in town again. Over at Johnny Lattners, the bartenders were opening another case of Bushmills and filling the glasses with Guiness, the dark, bitter stout with the thick, creamy head. The winter had been exceptionally cold, without much snow, but with bitterly constant subzero temperatures. The sun was warm as the cold wind still tore in off the lake, keeping the pavement and the streets icy. The bands and the whiskey and everyone crowding together kept the city warm.

As Bilandic led the parade down State Street, far from the Loop, on the northwest side of Chicago, Bill Burke, in his middle seventies, escorted his daughter down the aisle of Queen of All Saints Basilica. Janie had been a widow for nineteen years. She was nearly forty-five years old and had spent most of her life alone. She was marrying a man very different from her first husband. Jay McMullen was thirteen years older than Jane. He had been married twice. In order to be married in the Church, he had become a Catholic and his two marriages had been annulled—declared null and void, as if they had not existed, despite a son from his second marriage.

Jay had been a newspaperman for thirty years, covering City Hall for the now defunct *Chicago Daily News*. His thoughts could usually be summed up in one or two pithy sentences, which usually brought a laugh. He was very concerned with his sexual prowess and often made a point of alluding to his behavior and accomplishments in that area. In a time of heightened consciousness regarding the use of women as objects of lust, Jay appeared curiously out of step with the times.

Jane wore a crownlike white turban, gathered over her right ear, that completely covered her head. Attached was a cloth rose. Her uncle, Father Joe Burke, who was to marry the couple, whispered to his niece, "What happened to Janie? Did she get her hair shaved off?"

The queen had married the court jester. The king was dead, long live the king. While the queen was in exile, the kingdom was plundered by robber barons whom Jane called the "evil cabal," and she grieved over the rape and pillage of her fair city. As they receded down the aisle and out of the church, the music of *Camelot* played. The lyrics were a sinister warning to the evil men.

> Don't let it be forgot,
> That once there was a spot,
> For one, brief, shining, moment, That was known
> As Camelot.

The queen was about to restore the kingdom.

Three months before her marriage, Jane had addressed the Publicity Club of Chicago. After having reviewed the details of the taxi scandal and her firing, she stated:

There is a hunger abroad in the land. It's a hunger for clean, decent, and honest government. It was this hunger that brought down the Nixon-Ford administration. I believe this same hunger has spread to Chicago, and while Chicago may not be ready for reform, it's ready for a cleaner deal than it's getting in the administration of the present mayor. The nation rejected deceit, deviousness, and subterfuge. I predict that the voters will do that here. You can't take away their newfound gusto, their gusto for a fair deal in City Hall with impunity.

If Jane perceived a hunger in the land and in the city, it was because she, herself, had been shoved away from the table. Jane was out of the very center of power, power to which she had grown accustomed and which she liked, needed, and wanted. She had sat with Daley for ten years at the vortex of government and politics. Her identification with him had become so complete that she had begun to look like him. His power had become her power; his city was her city. He had shared with her the very chairmanship of the party. She was his heir apparent, his queen to rule after he was gone. The throne had been grabbed from her; the city was in bondage and would not be free until the "evil cabal" was banished and she was rightly placed on the throne.

While Daley was alive, Jane entertained no thoughts of ruling. If she had coveted the throne while he was still alive, he would have sensed it immediately and, in the blink of an eye, kicked her out. Only when Jane was on the outside could she begin to realize what the world looked like to others in a similar position: disenfranchised, on the outs, underdog—it was all the same. Jane had no power, and those without power were drawn to her like little metal scraps lunge toward a magnet.

Jane grew to symbolize all the little people in the city who have no power, who are laughed at, who get shoved away from the table by the big boys. The angry little woman in the blue cloth coat with the stiff wig became their spokesperson. She said loudly and clearly what they had always known and felt. She called the patronage system "playing with people's lives."

She said that she would raise money from the people and would not "make any sweetheart deals" with the big shots. She said she would not build a new stadium, new hotels, new high rises, but would fix up the neighborhoods, the very heart of Chicago's life.

On April 24, 1978, Jane officially announced her candidacy for mayor in the small hospitality suite of her apartment building:

> I am declaring my candidacy because I have been encouraged to do so by citizens from all walks of life, including many foot soldiers in the regular Democratic organization. Bilandic has lied to the people and is a part of the evil cabal dedicated to the perpetuation of its own power, to the enrichment of its inner ruling clique, and the prostitution of the forces of municipal government to selfish and purely personal ends. These sinister apostles of self-aggrandizement not only present a clear and present danger to good government, but they threaten to perpetuate themselves in the seats of the mighty, and I believe present a menace that calls for a united response from the citizens of Chicago.

Mayor Bilandic smiled. When asked how "Mayor McMullen"§ would sound, he retorted, "Of what? Peoria?" He said he was too busy running the city to be bothered about Jane but observed sadly, "She used to be one of the wonderful people." George Dunne smiled and said that "Jane Byrne has no significant political support that I can see." Bill Singer, the independent who had lost to Daley in 1975, said, "I'm convinced that Pucinski is seriously considering running for mayor." Alderman Vito Marzullo smiled, "They all think they can beat us, but they never will. But it's a free country. If she thinks she can beat us, let her run." Senator Richard Daley, speaking for the Daley family, smiled, "My brothers and I will support Mike

---

§Jane legally changed her name back to Byrne from McMullen because she was known politically as Jane Byrne.

Bilandic wholeheartedly. I offer no comment on Jane, but we believe Mike is doing a splendid job, and we're solidly behind him." And the papers continued to say that Jane was just front-running for Tom Tully, the "Irish bachelor who reformed the county assessor's office."

The politicians laughed. The press laughed. The people of Chicago did not laugh—they listened and understood what she was saying to them. And Jane listened to the people. The press stopped writing about her, for conventional wisdom dictated that Jane was a loser. Jane had her plan:

> To know my base, what I'll have in every ward, where every supermarket is in every ward, the churches I can rely on in the wards, the synagogues, community groups. Then I want to go, go, go to each one of those day in and day out. Then I want to start the telephone campaign, getting all the signatures and doing what is required by law. I'll do it just like I did it for Mayor Daley.

She did go to the people, block by block, neighborhood by neighborhood, to the churches, schools, block clubs, el plat-forms, stores, shopping centers—anywhere there were people. While the press and the politicians weren't looking, Jane was reaching the people.

Jane opened her headquarters in the Monadnock Building in the Loop. Elvin Bollett, who had been a New York taxi driver and who had organized the Drivers' Union in New York, was Jane's first volunteer. This was in May, 1978, ten months before the election. Bollett was to negotiate the police and fire depart-ment endorsement of her candidacy. Jane promised Bollett that he would be made Commissioner of Consumer Sales, Weights, and Measures after the election and that he would be reim-bursed for all out-of-pocket expenses.

The second call to volunteer was from Elena Martinez. When Jane picked up the phone and heard Elena's Spanish accent, she said, "This is from Heaven. God sent you to me." Jane needed a voice in the Latino community, and Elena was perfect for the job. Elena had left Cuba in 1961 after the Bay of

Pigs. Her family was relatively wealthy, with extensive real estate holdings. As a child, she had attended an American school staffed by the Dominican nuns. Because she had learned English at an early age, when she came to Chicago she did not have the language problem that many Latinos experience. She attended a Catholic high school in Evanston, graduated from Mundelein College in 1969, and received a Master's degree in social work from Jane Adams School of Social Work, University of Illinois, and was a member of the Academy of Certified Social Workers. Elena had received additional training in sexual dysfunction and child abuse and was employed full-time at the Catherine Wright Clinic of Illinois Masonic Hospital as a psychiatric social worker. Her caseload was not limited to the Spanish speaking but included blacks, whites, and Indians as well.

Elena believed in Jane Byrne. She was sick and tired of what she saw going on in the city, the little people squeezed out of the system. She had seen Jane on television and knew instinctively what Jane was saying. During the taxi scandal, Elena said to her mother, "If this woman runs for mayor, I'm going to back her." Elena was bright, educated, and believed that if individuals could change through therapy and counseling, then change could be made in the system through the political process. Jane said, "I don't believe in the myth of the incumbent's superior power. It is not that severe." Elena knew that Bilandic was beatable and that Jane Byrne was the one to do it.

For ten months Elena gave Jane Byrne every minute that was not demanded by her job. When there was a break in her schedule Elena went over to headquarters to give her time—weekends, evenings, nights. On the phone, scheduling appearances, fixing Jane's makeup, strategizing, bringing food over to her apartment, doing anything and everything to topple the system, to help Jane win. Jane told Elena that there would be a place for her in her administration after the election; Elena laughed and told Jane that she just wanted to see her win, that she wasn't looking for a job. It would be enough to see Bilandic go.

Volunteers began flocking to Jane's headquarters: blacks,

Latinos, gays, independents, young people and old; two women who had graduated from Barat College five years prior to Jane; suburbanites, north-siders, south-siders; people from the lake-front and the housing projects, Cabrini-Green and the Robert Taylor homes; students and members of Jane's own family. There was no pay, just an angry, persistent belief in the idea that Jane could and would win. Not for one moment did Jane doubt that she would win. On the day she announced her candidacy, April 24, 1978, a reporter asked Jane if she actually thought she would win. She looked at him incredulously, "I can't think of a reason why I won't win."

City Hall ignored her and the papers continued to disregard her campaign. Jane went into the neighborhoods in her modified school bus called the *Cannonball 2*. She said:

> The neighborhoods have pleaded with City Hall for aid. Instead of help, they get bond issues that enrich the big banks. The people ask for bread and they are given a stone. His heart is not with the people. His heart is with the bankers.

Jane said that the city was in a state of shock without Mayor Daley and issued a Charter for Chicago printed in the form of a parchment scroll, a Declaration of Independence from Fear, Distress, Corruption, Chaos. The preamble declared:

> Now be it declared that today's people of Chicago hold a covenant with all the generations who built Chicago. The people of Chicago owe a debt to the unborn generations who will inherit the city. We must not will them a city shrouded in fear. So be it resolved, this is our Charter for Chicago: Freedom to Work without Fear, Freedom to Play without Fear, Freedom to Live without Fear.
>
> Signed: Jane Byrne for
>   Mayor Committee

Jane understood, better than anyone else, the texture of

power and the fabric of fear. She knew all about banks and real estate and trade-offs and deals. She saw the little people who couldn't get into the system, who were cut off and cut out as she had been. She understood powerlessness, disenfranchisement, and fear. She knew that the incumbent was not very smart, was not a good politician, and she knew that he was vulnerable. He had been lucky—the right man at the right time, but his time was up. She had said that she was sick and tired of his jogging in the park, of "dancing with Mickey Mouse and cavorting with Bozo." She said that corruption sits on the fifth floor of City Hall and that the jackals are at the feast. For one brief shining moment in the city of Chicago under Richard Daley there had been goodness and peace and justice, and she was going to restore the kingdom.

She said that the city had a "caretaker mayor," taking care of the office until a *real* mayor could be found, but he was no longer even taking care. He couldn't give straight answers and when he stood in the sunlight he didn't cast a shadow. He was the man in the empty suit; no one was there. She said that when two doctors examined him, one peering into each of his ears, they saw each other. He was just a caretaker mayor who couldn't even take care.

On December 7, 1978, Jane appeared before the Democratic Mayoral Slate-making Committee at the Bismarck Hotel to ask them not only to endorse her, but to endorse all Democrats, all *bona fide* Democrats who deserved the party's stamp of approval. She told them that she felt like the spirit of Christmas past, for she had so recently sat at the head of the tables as their party co-chairman. They nudged each other. How sweet it was to see her begging. George Dunne had a little twinkle in his eyes. Richie Daley, like Mordred, Arthur's illegitimate son who came to destroy the kingdom of Camelot, snickered at the oblique reference to his father. Vito Marzullo shook his head, folding his arms tightly. He winked at Richie.

Jane didn't miss any of it. She told them that it was obsolete for a few so-called leaders to dictate to the party members who they shall work for, who they shall vote for, and to threaten swift reprisals to anyone who deviates from the hard party loyalty line. She ridiculed them for their disloyalty to Wilson Frost, for when he had claimed his rightful, legal position as temporary mayor after Daley died, the door to the mayor's office was slammed in his face "by the present usurper of the office." Jane said they flushed Parky Cullerton down the drain because he was getting old; they dumped John Marcin, city clerk, a "Democratic workhorse all these years," to get some more votes; Joe Bertrand got kicked aside like a piece of useless luggage, stripped of his manhood.

Jane attacked the banks, the lawyers, the real estate developers, and called it "The Gold Rush of '78, Chicago City Hall Style." She threatened that "the people will wreak a terrible vengeance, sooner or later. And their wrath will be heaped where it belongs—on the present leadership." The slate-makers smiled at little Jane Byrne. One man begrudgingly whispered, "My God, this woman has guts." Richie snickered again.

Two weeks later, on December 20, 1978, Jane Byrne filed her nominating petitions with John Marcin, the city clerk. It was the second anniversary of Mayor Daley's death. She had twenty thousand signatures; the mayor's brother, Nick Bilandic, delivered thirty thousand signatures to Marcin. Reporters asked Mayor Bilandic what he thought about Jane's challenge, now that she had officially filed her nominating petitions. He smiled a big watery smile and said that he really didn't have time to discuss such things because he had to run the city. The reporters understood. Wallace Johnson, an investment banker who had received the endorsement of the Republican party, filed seven thousand Republican signatures. When asked what he thought of Jane Byrne, he smiled and said that he didn't think she would make a very good mayor because she had her period every month. The reporters understood.

Jane looked straight into the television cameras and renewed her challenge to debate Bilandic:

> I'll debate him anywhere. I'd love to debate him in the Robert Taylor Homes. I'd love to debate him in Cabrini-Green, where

they have three rapes every two days and two murders a week.
I'd love to debate him in Uptown, where the houses are all
boarded up, or in Bridgeport, where the people are fed up with
the things that happen.

Bilandic would not debate her. Christmas came and went.
Jane was tired, but so many people believed in her. The family
never questioned for a moment, never second-guessed her
ambitions. Her niece, Caroline, was going to be making her
First Communion in May. Jane told Caroline that she would
pick her up at her Edgebrook home in her limousine and take
her to church for her first Holy Communion. Caroline was sure
Janie was going to be the new mayor of Chicago. Her mother
Mary Jill, Jane's sister, could not dispel Caroline's enthusiasm
and feared that her daughter was due for a painful disappoint-
ment. Some of the kids in her class laughed at her and at her
aunt, but Caroline knew and Janie knew.

December 31, 1978. Jane was standing, looking out over the
city from her apartment windows. In the twilight, she looked
at the Drake. Twenty-two years ago she and Bill had married.
Today would have been their twenty-second anniversary.
Twenty-two years ago they were getting ready to leave the
reception for the Morris Inn at Notre Dame. She thought of
their beautiful wedding, of the uniformed Marines, of Uncle Ed
who had been dead nearly four years, of her mother who had
been dead nearly five years. She thought of Bill and wondered
what he would have thought of all this. If he came back, she
probably wouldn't even know him and he probably wouldn't
recognize her. Today was also Kathy's twenty-first birthday.
Twenty years without a father. Kathy was in Cleveland celebrating with her grandmother. Jane wondered what their life
together would have been like, what he would have looked like
at forty-five, for he was only twenty-five when he was killed.
She saw a wedding party leave the Drake in a black limo as the
snow began to fall.

The snow got heavier. A light blanket began to stick to the
streets. The buses and cabs were slowing down. The snow came

down faster and thicker. Soon the streets were covered; Jane could no longer see them, just the trees outlined in little white Italian lights. Soon the trees began to fade; only the street lights were barely visible. Within a few minutes, there was nothing. Just snow. By morning, January 1, 1979, fifteen inches had fallen.

The city came to a halt. O'Hare Airport shut down. The Caretaker Mayor said that everything was fine, that the city had won an award for having the best airport last year and that it was going to win an award again this year. The planes did not move, and people slept in chairs and on suitcases.

Nothing moved. The mayor told the people to park in the school parking lots so that the city could clean the streets. When the people went to the schools, the lots were not plowed. Chicago was the city that works. It had stopped working.

On January 13, 1979, twenty more inches of snow fell. Aileen Byrne called Jane from Cleveland and said, "Janie, I'm praying that the snow will stop." Jane said, "Please don't do that. Pray that it keeps up."

Jane's campaign commercials began to air. On one of the commercials Mayor Daley's voice could be heard: "Jane Byrne is one of the most competent women I've ever known." The Caretaker Mayor was appearing more and more incompetent. The city was looking through his ears and seeing itself covered with snow. As the people, tired and cold, tried to get their cars out of the snow, Bilandic commercials began on television, showing him jogging during the summer along the lakefront, the parks green and warm.

Jane continued to visit the neighborhoods, the supermarkets, the churches. Bilandic was too busy to campaign. It wasn't necessary. It would only encourage her. Jane went on television and called Bilandic the abominable snowman. She said that all the snow and all the garbage that had not been collected should be piled up and called Mount Bilandic. The City Council called a special meeting to praise the mayor for his wonderful efforts at cleaning up the snow and to give him a special award. His

wife of recent vintage went on television and asked the voters
to vote for her marvelous husband who cared so much for the
wonderful people of Chicago.

The CTA trains weren't running and, when they did, they
ran right past the black neighborhoods on to the white areas. A
$90,000 consultant's report on snow removal, developed by
Bilandic's friend, Ken Sain, was revealed. It plagiarized a
Roosevelt University Master's thesis on snow removal plans for
the city. Jane called it the Great Sain Robbery. The people of
Chicago were in a rage—they knew when they had been had.
They knew the mayor was lying, deceiving them, and trying to
make fools of them. They knew that this just didn't happen in
Chicago, the city that works.

The politicians did not know what was happening in the city.
Neither did the press. Two weeks before the primary election,
the political editor for the *Chicago Tribune* wrote:

> Bilandic is indeed fortunate to have Jane Byrne as a primary
> opponent rather than someone with a more formidable power
> base. Those ethnic or ideological voters who backed Singer or
> Pucinski may see no appeal in Byrne's contention that she would
> be a mayor in the Daley mold. Moreover, some people just
> won't vote for a woman.

The Byrne for Mayor headquarters was completely disorga-
nized, people were walking in circles, bumping into each other.
It was an operation run by amateurs, yet somehow it worked.
Two women who had graduated from Barat were working for
Jane in the evenings. One had just put down the phone. An
angry black woman had just called to say that uniformed
policemen were working her high rise, passing out literature
for Bilandic, telling the people that they had better get out and
vote for the mayor.

Jane walked into the room. Three other volunteers were
standing around the coffee pot. Jane moved over to them and
they left the room. Jane closed the door after them. She stood
in front of Jamie Martin Lyons' desk and said in an even,

controlled voice: "Now listen. I want you to be the first to know. The CBS poll has just come out and I am ahead. Walter is going to announce it on the ten o'clock news." Jane showed no emotion. Jamie looked at Jane's pale hands, spread on her desk. "Jane, I know you are going to win." Jane nodded without smiling, turned on her heels, and walked quickly back to her office. Jane was ahead, 50 percent to 38 percent.

Bilandic knew he was in trouble. He gathered the ward committeemen, the precinct workers, the drones, and the workers, and spoke in a choked voice about Hitler and Moses and about all his troubles. As he cried and told them how evil people were trying to overthrow him, like they killed Jesus, Jane was busy showing reporters cracks in the support columns in the Monroe Street underground garage and said that it was in "imminent danger of collapsing." The garage stood, but Bilandic was about to give way.

The Democratic primary was held on February 27, 1979. That morning, Donna Fitzpatrick, Jane's younger sister, called a friend and said, "Janie gave it her all. She has nothing to be ashamed of. Even now, she still thinks she is going to win. That's Janie for you." The papers had endorsed Bilandic. Conventional wisdom still felt the incumbent had the election, but conventional wisdom was not going to the polls.

Jane received 51 percent of the vote in one of the most stunning upsets in Chicago history. That evening, in a hoarse voice, Jane told her supporters, "The people of Chicago freed themselves tonight." The next morning, a reporter asked her if she woke up and thought, "Did it really happen?" Jane stared at the reporter and said coolly, "No. I always thought I would win."

Jane turned to the party and said, "I'm a Democrat. I believe in the Democratic party. I never had a fight with you. I had a fight with one man and his administration, and that's all behind us now." The interim between the primary, February 27, and the regular election, April 3, was a time to heal party wounds, to plan, and to get rid of the superfluous. Jane Byrne was no longer the little woman in the blue cloth coat who had an ax to grind. The party regulars knew this and knew how to close ranks in order to present themselves as one to the world. The discipline of many years was not lost or forgotten.

The night of the primary, Democratic ward healer and city sewer bureau commissioner, Edward Quigley, had snarled: "Jane Byrne don't want me and I don't need Jane Byrne. I'll submit my resignation and walk, rather than work in her administration." Five days later, after a little stroking, Quigley said, "I love her. She's a great woman and I'm proud to be supporting her and to work for her after she's elected." As Jane came to present herself to the party regulars, Quigley dashed to her side, and kissed her like a long, lost sister.

George Dunne, perhaps a bit more reserved than Quigley, stated, "Recent events give us the sense that the underdog does come through. We will make accommodations for the young lady." Vito Marzullo, the *pater familias*, beamed, "Everything will be all right. She's coming back. No one walks alone in this world." A precinct captain warmed to the thought of Jane, "This is a hell of a homecoming for her. She's been around here in the background for a long time. Now, she's at center stage. She'll make a lovely candidate."

Neil Hartigan, 49th Ward committeeman, cried, "We can and we must get behind Jane Byrne, because she's our leader and there can be only one leader. She's done every rotten job there is to do, even when her name wasn't in the papers, like organizing three-hundred coffees over the years for Democratic candidates, not for glory but because of a belief in the principles and the Democratic party. And now she's the leader, she's the candidate, and we must get behind her." Jane nodded. "I hope to be elected mayor and I hope to keep myself busy with city government and I don't want to concern myself with politics."

She said that there would be no mass firings, that she did not want to play with people's lives, but that there would be changes. A new order was to come. "I was on the outside and I was fired. And I would walk down the streets and people I knew would turn their backs and walk the other way. The fear in this town can be terrible." There would be no mass firings. However, Sharon Gist, who had replaced Jane as Commissioner of Sales, Weights, and Measures, and whose secretary had grabbed Wanda Smolinski's chair, was given a warning: "I still get three hearts and two gizzards with my chicken."

Jane wanted to make changes, for the old order was gone. "I have no feelings about Bilandic. He's a zero to me." But what he had done to the city had to be eradicated. Jane called the best and the brightest to design the new order in which peace and justice would be the rule of the day. Louis H. Masotti, director of the Center for Urban Affairs at Northwestern University, headed the transition team. Independent aldermen, such as William Singer, Dick Simpson, Leon Depres; independent attorneys, academics, and urban strategists were all called to contribute their vision and their ideas to the New Chicago. These had been systematically excluded from city government, and Jane was giving them an opportunity to get in on the ground floor of the new structure she would be building. The coalition of the disenfranchised, the poor, the elderly and the sick, the ignorant and unschooled, the brown and black and red, the young, and the lame and the halt would all have their spokesmen. The coalition would be transformed. The coalition that had believed in Jane Byrne would not disintegrate, as coalitions do, but would be transformed into the body and blood of the new order.

Midway between the primary and the mayoral election, Alderman Vito Marzullo held his annual 25th Ward dinner dance, which is known as the best political affair of the year. In an informal way the transfer of power from Bilandic to Byrne was ritualized. Respect was given to the fallen leader; homage was paid to the new. In introducing Jane, Marzullo said that she had called him before the primary, asked for his support. He told her, "I cannot serve two masters. I support the ticket. If you win, call me and I will support you." She called Marzullo and he gave his support.

Jane looked at the group, who only weeks before had been laughing and snickering at her. "I have always been a Demo-

crat. This is my party. When I win, my office is open to all of
you. I need the help and advice of all of you, especially
Alderman Marzullo and Tom Keane." Marzullo responded,
"We are behind you. But get rid of those crackpots."‡

Jane's choices were clear. The coalition crackpots or the
party. She couldn't have it both ways; there could not be two
masters and she knew it. The powerless or the powerful. How
do you govern, how do you get things done with the powerless?
What had Singer or Masotti or Simpson ever really done? Spiro
Agnew called them "pointy-headed liberals." Eggheads. The
best and the brightest of what? How many votes did they get?
How many jobs could they give out? What did they really
know about anything?

On March 8, 1979, nine days after the primary, Elena Martinez presented Jane with a memo listing several issues that
concerned the Latino community, which Jane needed to address. Some of these were bilingual education, Latinos in the
police and fire departments, Latinos in key cabinet positions,
minority contracts, neighborhoods. Jane had not responded to
the memo. Elena had lost access to Jane. The day after the
primary two bodyguards were stationed outside of her office.
No one was allowed to stand around, much less approach her.
The bodyguards referred to Jane as the mayor. The Byrne for
Mayor Headquarters had been transformed overnight into a
City Hall.

Two weeks later, Elena finally stopped Jane in the hallway
and asked her what to do about the Latino issues, for Elena was
receiving calls asking her what Jane's position was. Jane said to
her, "What is this about? You can just go to them and say
anything you want." Elena said that she could not do that, for
Jane would have to determine her own policy; Elena was not
about to be the spokesperson to her own community if she felt
that what she was saying was not true. Jane grabbed the memo
from Elena, stabbing the paper with her fingernail, and said,
"I'm just not going to answer this. Just look at these. The

---

‡As reported by Milton Rakove, *Chicago Magazine*, May 1979.

Latinos did not vote for me, and I spent all that money there. I'll answer these when I'm good and ready."

Elena took the memo back and said softly, "Mrs. Byrne, I never asked you for a penny." Elena had never taken any money from Jane or from the campaign. She had cut her own clients to half and had taken out a $3,000 loan to make her house and car payments and to provide for her mother and foster children. Her out-of-pocket expenses came to $2,500. She had served notice at the Catherine Wright Clinic that she was quitting because Jane had told her many times that she wanted her to join her new administration. She went back to her office, dreading the hour when the Latinos would demand of Jane an answer and she would have none for them.

On March 23, ten days before the regular election, the West Town Concerned Citizens, a Latino coalition, picketed Jane's office. They barged in, demanding to know what she intended to do for the Latinos, where she stood on the issues, why they should support her. They had been asking for bread and were being given a stone. Elena stood next to Jane, while the Latinos filled her small office. It was an angry confrontation. The Latinos were tired of being used. Jane looked to Elena, her co-chairman of Latinos for Byrne, to respond to her own people. Housing? The police and fire? The schools and neighborhoods?

The men said loudly and clearly to Elena, "No hables! No hables! Tu no hables! No hables!"—Elena, keep your mouth shut and let her talk. Elena did not open her mouth. She had given Jane ample warning, and Jane had chosen not to address the issues. Elena was out. She was perceived as disloyal to Jane. She failed the test. There was no job waiting for Elena, despite the fact that she had quit her job at Jane's insistence.

There was no job for Elvin Bollett, who had been with Jane for ten months. There were no jobs waiting for the many, bright, angry volunteers who had believed in Jane, who had been on the margins and who felt that they could have contributed if they had been on the inside. The political world was either that of the party or that of the crackpots. Jane's decision was not difficult.

Jane had one final act to perform before she could take her vows. The Daleys. The 11th Ward. Jane had to pay homage, to banish any remnant of doubt, of rancor, of ill will, because the restoration of the kingdom could not withstand discord. Before Jane arrived, Bilandic spoke to the overflowing crowd at a Bridgeport school and dutifully asked the people to support her. He left immediately.

When Jane arrived, the people from Bridgeport shouted and cheered. Together with the Daley family and his Bridgeport neighbors, Jane watched a slide presentation of Mayor Daley, the king. Tears streamed down her face as she saw his big, beautiful face, his powerful eyes, and his strong smile.

Jane rose to speak before his wife, his children, his friends and neighbors, and her voice cracked:

> I hope you'll believe that I know to whom I owe everthing. I want you to know that you haven't really lost a mayor. As John Kennedy said, he knew from whence he came. He came from right here in this room. Whatever way we walk after April 3, I want to walk together with the Daleys and with the principles and beliefs and love that the late mayor of Chicago had for this city for which he gave his life. I won't let you down. I know how much he loved all of you.

The Daleys and the people of Bridgeport had not lost a mayor. The king was dead, long live the queen.

The people of Bridgeport and the Daley family did love her. The city loved her; those on the in and those on the out loved her.

April 3, 1979. Jane Byrne was swept into office by 82 percent of the vote. Jane said, "I'm pleased. I'm not overwhelmed." Jay McMullen said, "I'm glad my wife finally found work." They left the city for Palm Springs to rest before her inauguration.

Carpenters, painters, floor buffers, and city workers spent the week before the inauguration getting City Hall into shape. Walls were painted in ivory and lettuce-green; the tile floors looked like a dance floor. The traditional red carpet was discarded, and an emerald green one was rolled from the elevator door to the entrance to City Council chambers.

On the morning of her inauguration, April 16, 1979, Jane attended Mass at Holy Name Cathedral. She was radiant in her gray Pucci pinstripe suit and gray-blue blouse. The wig was gone, the makeup toned down. Jane was a winner—successful, wise and lovely, her skin sun-bronzed from the hours around the pool in Palm Springs. Her hair was soft and lovely. The city awaited the woman in the blue cloth coat whom they had grown to love.

Bilandic's last official act as mayor of Chicago was to dispatch the limousine to 111 E. Chestnut and to call the council to order. Vera Edwards sang the national anthem. John Cardinal Cody said the invocation. The roll call was taken by John Marcin, city clerk. He turned to Jane, wondering if he ought to cut the roll call short in the interest of time. She lifted her eyes and said, "Read the roll call, Mr. Marcin." Mr. Marcin read the roll call in its entirety. "Roti, Barnett, Kenner, Evans, Bloom . . . Volini, Orr, Stone."

The Honorable John Powers Crowley, U.S. District Court, Northern District of Illinois, administered the oath of office of mayor of the city of Chicago to Jane M. Byrne. She placed her hand on the Bible and swore before God, before his representatives, before the city officials, before her family and friends, before the people of Chicago, that she would administer her office justly and wisely and would do her duties as they were required.

She then turned and addressed the city as its mayor.

> As I stand here before you tonight, I am reminded of the simple words with which the late Mayor Richard Daley began his inaugural address. He would say that he was filled with "mingled feelings of humility and pride and with a sense of confidence to meet the challenges that lie ahead."
>
> That phrase best describes my own feelings at this moment. Like the late mayor, I love Chicago. It is where I have lived my

entire life and made some measures of contribution through public service to make it a better place in which to live.

But always I was a private citizen whose activities in government or political party were appointive. Tonight—by taking this solemn oath—I am no longer a private citizen but the mayor of the city of Chicago. I accept that responsibility and ask only that I be judged by any performance as its chief executive.

I can tell you that getting here wasn't easy.

Be assured that I did not become the mayor of Chicago to preside over its decline. I am here before you tonight to dedicate this administration to bringing a new renaissance of neighborhood life and community spirit, a renewal of confidence in the future of our city, and a revival of opportunity for all Chicago.

We must care. We must all care. And while I am working, while the government is working, so must the people also work.

Governments everywhere—at the national, state, and city levels—are in the throes of the revolution of rising expectations. The people ask much, often more than any government can give. We must resist the temptation to promise solutions to all problems. But we will set high goals and strive to achieve them. Reach for the stars . . . and if we fall short . . . look how high up we'll be anyway.

Grave problems confront us. The challenges they present are of sobering magnitude. They cry out for solution. So, with the help of God, let us begin.

After all the well-wishing and hand-shaking, after the relatives and friends, the politicians and hangers-on had gone, after the corridors of City Hall were emptied and the last lock turned for the night, after the long, black limo had brought her home, after the Pucci suit was hanging in her closet, Jane sat alone in the dark. It had been a long day. It had been a long year, she thought to herself. She smiled in the dark, remembering how they had thought she was such a fool. She lit a cigarette, watching it glow in the dark.

It was nice to be alone. So many people for so long, all

wanting a little piece of her. Shaking hands, smiling, being cordial and congenial. She was all alone with her power. She felt so good, so whole. Not fragmented and fearful. They wouldn't laugh at little Janie Byrne anymore. She laughed aloud to herself.

She looked out at the lake. A freighter was crawling on the water. She looked at the Drake, at Big John, at the Sears Tower, up and down Michigan Avenue. It was as familiar to her as the lines on her face. She knew every curb and mailbox, every street sign and traffic light. She knew the people and the wind, the parks and schools, the mood and ebb and tide of the city. She understood the pain of the city, the pain of little people, the pain of the big and powerful when they lose their power. She understood the anger and the humor of the city. She knew it and felt it. She loved it. She walked over to the window, pressing her nose against the cold glass. A streak of red appeared over the darkness of the lake, bringing the first light of dawn. She smiled to herself. "From now on, everything that goes wrong, that's my baby. From now on, it's all mine."

Afterword: Living with Jane Byrne—The Eye of a Hurricane

I have lived within my mind with Jane Byrne for two years. It was a most draining experience. Jane Byrne is not a simple person. She is hard and very difficult to live with. I began to see the world through her eyes, and could predict with a high degree of accuracy what she was thinking and what she would do and say. I began to sound like her; I imagined that I would begin to look like her.

Jane Byrne is a woman without prototype. There are no models to measure her against, except Richard Daley, and Daley is no longer a model; he is a legend. It is hardly fair to measure a novice against a legend.

Because there is no standard against which she can be measured, because there is no appropriate model of a successful Irish-American woman politician, people are nervous about her behavior and her performance as mayor. She may be destroying the city, as an irresponsible housewife would run her husband into bankruptcy; she may be creating one of the last, great, viable American cities; perhaps the truth may lie somewhere in the middle. Regardless of how history will judge her, there is

211

no doubt that she will deeply impact the city of Chicago and the lives of its citizens for many years. A rush to judgment is folly.

Because she is a woman, there is an instinctive response to view her within the context of the expectations and limitations society has set for women. She has her period every month, as Wallace Johnson reminded us; she is in her late forties, so she has probably hit menopause. She had her eyes tucked. She goes to Elizabeth Arden and gets into shape every once in a while. Her makeup is too bright or the wrong color; her clothing is not masculine enough. Her husband calls her "Janie Bird" and tells a national publication that she has gorgeous legs and a cute little ass, and then, indignantly, shouts that she is the victim of sexism. (It would be difficult to have imagined Mrs. Daley calling the Mayor "Dickie Boy" and saying that his little knees drove her wild.)

Yet, to say that Jane Byrne is simply the victim of sex discrimination is inadequate. If we as a society were to suspend the expectations and limitations we have set for women, and if we could judge her actions and behavior against a unisex background, we would still miss the mark.

The fact is that she is a woman, and society does have certain expectations of women. This is the decade of the 1980s in Chicago—traditional, midwestern, conservative. Yet if she is to be judged by the standards we as a society have set for women, so must she be understood within the context of the traditions and history of which she is a creation, with special emphasis placed on the fact that she is a woman, an Irish-American Catholic woman.

Catholic theology and traditions provide the basis for the manner in which Catholics exercise power. When this is joined to an understanding of the American Irish, a relatively clear blueprint emerges for predicting the behavior of a contemporary Catholic Irish-American politician. However, when this politician is a woman, a unique person emerges, who has no prototype within contemporary history. Jane Byrne is such a woman.

The Church has traditionally been an exclusively male domain, as has been politics. Within the last twenty-five years
women have entered the arena of politics. However, these
women have certain commonalities that have allowed them to
fit into the political world comfortably, as if there had been a
spot waiting for them. This is not meant to imply that these
women have not experienced their own unique difficulties,
cracking into the male world of politics, but once they have
been elected they seem to occupy a natural domain.

These women represent a prototype of the Earth Mother—
wise, nurturing, healing—maternal in a strong, disciplined,
selfless way. These women are usually mature, in their fifties or
sixties; they project a grandmotherly sort of image that speaks
on an unconscious level to the public and to their male counter-
parts as well. Such women are Golda Meir, Indira Ghandi, Ella
Grasso, Barbara Jordan, Bella Abzug, and Dixie Lee Ray. The
younger women, while not grandmotherly, are able to project a
young Earth Mother image—Dianne Feinstein, Elizabeth
Holtzman.

The Earth Mother is an intrinsic part of our American
culture and of many cultures. The concept of mother—the
nurturing, life-giving, protecting woman—is one most deeply
imbedded within us. We have feminized many of our institutions and our symbols. Our schools are called *alma mater*, loving
mother; the Church is referred to as Holy Mother Church, the
Spouse of Christ, the Whore of Babylon; ships and planes are
called *she*, the strong protective womb that will protect us on
the seas and in the skies; the Statue of Liberty is the strong,
welcoming woman, lighting the way for the orphans of the
world; Justice is a woman, her eyes blindfolded, as she brings
equity and righteousness to the wronged. The Romans named
their conquered lands with the names of women—Iberia, Brit-
tanica, Italia, Germania, Gallia. Old Mother England; Mother
Russia.

Within the Irish culture there is no nurturing mother, no
Earth Mother concept. Studies on the Irish by Andrew Greely
show that the Irish women, especially the American-Irish, are

the least tolerant, most severe, unaffectionate of sociological groups. Irish-American women do not physically touch their children often and are more severe in their discipline and more rigorous in their methods of control. (Interestingly, Irish-American men are most tolerant and least severe of men studied.)

In Irish mythology the women depicted are the virgin maiden—Kathleen ni Houlihan, the Dark Rosaleen—and the old woman. The concept of nurturing mother is simply not there. Ireland herself is pictured as the sow who eats her young. While this is certainly not true of all Irish women, many are as cold as the sharp winds off the North Atlantic, tearing away at the west coast of Ireland. Many are as strong and bitter as a steaming cup of Irish tea. The Irish woman is strong, alone, tragic; if she is tied to a man, she is tied obliquely.

The Irish woman is able to contain within herself contradictions that defy analysis: she can be publicly warm, privately cold; her compulsion for survival is balanced by a pervasive self-destruction; she can punish unmercifully, while protecting selflessly; she is insightful on an almost mystic level, while retaining an obtuseness about human relationships; her degree of mortification is matched only by her capacity for self-indulgence. The Irish woman is full of contradictions, keeping those around her ever vigilant for a shift in the wind, a turn of the tide, that happens without warning. This unpredictability is perhaps her most successful method of control. Jane Byrne, as woman, springs from this ancient Celtic tradition.

Jane Byrne is in accord with another deeply imbedded Irish tradition—the overt use of power. She has no time for subtlety. Her system of rewards and punishments is up front, out in the open for everyone to view and to fear. There has emerged within the American traditions a notion that the exercise of power is akin to sin. We want power to be just, for the common good, and equitable. We use such value-loaded words as *exploit* and *manipulate* to express the raw use of power. Our Puritan ethic demands that the raw use of power be denied, or at least put out of view. The use of such terms as *smoke-filled rooms, behind the scenes, undercover* all attest to the belief that the exercise of power is not very nice; if it has to be done at all, it ought to be done privately, much as one closes a bathroom door.

Catholics—Irish Catholics—take quite literally the scriptural imperative to render to Caesar the things that are Caesar's and to God the things that are God's. The concept of Christ in the marketplace, let alone in City Hall, has no place in the Irish mind. Things have to get done; decisions have to be made; some people are going to have to come up with the short end of the stick; and that's all there is to it. This is earth, not heaven. The entire decision-making process involves much more than a committee sitting along a dark, mahogany table, nodding in unison. It involves much more than a chief executive, retiring gracefully to his or her chambers, praying for inspiration, and emerging with a wise, impartial, just decision.

Mr. Dooley said, "Politics ain't no beanbag." Politics involves the change and distribution of the goods of society—health, jobs, education, safety, property, money—by ones authorized to do so. These changes and distributions do not happen within a vacuum, a sanctuary. Power involves trading, bargaining, negotiating; it demands movers and shakers, wheelers and dealers, power elites who can play poker with a straight face. Irish politicians know this. Jane knows this, and it does not embarrass her.

She felt an absolute loathing for a President who was afraid of his powers, who spoke as if the political matrix spun around morality and not around power. She felt utter contempt for a President who felt it beneath him to twist congressional arms and who vowed never to lie to the people. Carter's fear of his power was eminently clear, for when he delivered an ominous note to the American public, he would smile a smile of purity and innocence, reassuring the people that his hands were as clean as the desires of his heart. She called it "lack of leadership," but she knew it was impotency of a great magnitude.

Our politicians know well the public expectation that they appear righteous and humble in the face of such awesome power. Lyndon Johnson, perhaps the most successful, adroit politician of the last fifty years, understood this, and in response to what he felt the public wanted, made a caricature of himself, affecting a somewhat pious, righteous pose when addressing the public. Stories that flowed from the White House about his bending and breaking of his enemies and whipping Congress into line and making them jump through hoops did not mesh with his public projection of himself.

Jane Byrne does not suffer from a need to project public piety; her public display of power is in harmony with her actual exercise of it. She loves power and relishes the use of it. It does not make her blush or smile apologetically or make her feel that she has to garb it in piety and grace. Politics and power are her life, her first love, her essence. That unabashed lust for power makes people nervous, embarrassed, angry.

For better or for worse, this work is what Jane Byrne is to me—fascinating, infuriating, intriguing. No one who came before has been anything like her. She is her own self—proud, controlling, with a love for Chicago that is matched only by her love for power. She springs from a deep, rich culture, and she is true to that culture.

When God told Solomon that he wanted to reward him for being such a wise king, Solomon asked God for an understanding heart with which to judge his people. I have asked for that, for if we must judge her, we must first understand.

Notes on Research

The prime source of data for this book came through in-depth interviews with nearly three hundred persons. Some of these people were interviewed a number of times. Mary Agnes Dalton assisted in this interviewing.

Background material on the chapter dealing with Monsignor Edward Burke was provided by Monsignor Harry Koenig and Father Mencelaus J. Madaj, archdiocese of Chicago archivists, and by Father Roger Coughlin, archdiocesan historian. Approximately fifteen other priests were interviewed regarding Monsignor Burke, as well as many laypersons.

Chapter 5 on Barat College was written in the college library. Beth Lucas, director of public relations; Joan Dolan, alumnae director; Sisters Marguerite Green, Sophie Cooney, and Margaret Burke provided material and insight into the history of Barat College in the 1950s.

Information on the University of Notre Dame was provided by Dick Conklin, public relations director, and David Schlaver, CSC. Dick Burke, president, class of '55, provided me with contacts to friends of Bill Byrne during his years at Notre

Dame. Approximately twenty of these men were interviewed.

Chapters 8 and 9 deal with Bill Byrne's death. Material used in the section derives from the *Judge Advocacy General's (JAG) Manual* (#132664), Department of the Navy. This report involved sworn statements taken by the Navy with those who had been with Lieutenant Byrne immediately prior to his death as well as the transcript of his conversation with the ground controller. Joe Lucas and Carol Larson, both FAA-licensed pilots, assisted in the interpretation of technicalities of aviation. Conclusions of the JAG report had been deleted from the report by the Navy before it was sent to me. In other words, what happened to Lieutenant Byrne was reported, but the purported reasons for his death were omitted. Senator Charles H. Percy of Illinois attempted to obtain the release of this information from the Department of the Navy but was unsuccessful. Michael J. Regan, attorney at law, advised me of the legal ramifications of the Freedom of Information Act, as well as of case law precedent regarding the release of such material. It is relatively safe to say that no one will ever really know the cause of Lieutenant Byrne's death.

Bibliography

Adler, Norman, and Charles Harrington. *The Learning of Political Behavior.* Glenview, Illinois: Scott, Foresman and Co., 1970.

Bardwick, Judith M. *In Transition.* New York: Holt, Rinehart and Winston, Inc., 1979.

Beaty, Gene R. "Disclosure of the Air Force Human Factors Investigation." *Journal of Law and Commerce,* 1977, pp. 385–402.

Begley, Kathleen. "My Years with Mayor Daley." *Chicago Daily News,* January 17–20, 1978.

Bowlby, John. *Attachment and Loss,* Vols. 1, 2 & 3. New York: Basic Books, 1969, 1973, 1980.

Bradlee, Benjamin C. *That Special Grace.* New York: J. B. Lippincott Co., 1963–64.

———. *Conversations with Kennedy.* New York: W. W. Norton Co., 1975.

Bryant, Betty. *Leaning into the Wind: Wilderness of Widowhood.* Philadelphia: Fortress Press, 1975.

Burns, James MacGregor. *Leadership.* New York: Harper and Row, 1979.

Christie, Richard, and Florence L. Geis. *Studies in Machiavellianism*. New York: Academic Press, 1970.

Cole, Mary. *Summer in the City*. New York: P. J. Kennedy & Sons, 1967.

Cross, Robert. "Jane Byrne: Muscle in the Marketplace, Power in Politics." *Chicago Tribune Magazine*, July 13, 1975, pp. 10-13, 24, 26-28.

Elms, Alan C. *Personality in Politics*. New York: Harcourt Brace Jovanovich, Inc., 1976.

Fish, John Hall. *Black Power, White Control*. Princeton, New Jersey: Princeton University Press, 1973.

Fleming, Thomas. *Rulers of the City*. New York: Warner Books, 1977.

Gleason, Bill. *Daley of Chicago: The Man, the Mayor, and the Limits of Constitutional Politics*. New York: Simon and Schuster, 1970.

Gleason, Philip, ed. *Catholicism in America*. New York: Harper and Row, 1970.

Glick, I. D., R. S. Weiss, and C. Murray Parks. *The First Years of Bereavement*, New York: J. Wiley & Sons, 1974.

Greeley, Andrew M. "Take Heart from the Heartland." *The New Republic*, December 12, 1970, pp. 16-19.

——. *That Most Distressful Nation*. Chicago: Quadrangle Books, 1972.

——. *Ethnicity in the United States: A Preliminary Reconnaissance*. New York: John Wiley and Sons, 1974.

Hanna, Mary T. *Catholics and American Politics*. Cambridge, Massachusetts: Harvard University Press, 1979.

Harragan, Betty L. *Games Mother Never Taught You: Corporate Gamesmanship for Women*. New York: Rawson Associates Publishers, Inc., 1977.

Heise, Kenan. *Chicago: Is There Only One*. Richmond, Virginia: Westover Publishing Co., 1973.

Hennig, Margaret, and Anne Jardim. *The Managerial Woman*. New York: Doubleday and Company, Inc., 1976.

Instrument Flying Handbook. Department of Transportation, Federal Aviation Administration, Revised, 1971.

Jaquette, Jane S., ed. *Women in Politics*. New York: John Wiley and Sons, 1974.

Jilke, Camille Stagg. "Jane Byrne: Our Lady of Open Coding." *The Chicago Guide*, March 1973, pp. 95-96, 98-101.

Johnson, Paula B., and Jacqueline D. Goodchilds. "How Women Get Their Way." *Psychology Today*, October 1976, pp. 69-70.

Jones, Richard H., and William E. Findler. "The Freedom of Information Act in Military Aircrash Cases." *Journal of Air Law and Commerce*, 1977, pp. 535-553.

Kanter, Rosabeth Moss. "Corporate Success: You Don't Have to Play by *Their* Rules." *Ms.*, October 1979, pp. 63-64, 107-109.

Kelly, Msgr. George A. *The Battle for the American Church*. Garden City, New York: Doubleday and Company, Inc., 1979.

Kelly, Rita Mae and Mary Boutilier. *The Making of Political Women*. Chicago: Nelson Hall, 1978.

Kelly, Tom. "Mayor Daley's Smart, But What Else?" *The New Republic*, December 26, 1970, pp. 9-11.

Kennedy, Eugene. *Himself: The Life and Times of Mayor Richard J. Daley*. New York: The Viking Press, 1978.

————. "Jane Byrne: Hard Times in Chicago." *The New York Times Magazine*, March 9, 1980, pp. 20-24, 32, 34, 73, 75, 77.

Kirkhorn, Michael. "Chicago Looks Beyond Daley." *The Nation*, June 29, 1974, pp. 809-812.

Kolbenschlag, Madonna. *Kiss Sleeping Beauty Good-Bye: Breaking the Spell of Feminism Myths and Models*. New York: Doubleday and Company, Inc., 1979.

Korda, Michael. *Power: How to Get It, How to Use It*. New York: Random House, 1975.

Kotker, Zane. "The 'Feminist' Behavior of Powerless People." *Savvy*, March 1980, pp. 36-42.

Kubler-Ross, Elizabeth. *On Death and Dying*. New York: Mac-Millan Publishing Co., 1969.

Leonard, Martha. "The Many Faces of Jane Byrne." *Chicago*

Tribune Magazine, July 13, 1980, pp. 10-14, 18, 20-27.

Levine, Edward M. *The Irish and Irish Politicians: A Study of Cultural and Social Alienation*. Notre Dame, Indiana: University of Notre Dame Press, 1966.

Lewis, C. S. *A Grief Observed*. New York: Seabury Press, Inc. 1961.

Love, Ann Burnside. "Surviving Widowhood." *Ms.*, October 1974, pp. 87-91.

Machiavelli. *The Prince*. Great Britain: Penguin Classics, 1961.

MacPherson, Myra. "The Daley Disciple Who's Taken Chicago by Storm." *The Washington Post*, March 11, 1979, pp. G1, G3-G5.

Maddison, D. C. and W. L. Walker. "Factors Affecting the Outcome of Conjugal Bereavement," *British Journal of Psychiatry*, Vol. 113, pp. 1057 ff, 1967.

Markoutsas, Elaine. "105 Minutes with Jane Byrne." *Chicago Faces*, June, 1979, pp. 24-27.

McGrath, Paul. "How I Got Involved." *Chicago*, April 1979, pp. 126-130, 164-166, 170-171.

Novak, Michael. "Catholics and Power." *Notre Dame Magazine*, February 1980, pp. 12-15.

O'Connor, Len. *Clout: Mayor Daley and His City*. Chicago: Henry Regnery Co., 1975.

————. *Requiem: The Decline and Demise of Mayor Daley and His Era*. Chicago: Contemporary Books, 1977.

O'Donnell, Kenny, Dave Powers. *Johnny We Hardly Knew Ye*. Boston: Little Brown and Co., 1970-72.

Parkes, C. M. *Bereavement: Studies of Grief in Adult Life*, New York: International University Press, 1972.

Parmet, Herbert S. *Jack: The Struggles of John F. Kennedy*. New York: Dial Press, 1980.

Patchter, Marc, ed. *Telling Lives*. Washington, D. C.: New Republic Books, 1979.

The People of Chicago: Who We Are and Who We Have Been. City of Chicago Department of Development and Planning, 1976.

Rakove, Milton L. *Don't Make No Waves, Don't Back No Losers:*

An Insider's Analysis of the Daley Machine. Bloomington, Indiana: Indiana University Press, 1975.

―――. "A Transfer of Power." *Chicago*, May 1979, pp. 180, 182.

―――. *We Don't Want Nobody Nobody Sent: An Oral History of the Daley Years*. Bloomington, Indiana: Indiana University Press, 1979.

Reese, Mary Ellen. *Moving On*. New York: Wyden Books, 1979.

Reeves, Richard. "Carter, Kennedy and Brown: How Religion Shapes Their Politics." *Notre Dame Magazine*, February 1980, pp. 9-11.

Renshon, Stanley Allen. *Psychological Needs and Political Behavior: A Theory of Personality and Political Efficacy*. New York: The Free Press, 1974.

Royko, Mike. *Boss: Richard J. Daley of Chicago*. New York: Signet, 1971.

Sax, Shirley. "After a Time, We Must Accept the Loss of a Loved One." *Chicago Sun-Times*, July 23, 1980.

Scarf, Maggie. *Unfinished Business: Pressure Points in the Lives of Women*. New York: Doubleday, 1980.

Schlaver, David Edward. *The Notre Dame Ethos: Student Life in a Catholic Residential University*. Unpublished dissertation, University of Michigan, 1979.

Schlereth, Thomas J. *The University of Notre Dame: A Portrait of Its History and Campus*. Notre Dame, Indiana: University of Notre Dame Press, 1976.

Schoen, Douglas. *Pat Moynihan*. New York: Harper and Row, 1979.

Schoenberg, Bernard, ed. *Bereavement: Its Psychosocial Aspects*. New York: Columbia University Press, 1975.

Shannon, William V. *The American Irish: A Political and Social Portrait*. New York: Collier Books, 1966.

Smith, Joseph. "Identification Styles in Depression and Grief, *International Journal of Psychoanalysis*, Vol. 52, pp. 259, 1973.

Snyder, Mark. "The Many Me's of the Self-Monitor." *Psychology Today*, March 1980, pp. 33-34, 36, 39-40, 92.

Soll, Rick. "Jane Byrne: She Is Woman, Watch Her Roar."

Chicago Sun-Times/Chicago Style, April 13, 1980, pp. 8-10, 18-19, 23.

Switzer, David K. *The Dynamics of Grief*. Nashville, Tennessee: Abingdon, 1970.

Tolchin, Susan and Martin. *Clout: Women, Power and Politics*. New York: Howard McCann and Geographic Inc., 1973-74.

Trahey, Jane. *On Women and Power: Who's Got It, How to Get It*. New York: Avon Books, 1977.

Index